Simple Steps

Grade
6

for Sixth Grade

D1449935

Thinking Kids™
An imprint of Carson-Dellosa Publishing LLC
P.O. Box 35665
Greensboro, NC 27425 USA

Thinking Kids™
Carson-Dellosa Publishing LLC
P.O. Box 35665
Greensboro, NC 27425 USA

ISBN 978-1-4838-2676-9

Table of Contents

Simple Steps

Table of Contents

Simple Steps

MATH

Math Introduction

Simple Steps for Sixth Grade uses a combination of step-by-step examples and color coding designed to build students' math skills and deepen their understanding of math concepts.

Instructions

The instructional sections of this book are organized around step-by-step examples. In these sections, key math concepts and terms are assigned colors. This can help students visualize a connection between the skill they are learning and the way that it is applied.

1. The left side explains each step of the math skill being taught.

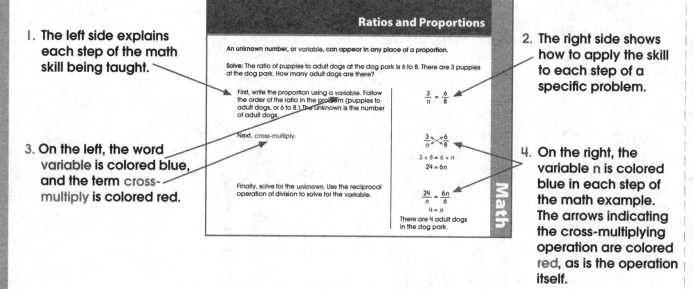

2. The right side shows how to apply the skill to each step of a specific problem.

3. On the left, the word variable is colored blue, and the term cross-multiply is colored red.

4. On the right, the variable n is colored blue in each step of the math example. The arrows indicating the cross-multiplying operation are colored red, as is the operation itself.

Practice

Practice problems follow the concepts after they are explained, giving students an opportunity to work with what they have just learned.

Review

Review sections are included throughout each chapter, along with a chapter review section at the end of each chapter and an overall math review at the end of the math section.

Multiplication is the way to find the sum of equal groups of numbers. Follow these steps to multiply numbers with more than one digit.

Solve: 3263 × 43

First, write the problem vertically. Place the factor with the most digits on top.	$\begin{array}{r} 3263 \\ \times\ \ 43 \\ \hline \end{array}$	
Next, use **place value** to break the smaller factor up. 43 can be broken up into 40 and 3.	$\begin{array}{r} 3263 \\ \times\ \ 40 \\ \hline \end{array}$	$\begin{array}{r} 3263 \\ \times\ \ \ \ 3 \\ \hline \end{array}$
Then, **multiply** 3263 by 40 and then by 3. Work from right to left.	$\begin{array}{r} 3263 \\ \times\ \ 40 \\ \hline 130520 \end{array}$	$\begin{array}{r} 3263 \\ \times\ \ \ \ 3 \\ \hline 9789 \end{array}$
Finally, add the results to find the final product.	$\begin{array}{r} 130520 \\ +\ \ 9789 \\ \hline 140309 \end{array}$	$\begin{array}{r} 3263 \\ \times\ \ 43 \\ \hline 140,309 \end{array}$

Math

Practice

Solve the following problems.

1. $\begin{array}{r} 324 \\ \times\ \ 27 \\ \hline \end{array}$

2. $\begin{array}{r} 5150 \\ \times\ \ 22 \\ \hline \end{array}$

3. $\begin{array}{r} 886 \\ \times\ 374 \\ \hline \end{array}$

4. $\begin{array}{r} 763 \\ \times\ 618 \\ \hline \end{array}$

5. $\begin{array}{r} 2186 \\ \times\ 342 \\ \hline \end{array}$

6. $\begin{array}{r} 1898 \\ \times\ 475 \\ \hline \end{array}$

Multi-Digit Division

Division is the way to subtract equal groups of numbers from one larger number. Follow these steps to divide numbers with more than one digit.

Solve: $983 \div 28$

First, divide the first digit of the **dividend** by the **divisor**. If the divisor will not go into the first digit, use both the first and second digit.

$$\text{divisor} \leftarrow 28\overline{)983} \rightarrow \text{dividend}$$
$$\begin{array}{r} 3 \\ 28\overline{)983} \\ -84 \\ \hline 14 \end{array}$$

Next, subtract the result from the first two digits in the dividend. Bring down the final digit in the dividend and write it beside the difference. Divide this number by the **divisor** and repeat the same steps as for the first digit.

$$\begin{array}{r} 35 \\ 28\overline{)983} \\ -84 \\ \hline 143 \\ -140 \\ \hline 3 \end{array}$$

Finally, write the final difference, or **remainder**, as part of the quotient at the top of the answer line following the letter **r**. Make sure that this remainder is not divisible by the the divisor.

$$\begin{array}{r} 35\ r3 \\ 28\overline{)983} \\ -84 \\ \hline 143 \\ -140 \\ \hline 3 \end{array}$$
→ quotient with remainder

Practice

Solve the following problems.

1. $18\overline{)94}$

2. $43\overline{)88}$

3. $12\overline{)125}$

4. $27\overline{)815}$

5. $54\overline{)725}$

6. $45\overline{)880}$

Reciprocal operations are opposite operations. Multiplication and division are reciprocal operations, just like addition and subtraction are reciprocal operations. You can use reciprocal operations to check your answers when you solve math problems.

Solve: 392 × 22

First, multiply the two factors together to find the product.

```
    3 9 2
  ×   2 2
    7 8 4
+ 7 8 4 0
  8,6 2 4
```

Next, use the reciprocal operation of multiplication to check your work. The opposite of multiplication is division, so divide the product by one of the factors. The quotient should be the other factor in your original multiplication problem.

```
          3 9 2 ⟶ quotient
    2 2) 8 6 2 4
       − 6 6
         2 0 2
       − 1 9 8
           4 4
         − 4 4
             0
```

Finally, check your work. It should match your original problem.

392 × 22 = 8,624

Practice

Solve the following problems.

1.
```
    9 3 1
  ×   7 7
```
Check:

2. 3 2) 4 8 3 2   Check:

3.
```
    9 7 2
  ×   9 3
```
Check:

4. 4 1) 4 4 6 9   Check:

Multiplying Decimals

When multiplying decimals, the number of digits to the right of the decimal point in the product is the sum of the number of digits to the right of the decimal point in both factors.

Solve: 0.4×0.2

First, **multiply** the numbers without their decimal points. Line up the numbers by place value, NOT by decimal points.

$$\begin{array}{r} 0.4 \\ \times\ 0.2 \\ \hline 8 \end{array}$$

Think: $4 \times 2 = 8$.

Next, count the **decimal places** in each factor.

$$\begin{array}{r} 0.4 \longrightarrow \text{I decimal place} \\ \times\ 0.2 \longrightarrow \text{I decimal place} \\ \hline 8 \end{array}$$

Then, add them to find out how many **decimal places** the product will have. This is how many numbers will be to the **right** of the decimal point in your answer.

$$\begin{array}{r} \text{I decimal place} \\ +\ \text{I decimal place} \\ \hline 2 \text{ decimal places} \end{array}$$

Finally, write the decimal point in the product. If needed, write zeros as place holders.

$$\begin{array}{r} 0.4 \\ \times\ 0.2 \\ \hline 0.08 \longrightarrow \end{array}$$ 2 numbers to the right of the decimal

---

Practice

Solve the following problems.

1. $\begin{array}{r} 0.08 \\ \times\ \ 0.5 \\ \hline \end{array}$

2. $\begin{array}{r} 0.7 \\ \times\ \ \ 8 \\ \hline \end{array}$

3. $\begin{array}{r} 0.5 \\ \times\ 0.6 \\ \hline \end{array}$

4. $\begin{array}{r} 0.03 \\ \times\ \ 0.4 \\ \hline \end{array}$

5. $\begin{array}{r} 0.6 \\ \times\ 0.06 \\ \hline \end{array}$

6. $\begin{array}{r} 0.09 \\ \times\ \ 0.7 \\ \hline \end{array}$

You can multiply a larger decimal and a whole number by a decimal by following these steps.

Solve: 2.8×0.6

First, multiply the numbers without their decimal points. Line up the numbers by place value, NOT by decimal points.

$$\begin{array}{r} 2.8 \\ \times\ 0.6 \\ \hline 168 \end{array}$$

Think: $28 \times 6 = 168$

Next, count the decimal places in each factor.

$$\begin{array}{rl} 2.8 & \rightarrow \text{I decimal place} \\ \times\ 0.6 & \rightarrow \text{I decimal place} \\ \hline 168 \end{array}$$

Then, add them to find out how many decimal places the product will have. This is how many numbers will be to the right of the decimal point in your answer.

$$\begin{array}{r} \text{I decimal place} \\ +\ \text{I decimal place} \\ \hline 2 \text{ decimal places} \end{array}$$

Finally, write the decimal point in the product. If needed, write zeros as place holders.

$$\begin{array}{r} 2.8 \\ \times\ 0.6 \\ \hline 1.68 \end{array} \rightarrow 2 \text{ decimal places}$$

Practice

Solve the following problems.

1.
$$\begin{array}{r} 1.68 \\ \times\quad 8 \\ \hline \end{array}$$

2.
$$\begin{array}{r} 25 \\ \times\ 0.7 \\ \hline \end{array}$$

3.
$$\begin{array}{r} 9.806 \\ \times\quad 31 \\ \hline \end{array}$$

4.
$$\begin{array}{r} 895 \\ \times\ 0.63 \\ \hline \end{array}$$

5.
$$\begin{array}{r} 27.1 \\ \times\ 3.54 \\ \hline \end{array}$$

6.
$$\begin{array}{r} 76.4 \\ \times\ 3.6 \\ \hline \end{array}$$

Dividing Decimals

You can divide a decimal by a whole number by following these steps.

Solve: $25.84 \div 4$

First, write the problem in long division form.

$$4\overline{)25.84}$$

Next, write the **decimal point** in the quotient line directly above the decimal point in the dividend.

$$4\overline{)25.84}$$

Finally, divide the numbers.

$$
\begin{array}{r}
6.46 \\
4\overline{)25.84} \\
-24 \\
\hline
18 \\
-16 \\
\hline
24 \\
-24 \\
\hline
0
\end{array}
$$

Math

Practice

Solve the following problems.

1. $3\overline{)37.08}$

2. $8\overline{)9.976}$

3. $2\overline{)0.0214}$

4. $11\overline{)20.614}$

5. $16\overline{)376.32}$

6. $12\overline{)230.16}$

You can divide a decimal by another decimal. Multiply the divisor and dividend by a power of ten (10, 100, or 1,000) so that the divisor is a whole number.

Solve: $14 \div 3.5$

First, change the divisor to a whole number by multiplying by a power of ten. Multiply the dividend by that *same* power of ten.

$3.5 \times 10 = 35$

$14 \times 10 = 140$

Next, write the division problem with the "new" numbers.

$35\overline{)140}$

Finally, solve the problem.

$$\begin{array}{r} 4 \\ 35\overline{)140} \\ -140 \\ \hline 0 \end{array}$$

Practice

Solve the following problems.

1. $2.3\overline{)5.06}$

2. $7.2\overline{)10.8}$

3. $0.22\overline{)1.166}$

4. $0.015\overline{)0.45}$

5. $0.85\overline{)5.1}$

6. $0.035\overline{)7.7}$

Problem Solving

You can use the multiplication and division strategies you have learned so far to solve more difficult problems.

First, underline the <u>important information</u> that you will need to solve the problem.

A package weighs <u>2.6</u> pounds. How much do <u>8</u> of the <u>same-sized</u> packages weigh?

Next, determine which operation is best for solving the problem.

We will use multiplication because finding 8 of the same-sized groups means to multiply.

Then, write a math sentence using the information.

2.6 pounds × 8 = total weight of packages

Finally, solve the problem.

$$\begin{array}{r} 2.6 \\ \times\ \ 8 \\ \hline 20.8 \text{ pounds} \end{array}$$

Practice

Solve the problems. Show your work in the space provided.

1. A collection of nickels is worth $18.60. How many nickels are in the collection?

   1.

2. A box of grass seed weighs 0.62 pounds. How much does a box containing 0.75 times as much grass seed weigh?

   2.

3. Each prize for a carnival booth costs $0.32. How many prizes can you buy with $96?

   3.

Use all of the multiplication and division skills you have learned so far to solve the problems.

Solve the problems.

1.
$$213 \times 362$$

2.
$$248 \times 231$$

3.
$$2851 \times 261$$

4.
$$3732 \times 531$$

5. $76\overline{)6308}$

6. $45\overline{)8329}$

7. $26\overline{)45702}$

8. $86\overline{)99588}$

Solve the following problems and use the reciprocal operation to check your work.

9.
$$465 \times 26$$ Check:

10. $23\overline{)9798}$ Check:

Solve the problems.

11.
$$365.3 \times 5.2$$

12.
$$0.76 \times 0.53$$

13.
$$\$67.45 \times 23$$

14.
$$4.26 \times 7.62$$

15. $0.6\overline{)78}$

16. $0.09\overline{)738}$

17. $0.07\overline{)50.4}$

18. $18\overline{)\$13.50}$

Math

Greatest Common Factor

A factor is a divisor of a number. A common factor is a factor that two or more numbers have in common. The greatest common factor is the largest factor that the numbers have in common. Use the following steps to find the greatest common factor of two numbers.

Solve: Find the greatest common factor of 32 and 40.

First, list all of the factors of each number in order.	Think: 1 × 32, 2 × 16, and 4 × 8. Factors of 32: 1, 2, 4, 8, 16, 32 Think: 1 × 40, 2 × 20, and 4 × 10, and 5 × 8. Factors of 40: 1, 2, 4, 5, 8, 10, 20, 40
Next, underline the common factors of the numbers.	Factors of 32: <u>1</u>, <u>2</u>, <u>4</u>, <u>8</u>, 16, 32 Factors of 40: <u>1</u>, <u>2</u>, <u>4</u>, 5, <u>8</u>, 10, 20, 40
Finally, circle the greatest common factor of the numbers.	Factors of 32: 1, 2, 4, 8, 16, 32 Factors of 40: 1, 2, 4, 5, 8, 10, 20, 40

The greatest common factor of 32 and 40 is 8.

Practice

Find the greatest common factor of the following numbers.

1. 8 _____
   12 _____

2. 6 _____
   18 _____

3. 24 _____
   15 _____

4. 4 _____
   6 _____

5. 5 _____
   12 _____

6. 16 _____
   12 _____

A multiple is a product of a number multiplied by another number. A common multiple is a multiple that two or more numbers have in common. The least common multiple is the smallest multiple that the numbers have in common. Use the following steps to find the least common multiple of two numbers.

Solve: Find the least common multiple of 3 and 6.

First, list some multiples of each number in order.	Multiples of 3: 3, 6, 9, 12, 15, 18, 21, 24... Multiples of 6: 6, 12, 18, 24, 30, 36, 42...
Next, underline the common multiples of the numbers.	Multiples of 3: 3, 6, 9, 12, 15, 18, 21, 24... Multiples of 6: 6, 12, 18, 24, 30, 36, 42...
Finally, circle the least common multiple of the numbers.	Multiples of 3: 3, 6, 9, 12, 15, 18, 21, 24... Multiples of 6: 6, 12, 18, 24, 30, 36, 42...

The least common multiple of 3 and 6 is 6.

Math

Practice

Find the least common multiple of the following numbers.

1. 8 _____

    12 _____

2. 12 _____

    16 _____

3. 4 _____

    7 _____

4. 2 _____

    10 _____

5. 5 _____

    7 _____

6. 4 _____

    9 _____

Multiplying Fractions

Multiply a fraction by another fraction by following these steps.

Solve: $\frac{3}{8} \times \frac{2}{3}$

First, multiply the numerators.

$$\frac{3}{8} \times \frac{2}{3} = \frac{3 \times 2}{\boxed{}} = \frac{6}{\boxed{}}$$

Next, multiply the denominators.

$$\frac{3}{8} \times \frac{2}{3} = \frac{3 \times 2}{8 \times 3} = \frac{6}{24}$$

Finally, simplify. To simplify, divide the numerator and the denominator by the greatest common factor.

$$\frac{6}{24} = \frac{1}{6}$$

The greatest common factor of 6 and 24 is 6.

$$6 \div 6 = 1$$
$$24 \div 6 = 4$$

Practice

Solve the following problems. Write the answers in simplest form.

1. $\frac{2}{5} \times \frac{2}{3}$

2. $\frac{3}{4} \times \frac{5}{6}$

3. $\frac{7}{8} \times \frac{5}{7}$

4. $\frac{2}{3} \times \frac{8}{9}$

5. $\frac{3}{4} \times \frac{3}{7}$

6. $\frac{11}{12} \times \frac{2}{3}$

When you multiply with fractions, you are finding a piece of a piece. Follow these steps to multiply a fraction by a whole number.

Solve: $\frac{2}{3} \times 5$

First, rewrite the whole number as a fraction.	$5 = \frac{5}{1}$
Next, multiply the numerators.	$\frac{2}{3} \times \frac{5}{1} = \frac{2 \times 5}{\boxed{}} = \frac{10}{\boxed{}}$
Then, multiply the denominators.	$\frac{2}{3} \times \frac{5}{1} = \frac{2 \times 5}{3 \times 1} = \frac{10}{3}$
Finally, simplify.	$\frac{10}{3} = 3\frac{1}{3}$

Practice

Solve the following problems. Write the answers in simplest form.

1. $\frac{3}{4} \times 4$

2. $\frac{7}{8} \times 6$

3. $3 \times \frac{2}{5}$

4. $\frac{5}{12} \times 3$

5. $9 \times \frac{3}{5}$

6. $\frac{10}{11} \times 12$

Math

Multiplying Mixed Numbers

A mixed number is a whole number with a fractional part. You can multiply a mixed number by another mixed number by rewriting them both as improper fractions. Follow these steps to multiply mixed numbers.

Solve: $2\frac{3}{4} \times 3\frac{1}{3}$

First, rewrite each mixed number as an improper fraction. An improper fraction is a fraction greater than one. Its numerator is greater than its denominator.

$$2\frac{3}{4} = \frac{11}{4} \qquad 3\frac{1}{3} = \frac{10}{3}$$

Next, multiply the numerators and then multiply the denominators.

$$\frac{11}{4} \times \frac{10}{3} = \frac{110}{12}$$

Finally, simplify.

$$\frac{110}{12} = \frac{55}{6} = 9\frac{1}{6}$$

Practice

Solve the following problems. Write the answers in simplest form.

1. $1\frac{1}{3} \times 2\frac{1}{8}$

2. $2\frac{1}{2} \times 1\frac{3}{4}$

3. $2\frac{5}{8} \times 2\frac{3}{5}$

4. $1\frac{1}{2} \times 2\frac{2}{3}$

5. $3\frac{1}{5} \times 5\frac{2}{3}$

6. $4\frac{1}{2} \times 4\frac{1}{2}$

7. $2\frac{1}{3} \times 3\frac{1}{4}$

8. $2\frac{4}{5} \times 3\frac{1}{8}$

Fraction bars can help you divide fractions. Follow these steps to divide fractions.

Solve: $\dfrac{1}{3} \div \dfrac{1}{6}$

First, determine how many groups of the **divisor** are in the **dividend**.

$\dfrac{1}{3}$ is the dividend and $\dfrac{1}{6}$ is the divisor. How many sixths are in $\dfrac{1}{3}$?

Next, line up fraction bars and divide them into equal-sized pieces to match the problem.

$\dfrac{1}{3}$		

$\dfrac{1}{6}$					

Then, count **how many** of the bottom pieces equal the top piece.

Two one-sixth pieces are equal to the top one-third piece. So,

$\dfrac{2}{6} = \dfrac{1}{3}$.

$\dfrac{1}{3}$		

$\dfrac{1}{6}$	$\dfrac{1}{6}$				

Finally, solve the problem.

$\dfrac{1}{3} \div \dfrac{1}{6} = 2$

Practice

Use the fraction bars to solve the problems.

1. $\dfrac{1}{2} \div \dfrac{1}{4}$

2. $\dfrac{2}{3} \div \dfrac{1}{6}$

Math

Dividing Fractions

Dividing fractions means to find how many groups of the **divisor** are in the **dividend**. To divide a fraction by another fraction, follow these steps.

Solve: $\dfrac{4}{5} \div \dfrac{8}{9}$

First, change the **divisor** into its reciprocal. The **divisor** is the second fraction in the problem. A reciprocal is when you switch the numerator and denominator.

The reciprocal of $\dfrac{8}{9}$ is $\dfrac{9}{8}$.

Then, multiply the **dividend** by the reciprocal.

$$\dfrac{4}{5} \div \dfrac{8}{9} = \dfrac{4}{5} \times \dfrac{9}{8} = \dfrac{36}{40}$$

Finally, simplify. The greatest common factor of 36 and 40 is 4, so divide both the numerator and the denominator by 4.

$$\dfrac{36}{40} = \dfrac{9}{10}$$

Practice

Divide the fractions. Write the answers in simplest form.

1. $\dfrac{1}{2} \div \dfrac{3}{5}$

2. $\dfrac{1}{2} \div \dfrac{7}{8}$

3. $\dfrac{7}{8} \div \dfrac{1}{3}$

4. $\dfrac{3}{5} \div \dfrac{2}{3}$

5. $\dfrac{3}{4} \div \dfrac{1}{6}$

6. $\dfrac{1}{7} \div \dfrac{1}{2}$

You can divide a fraction by a whole number and a whole number by a fraction by following these steps.

Solve: $12 \div \dfrac{1}{5}$

First, rewrite the whole number as a fraction.

$$12 = \dfrac{12}{1}$$

Next, multiply the whole number in its fraction form by the reciprocal of the second fraction.

The reciprocal of $\dfrac{1}{5}$ is $\dfrac{5}{1}$.

$$\dfrac{12}{1} \times \dfrac{5}{1} = \dfrac{60}{1}$$

Finally, simplify.

$$\dfrac{60}{1} = 60$$

$$12 \div \dfrac{1}{5} = 60$$

Practice

Divide. Write the answers in simplest form.

1. $2 \div \dfrac{2}{3}$

2. $5 \div \dfrac{1}{4}$

3. $\dfrac{1}{4} \div 3$

4. $\dfrac{1}{6} \div 4$

5. $7 \div \dfrac{1}{3}$

6. $\dfrac{3}{7} \div 6$

Dividing Mixed Numbers

You can divide a **mixed number** by another mixed number by following these steps.

Solve: $4\frac{1}{3} \div 2\frac{3}{4}$

First, rewrite each mixed number as an **improper fraction**.	$4\frac{1}{3} \div 2\frac{3}{4} = \frac{13}{3} \div \frac{11}{4}$
Next, multiply the dividend by the **reciprocal** of the divisor.	$\frac{13}{3} \times \frac{4}{11} = \frac{52}{33}$
Finally, simplify.	$\frac{52}{33} = 1\frac{19}{33}$

Practice

Divide. Write the answers in simplest form.

1. $2\frac{1}{2} \div 3\frac{1}{3}$

2. $4\frac{1}{2} \div 1\frac{1}{6}$

3. $6 \div 2\frac{1}{2}$

4. $3\frac{3}{5} \div 4$

5. $4\frac{5}{6} \div 2\frac{2}{5}$

6. $4\frac{1}{3} \div 6$

7. $1\frac{1}{2} \div 3\frac{1}{8}$

8. $3\frac{1}{3} \div 2\frac{3}{8}$

You can use the multiplication and division strategies you have learned so far to solve more difficult problems.

First, underline the <u>important information</u> that you will need to solve the problem.	Sam and Jose mowed $\frac{2}{3}$ of the yard. Jose mowed $\frac{3}{4}$ of that amount. <u>What part of the yard did Jose mow</u>?
Next, determine which **operation** is best for solving the problem.	We will use **multiplication** because finding $\frac{3}{4}$ of $\frac{2}{3}$ means to **multiply**.
Then, write a **math sentence** using the information.	$\frac{3}{4} \times \frac{2}{3}$ = the part of the yard that Jose mowed
Finally, solve the problem.	$\frac{3}{4} \times \frac{2}{3} = \frac{6}{12} = \frac{1}{2}$

Practice

Solve the problems. Show your work in the space provided.

1. Maria practices the piano $\frac{5}{6}$ of an hour every day. How many hours does she practice in 4 days?

   Maria practices _____ hours.

2. A container holding $6\frac{2}{3}$ pints of juice will be divided equally among 5 people. How much juice will each person get?

   Each person will get _____ pints.

1.

2.

Use everything you have learned so far about factors, multiples, and multiplying and dividing fractions to solve the problems.

Find the greatest common factor of each set of numbers.

1. 40, 4
2. 30, 12
3. 4, 10
4. 20, 24
5. 3, 10

_____   _____   _____   _____   _____

Find the least common multiple of each set of numbers.

6. 30, 15
7. 15, 5
8. 20, 4
9. 3, 8
10. 5, 12, 10

_____   _____   _____   _____   _____

Multiply the fractions. Write the answers in simplest form.

11. $\dfrac{2}{3} \times \dfrac{3}{4}$

12. $\dfrac{2}{3} \times 5$

13. $3\dfrac{1}{8} \times 4$

14. $2\dfrac{1}{2} \times 3\dfrac{1}{3}$

Write the reciprocal of each fraction.

15. $\dfrac{3}{8}$ _____

16. 5 _____

17. $\dfrac{12}{5}$ _____

18. $\dfrac{4}{7}$ _____

Divide. Write the answers in simplest form.

19. $5 \div \dfrac{2}{3}$

20. $\dfrac{2}{3} \div \dfrac{4}{5}$

21. $\dfrac{7}{8} \div 2$

22. $3\dfrac{1}{8} \div 2\dfrac{1}{2}$

23. $4\dfrac{2}{3} \div 3\dfrac{1}{2}$

24. $2\dfrac{3}{4} \div 2\dfrac{3}{4}$

Multiply or divide. Use the reciprocal operation to check your work.

1. $\begin{array}{r} 258 \\ \times\ \ 37 \end{array}$ Check:

2. $\begin{array}{r} 674 \\ \times\ \ 83 \end{array}$ Check:

3. $45\overline{)6950}$ Check:

4. $78\overline{)40794}$ Check:

Multiply or divide to solve the word problems.

5. At West Side Middle School, there are 42 classrooms with 28 desks in each. How many desks are there in the whole school?

5.

6. There are 1,104 books to be shelved in the library. Each shelf holds 23 books. How many shelves will be used?

6.

Multiply or divide with decimals.

7. $\begin{array}{r} 2.86 \\ \times\ \ 0.3 \end{array}$

8. $\begin{array}{r} \$78.53 \\ \times\ \ \ \ \ 16 \end{array}$

9. $\begin{array}{r} 3.21 \\ \times\ 8.72 \end{array}$

10. $0.08\overline{)64}$

11. $0.3\overline{)726}$

12. $14\overline{)\$7.70}$

Chapter Review

Find the greatest common factor of each set of numbers.

13. 15, 20 _____

14. 12, 36 _____

15. 72, 60 _____

16. 65, 39 _____

17. 95, 76 _____

18. 96, 112 _____

Find the least common multiple of each set of numbers.

19. 12, 3 _____

20. 4, 7 _____

21. 12, 6 _____

22. 3, 5 _____

23. 15, 3 _____

24. 6, 10 _____

Multiply. Write each answer in simplest form.

25. $\dfrac{7}{8} \times \dfrac{3}{4}$

26. $9 \times \dfrac{3}{8}$

27. $\dfrac{5}{8} \times 5$

28. $5\dfrac{3}{4} \times 2\dfrac{1}{3}$

Solve the word problems.

29. Jen and Gina together raked $\dfrac{7}{8}$ of the yard. Jen raked $\dfrac{3}{5}$ of that amount. What part of the yard did Jen rake?

    Jen raked _____ of the yard.

    29.

30. Felipe has track practice for $\dfrac{5}{8}$ of an hour after school each day. How many hours does he have track practice in 6 days?

    Felipe has track practice for _____ hours.

    30.

Divide. Write the answers in simplest form.

31. $8 \div \dfrac{2}{3}$

32. $\dfrac{4}{5} \div 3$

33. $10 \div \dfrac{3}{8}$

34. $\dfrac{4}{5} \div \dfrac{7}{8}$

35. $\dfrac{2}{3} \div \dfrac{5}{6}$

36. $\dfrac{3}{8} \div \dfrac{7}{8}$

37. $2\dfrac{3}{4} \div 3\dfrac{1}{8}$

38. $7 \div 3\dfrac{1}{4}$

39. $7\dfrac{3}{8} \div 9$

Solve the word problems.

40. Nadia has a stack of 7 books on her desk. Each book is $1\dfrac{7}{8}$ inches thick. How tall is the stack?

The stack is _____ inches tall.

40.

41. Jamie divided $6\dfrac{2}{5}$ ounces of popcorn into equal amounts. He put the popcorn into containers that hold $2\dfrac{2}{3}$ ounces each. How many containers will be filled?

_____ containers will be filled.

41.

Math

Ratios

A ratio compares two numbers. Follow these steps to learn three ways to write a ratio.

Solve: Write a ratio to compare 4 cups of flour to 2 cups of sugar.

First, write the ratio in **words**. The first number in the problem is written first, and the second is written second. Write "to" between the numbers when comparing different groups. Write "out of" when comparing numbers from the same group.

4 to 2

Next, write the ratio with a **symbol**. The symbol is called a **colon**. This ratio is read as "4 to 2."

4:2

Finally, write the ratio as a **fraction**. The numerator is the first number in the ratio, and the denominator is the second number. This ratio is also read as "4 to 2." Written in simplest form, it is "2 to 1."

$$\frac{4}{2} = \frac{2}{1}$$

Practice

Write each ratio in three ways.

1. 5 pounds to 35 pounds _____

2. 15 students out of 30 students _____

3. 10 dogs to 12 cats _____

4. 24 rainy days out of 60 days _____

5. 2 sports out of 19 sports _____

Ratios can be used to compare two different groups of numbers. The order of the numbers in the ratio depends on which ratio the problem is asking you to find.

Solve: There are 2 bottles of sports drink and 5 bottles of water in the refrigerator. Write the ratio of sports drinks to waters.

First, read which ratio the problem is asking you to find. This ratio is the number of sports drinks to the number of waters. Write the ratio in words.	2 to 5
Next, write the ratio with the ratio symbol.	2:5
Finally, write the ratio as a fraction.	$\frac{2}{5}$

Practice

Express each ratio in word form, with a symbol, and as a fraction in simplest form.

1. There are 2 cubes and 15 spheres in a geometry box. Write the ratio of spheres to cubes.

   _____

2. There are 5 cars and 4 vans in a parking lot. Write the ratio of vans to cars.

   _____

3. There are 28 red bikes out of 40 bikes. Write the ratio of red bikes to the total number of bikes.

   _____

4. There are 12 apples and 15 oranges in a fruit basket. Write the ratio of apples to oranges.

   _____

Ratios and Proportions

You can use proportions to solve ratio problems. A proportion uses a variable, or an unknown number.

Solve: The ratio of apples to oranges is 4 to 5. There are 20 oranges in the basket. How many apples are there?

First, write the proportion using a **variable**. A variable is a letter or a symbol that stands for an **unknown value**. The *n* stands for the unknown number of apples.

$$\frac{4}{5} = \frac{n}{20}$$

Next, **cross-multiply**. That means multiply the first numerator with the second denominator, and the second numerator with the first denominator. Notice how the arrows of cross-multiplication make an "X" like a multiplication symbol

$$\frac{4}{5} \diagdown\!\!\!\!\diagup \frac{n}{20}$$

$$4 \times 20 = 5 \times n$$
$$80 = 5n$$

Finally, solve for the **unknown**. Use the reciprocal operations of division to solve for the **variable**. Since 5*n* means "5 times *n*," divide both sides of the equation by 5 to get the variable alone on one side of the equation.

$$\frac{80}{5} = \frac{5n}{5}$$
$$16 = n$$

There are 16 apples in the basket.

Practice

Solve to find the value of the variable.

1. $\dfrac{1}{3} = \dfrac{n}{24}$

2. $\dfrac{4}{9} = \dfrac{n}{36}$

3. $\dfrac{3}{5} = \dfrac{n}{15}$

4. $\dfrac{7}{12} = \dfrac{n}{36}$

An unknown number, or variable, can appear in any place of a proportion.

Solve: The ratio of puppies to adult dogs at the dog park is 6 to 8. There are 3 puppies at the dog park. How many adult dogs are there?

First, write the proportion using a **variable**. Follow the order of the ratio in the problem (puppies to adult dogs, or 6 to 8.) The unknown is the number of adult dogs.	$$\frac{3}{n} = \frac{6}{8}$$
Next, **cross-multiply**.	$$\frac{3}{n} \diagdown \frac{6}{8}$$ $$3 \times 8 = 6 \times n$$ $$24 = 6n$$
Finally, solve for the **unknown**. Use the reciprocal operation of division to solve for the **variable**.	$$\frac{24}{n} = \frac{6n}{6}$$ $$4 = n$$ There are 4 adult dogs in the dog park.

Math

Practice

Solve to find the value of the variable.

1. $\dfrac{n}{3} = \dfrac{3}{9}$

2. $\dfrac{15}{30} = \dfrac{2}{n}$

3. $\dfrac{6}{n} = \dfrac{15}{20}$

4. $\dfrac{7}{9} = \dfrac{n}{63}$

5. $\dfrac{35}{n} = \dfrac{4}{8}$

6. $\dfrac{3}{27} = \dfrac{4}{n}$

Ratios and Proportions

You can solve ratio and proportion problems by following these steps.

Solve: The ratio of boys to girls in the swim club is 3 to 5. There are 10 girls in the swim club. How many boys are there?

First, write the ratio as a proportion with a variable. Reread the problem to decide where to place each number in the proportion. Since the problem is about a ratio of "boys to girls," that is the order you will write the ratio and proportion. The unknown variable is the number of boys.

$$\frac{boys}{girls} = \frac{3}{5} = \frac{n}{10}$$

Next, cross-multiply.

$$\frac{3}{5} = \frac{n}{10}$$
$$3 \times 10 = 5 \times n$$
$$30 = 5n$$

Finally, solve to find the value of the **variable**. Use the reciprocal operation of division to get the variable alone on one side of the equation.

$$\frac{30}{5} = \frac{5n}{5}$$
$$6 = n$$

There are 6 boys in the swim club.

Practice

Solve to find the unknown variable.

1. The ratio of fish to tanks is 5 to 3. There are 15 fish. How many tanks are there?

   1.

2. The ratio of sunflowers to daisies is 4 to 6. There are 24 daisies. How many sunflowers are there?

   2.

3. The ratio of baseballs to softballs is 1:4. There are 2 baseballs. How many softballs are there?

   3.

Math

Tables can be used to help find missing values in **ratio** problems.

Solve: A car uses 2 gallons of gas to drive 60 miles. Create a table to find out how many miles the car can travel on 10 gallons of gas.

First, find the **ratio** in the problem.

If the car uses 2 gallons of gas to drive 60 miles, that means the ratio of gas to miles is **2 to 60**.

Next, draw a table using the **ratio**. Extend the table to the number the problem is asking you to find. In this case, extend it to 10 gallons of gas.

Gas (gallons)	2	4	6	8	10
Miles	60				

Finally, complete the table following the pattern of equivalent ratios. An equivalent ratio is a ratio that is equal to the original ratio. Use the ratio $\frac{2}{60}$ to find the equivalent ratios.

Think: For every 2 gallons of gas, the car drives 60 miles.

$$\frac{2}{60} \frac{\times 2}{\times 2} = \frac{4}{120} \qquad \frac{2}{60} \frac{\times 3}{\times 3} = \frac{6}{180}$$

$$\frac{2}{60} \frac{\times 4}{\times 4} = \frac{8}{240} \qquad \frac{2}{60} \frac{\times 5}{\times 5} = \frac{10}{300}$$

Gas (gallons)	2	4	6	8	10
Miles	60	120	180	240	300

The car can travel 300 miles on 10 gallons of gas.

Math

Practice

Complete the table to solve the ratio problem.

Lydia can solve 21 math problems in 3 hours. At this rate, how many problems could she solve in 9 hours?

Math problems	21		
hours	3 hours	6 hours	9 hours

Tables and Ratio Problems

Practice

Complete the tables to solve the ratio problems.

1. You can buy 4 cans of green beans at the market for $2.25. How much will it cost to buy 12 cans of beans?

Cans	4 cans	8 cans	12 cans
Cost	$2.25		

2. An ice-cream factory makes 180 quarts of ice cream in 2 hours. How many quarts could be made in 12 hours?

Ice Cream (quarts)	180					
Hours	2	4	6	8		

3. A jet travels 650 miles in 3 hours. At this rate, how far could the jet fly in 9 hours?

Distance (miles)	650		
Hours	3		

4. A bakery can make 640 bagels in 4 hours. How many can they bake in 16 hours?

Bagels	640			
Hours	4			

A rate is a special ratio that compares quantities of two different units, such as 340 miles per 10 gallons. In a unit rate, one of those quantities is 1, such as 34 miles per gallon.

Solve: If there are 160 students and 4 buses, how many students should go on each bus?

First, write the ratio in the problem as a fraction.	$\dfrac{160}{4}$
Next, write the equivalent unit rate as a variable over one. Use a variable as the numerator, and 1 as the denominator. Here, we will use **s** for students.	$\dfrac{160}{4} = \dfrac{s}{1}$
Finally, cross-multiply and solve to find the unit rate.	$4s = 160$ $s = 40$ The unit rate is $\dfrac{40}{1}$, or 40 students per bus.

Math

Practice.

Solve each problem by finding the unit rate.

1. John can create 20 paintings in 4 weeks. How many paintings can he create each week?

    1.

2. Sasha can walk 6 miles in 3 hours. If she has to walk 1 mile, how long will it take her?

    2.

3. Victoria can make 8 necklaces in 4 days. How long does it take her to make one necklace?

    3.

Unit Rates

You can use unit rates to solve real-world problems. Extend the unit rate to solve the problem.

Solve: Chelsea walked a total of 6 miles making 3 trips to school. How many trips to school will Chelsea have to make to walk a total of 10 miles?

First, find the unit rate.	$\dfrac{6 \text{ miles}}{3 \text{ trips}} = 2$ miles per trip
Next, use the unit rate to solve the problems.	10 total miles ÷ 2 miles per trip = 5 trips

Practice

Solve each problem by finding the unit rate.

1. Charlie downloads 3 songs for $3.90. If each song costs the same amount, how much would he pay to download 5 songs?

   1.

2. Kendra read 40 pages in 2 hours. At this rate, in how many hours will she have read 100 pages?

   2.

3. Jaxon buys 5 cheeseburgers for $15.00. How many cheeseburgers can he buy with $24.00?

   3.

4. Carli knits 3 scarves in 6 weeks. How many weeks will it take her to knit 7 scarves?

   4.

5. Mateo baked a dozen muffins with 3 cups of flour. How many cups of flour will he need to bake 36 muffins?

   5.

You can graph a ratio on a coordinate grid.

Solve: Tom deposits $10 into his savings account each week. Complete the table to show the **ratio** of dollars to weeks, then graph the ratio.

First, determine the **ratio**.

Next, complete the table following the ratio.

In one week, Tom saves $10. The ratio of weeks to dollars is 1:10.

Weeks (x-values)	Dollars (y-values)
1	10
2	20
3	30
4	40
5	50

Then, graph the **points** on the coordinate grid. The points are in (x,y) order, or (weeks, dollars).

Math

Practice

Solve the problem.

1. For her business, Carey's Roses, Carey buys a box of two dozen roses wholesale for $20. Make a table and graph of her costs for 2, 4, 6, and 8 boxes of roses. Be sure to label the x-axis and y-axis on your graph.

   What would Carey's cost be for 20 dozen roses?

   _____

Boxes (x-values)	Dollars (y-values)

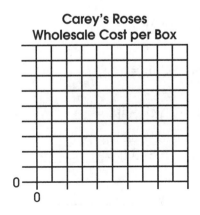

Carey's Roses
Wholesale Cost per Box

Converting Measurements

You can use what you know about ratios to convert measurements. Use the conversion chart to write the equivalent measurements.

Solve: How many feet are equal to 24 inches?

1 foot (ft.) = 12 inches (in.)	1 in. = $\frac{1}{12}$ ft.
1 yard (yd.) = 3 ft.	1 ft. = $\frac{1}{3}$ yd.
1 yd. = 36 in.	1 in. = $\frac{1}{36}$ yd.
1 mile (mi.) = 5,280 ft.	1 mi. = 1,760 yd.

First, set up a **proportion** with the two measurements.

$$1 \text{ inch} = \frac{1}{12} \text{ ft.}$$

Next, use a **variable** to set up the proportion.

$$24 \text{ in.} = n \text{ ft.}$$

Finally, decide if you need to multiply or divide to solve. Since 1 inch is equal to $\frac{1}{12}$ of a foot, 24 inches is $24 \times \frac{1}{12}$ feet.

$$24 \text{ in.} = \left(24 \times \frac{1}{12}\right) \text{ ft.}$$

$$24 \text{ in.} = 2 \text{ ft.}$$

Practice

Complete the following measurement conversions.

1. 7 ft. = _____ in.

2. 72 in. = _____ ft.

3. 15 yd. = _____ ft.

4. 108 in. = _____ yd.

5. 4 mi. = _____ ft.

6. 4 mi. = _____ yd.

7. 3 yd. = _____ ft.

8. 120 in. = _____ ft.

9. 42 ft. = _____ yd.

10. 4 ft. 7 in. = _____ in.

11. 2 yd. 9 in. = _____ in.

12. 30 in. = _____ ft.

13. 15,840 ft = _____ mi.

14. 6 yd. = _____ ft.

15. 6 yd. = _____ in.

16. 2,640 ft. = _____ mi.

You can use the strategies about ratios and proportion you have learned so far to solve more difficult problems.

First, underline the <u>important information</u> that you will need to solve the problem.	Peaches are <u>8 for $2</u>. Jill bought <u>12 peaches</u>. <u>How much did she spend</u>?
Next, determine which operation is best for solving the problem.	The ratio is $2 for 8 peaches, or 2 to 8, or $\dfrac{\$2}{8 \text{ peaches}}$. Divide to find the unit rate, or the cost of one peach.
Then, write a math sentence using the information.	$\dfrac{\$2}{8 \text{ peaches}} = \$0.25$ per peach 12 peaches × cost per peach = total spent
Finally, solve the problem.	$12 \times 0.25 = 3$ Jill spent $3 on 12 peaches.

Practice

Solve the problems. Show your work in the space provided.

1. A frozen-yogurt factory makes 100 quarts of frozen yogurt in 5 hours. How many quarts could be made in 36 hours? What was the rate per day?

   1.

2. A jet travels 590 miles in 5 hours. At this rate, how far could the jet fly in 10 hours? What is the rate of speed of the jet?

   2.

3. You can buy 5 cans of green beans at Village Market for $2.30, or you can buy 10 of them at Best Food for $5.10. Which place has the better deal?

   3.

Review

Use everything you have learned so far about ratios, proportions, unit rates, ratio graphing, and measurement conversion to solve the problems.

Complete the proportion equations.

1. $\dfrac{\square}{12} = \dfrac{5}{4}$

2. $\dfrac{15}{21} = \dfrac{\square}{7}$

3. $\dfrac{5}{\square} = \dfrac{20}{24}$

4. $\dfrac{\square}{10} = \dfrac{21}{15}$

Solve each problem.

5. A ferris wheel can accommodate 55 people in 15 minutes. How many people could ride the ferris wheel in 2 hours? What is the rate per hour?

6. Laura earns $7 per hour babysitting for her neighbor. How much will Laura make if she babysits for 4 hours?

7. Sweaters are 3 for $50. Leslie and her mother spent $100 on sweaters. How many did they buy?

8. Jamal can ride his bike 5 miles in 2 hours. At this rate, how long will it take him to ride 20 miles? Complete the table to solve.

Miles	5			20
Hours	2			

9. Genny can make 7 bracelets in 3 hours. At this rate, how many bracelets can she make in 9 hours? Complete the table to solve.

Bracelets	7		
Hours	3		9

5.

6.

7.

9.

10.

A percent is a part of 100. The symbol % (percent) means $\frac{1}{100}$ or 0.01 (one hundredth). Use the following steps to find the percent as a fraction and as decimal.

Solve: Write 7% as a fraction and as a decimal.

First, write the percent as a fraction over 100. Write it in simplest form.	$7\% = 7 \times \frac{1}{100}$ $= \frac{7}{1} \times \frac{1}{100}$ $= \frac{7}{100}$
Next, write the percent as a decimal in the hundredths place.	$7\% = 7 \times 0.01$ $= 0.07$

Practice

Write each percent as a fraction and as a decimal.

	Percent	Fraction	Decimal
1.	2%	_____	_____
2.	8%	_____	_____
3.	27%	_____	_____
4.	13%	_____	_____
5.	68%	_____	_____
6.	72%	_____	_____
7.	56%	_____	_____
8.	11%	_____	_____

Percents and Fractions

You can find a **percent** of a number by multiplying fractions.

Solve: Find 35% of 60.

First, write the **percent** as a fraction over 100.

$$35\% = \frac{35}{100}$$

Next, multiply the **fraction** by the **whole number**. The word "of" tells us to multiply because we are finding a part "of" a whole.

$$\frac{35}{100} \times 60 = \frac{35}{100} \times \frac{60}{1}$$

Finally, solve and write the answer in simplest form. You can simplify the **fraction** *before* you multiply for an easier problem.

$$\frac{35}{100} = \frac{7}{20}$$

$$\frac{7}{20} \times \frac{60}{1} = \frac{420}{20} = \frac{42}{2} = 21$$

$$35\% \text{ of } 60 = 21$$

Practice

Solve the following problems. Write the answers as fractions in simplest form.

1. 40% of 20 = _____

2. 80% of 80 = _____

3. 40% of 32 = _____

4. 8% of 65 = _____

5. 30% of 32 = _____

6. 90% of 60 = _____

7. 28% of 7 = _____

8. 12% of 40 = _____

9. 45% of 50 = _____

10. 18% of 45 = _____

11. 36% of 80 = _____

12. 27% of 60 = _____

13. 14% of 70 = _____

14. 38% of 50 = _____

You can find a percentage of a number by multiplying decimals.

Solve: Find 26% of 73.2.

First, write the percent as a decimal in the hundredths place.	26% = 0.26
Next, multiply the decimal by the number you're trying to find the percentage of. This number could be a decimal or a whole number.	0.26 × 73.2

Finally, solve the problem.

$$\begin{array}{r} 73.2 \\ \times\ 0.26 \\ \hline 4392 \\ +1464 \\ \hline 19.032 \end{array}$$

26% of 73.2 = 19.032

Practice

Solve the following problems.

1. 40% of 95 = _____

2. 12% of 200 = _____

3. 26% of 40 = _____

4. 73% of 8.4 = _____

5. 49% of 7.6 = _____

6. 88% of 32.5 = _____

7. 55% of 55.55 = _____

8. 99% of 45.8 = _____

9. 78% of 48 = _____

10. 36% of 72 = _____

11. 21% of 9.9 = _____

12. 56% of 41 = _____

Finding Percents

Follow these steps to find out what percent a number is of another number.

Solve: 50 is what percent of 80?

First, write the problem as an equation with a **variable**.

$$50 = n\% \times 80$$

$$50 = \frac{n}{100} \times 80$$

Next, solve to find the value of the **variable**. Use the reciprocal operation to get the variable alone on one side of the equation. The reciprocal operation of division is multiplication. **Multiply** both sides of the equation by 100 and then **divide** by 80 to get the *n* variable alone.

$$50 = \frac{80n}{100}$$

$$50 \times 100 = \frac{80n}{100} \times 100$$

$$5,000 = 80n$$

$$5,000 \div 80 = 80n \div 80$$

$$62.5 = n$$

50 is 62.5% of 80.

Practice

Solve the following problems.

1. 15 is _____ % of 100.

2. 12 is _____% of 20.

3. 48 is _____% of 64.

4. 19 is _____% of 95.

5. 12 is _____% of 32.

6. 35 is _____% of 56.

7. 27 is _____% of 90.

8. 18 is _____% of 45.

9. 32 is _____% of 40.

10. 21 is _____% of 24.

11. 42 is _____% of 56.

12. 63 is _____% of 90.

Math

Follow these steps to find out what percent a number is of a fraction or a decimal.

Solve: $\frac{1}{4}$ is what percent of $\frac{5}{8}$?

First, write the problem as an equation with a **variable**.

$$\frac{1}{4} = n\% \times \frac{5}{8}$$

$$\frac{1}{4} = \frac{n}{100} \times \frac{5}{8}$$

Next, solve to find the value of the **variable**. Use the reciprocal operation to get the variable alone on one side of the equation. The reciprocal operation of division is multiplication. **Multiply** both sides of the equation by 800 and then **divide** by 5 to get the *n* variable alone.

$$\frac{1}{4} = \frac{5n}{800}$$

$$\frac{1}{4} \times 800 = \frac{5n}{800} \times 800$$

$$\frac{800}{4} = 5n$$

$$200 = 5n$$

$$200 \div 5 = 5n \div 5$$

$$40 = n$$

$\frac{1}{4}$ is 40% of $\frac{5}{8}$.

Math

Practice

Solve the following problems.

1. $\frac{1}{3}$ is _____% of $\frac{5}{6}$.

2. 1.8 is _____% of 6.

3. 0.9 is _____% of 4.5.

4. $\frac{1}{5}$ is _____% of $\frac{8}{10}$.

5. 2.4 is _____% of 16.

6. 0.72 is _____% of 1.2.

Problem Solving

You can use the percent strategies you have learned so far to solve more difficult problems.

First, underline the <u>important information</u> that you will need to solve the problem.

The sales tax on the purchase of a refrigerator that costs <u>$695</u> is <u>7 percent</u>. <u>What is the amount of sales tax?</u>

Next, determine which operation is best for solving the problem.

Multiply to find 7% of 695. The word "of" tells us we will multiply.

Then, write a math sentence using the information.

$0.07 \times 695 =$ amount of sales tax

Finally, solve the problem.

$$\begin{array}{r} 695 \\ \times\ 0.07 \\ \hline \$48.65 \end{array}$$

The 7% sales tax of $695 is $48.65.

Practice

Solve the problems. Show your work in the space provided.

1. In math class, 60% of the students are males. There are 30 students in the class. How many students are males?

   1.

2. Lauren is saving for gymnastics camp. Camp costs $225 to attend. She has 40 percent of the money saved. How much money has she saved?

   2.

3. East Side Middle School has 1,500 students. Thirty-two percent of them are in sixth grade. How many sixth-grade students are there?

   3.

Use everything you have learned so far about percents to solve the following problems.

Write the equivalent decimal and fraction for each percent.

	Percent	Decimal	Fraction
1.	6%	_____	_____
2.	37%	_____	_____
3.	110%	_____	_____

For each fraction or decimal, write the equivalent percent.

4. $\frac{4}{25}$ _____

5. 0.05 _____

6. $\frac{3}{5}$ _____

7. 0.8 _____

8. $\frac{7}{8}$ _____

9. 1.3 _____

Solve the problems.

10. 24 is 30% of _____.

11. 20% of 75 is _____.

12. 6.2 is _____% of 124.

13. 42 is _____% of 50.

14. 112 is 70% of _____.

15. 9 is 12.5% of _____.

Math

Chapter Review

Write the ratios in three different ways.

1. 15 feet out of 36 feet

   _____

2. 10 pints to 20 pints

   _____

3. 28 red bikes to 40 bikes

   _____

4. 18 beetles out of 72 insects

   _____

Express each ratio as a fraction in simplest form.

5. There are 5 blue marbles and 16 red marbles in a box. Write the ratio of blue marbles to red marbles.

   5.

6. There are 6 pennies and 10 dimes in a jar. Write the ratio of pennies to dimes.

   6.

7. There are 12 dogs and 7 cats in a park. Write the ratio of cats to dogs.

   7.

8. There are 24 butterflies and 16 snails on the ground. Write the ratio of butterflies to snails.

   8.

Solve to find the value of the variable.

9. $\dfrac{7}{12} = \dfrac{n}{36}$

10. $\dfrac{9}{2} = \dfrac{27}{n}$

11. $\dfrac{7}{1} = \dfrac{n}{3}$

12. $\dfrac{35}{n} = \dfrac{4}{8}$

13. $\dfrac{n}{12} = \dfrac{25}{30}$

14. $\dfrac{7}{n} = \dfrac{21}{12}$

Solve the word problems.

15. Corn costs $2 for 6 ears. Carmen bought 24 ears of corn. How much did she spend?

15. _____

16. Tomatoes are 5 for $2. Keith spent $8 on tomatoes. How many tomatoes did he get?

16. _____

17. A recipe calls for 2 cups of sugar to 3 cups of flour. How much sugar will you use if you triple the recipe and use 9 cups of flour?

17. _____

18. Malik scores 24 goals in 8 soccer games. At that rate, how many goals will he score in 15 games?

18. _____

Solve the problem.

19. Ms. Rivera recorded her students' average study hours per week and their grade in the class, as shown in the table. Make a graph of the data. Label the x- and y-axis.

Student	Study hours per Week	Grade in the Class
Sheree	5	98
Paul	1.5	60
Tim	4	90
Marcus	4.5	93
Linda	2	70
Alicia	3	84
Pat	2	65

Study Hours and Grade in the Class

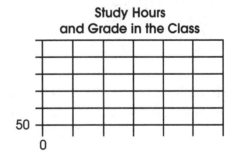

Based on your graph, how are number of study hours related to grade?

_____

Complete the following measurement conversions.

20. 7 yd. 2 ft. = _____ ft.

21. 7 yd. 2 ft. = _____ in.

22. 24 ft. = _____ yd.

23. 11 ft. 9 in. = _____ in.

Solve the percent problems. Where needed, write answers using decimals.

24. 25% of 28 = _____

25. 10% of 38 = _____

26. 9% of 60 = _____

27. 80% of 256 = _____

28. 7.5% of 60 = _____

29. 1.2% of 385 = _____

30. 12 is _____% of 32.

31. 64 is _____% of 51.2.

32. 5.6 is _____% of 2.8.

33. 68 is _____% of 80.

Solve the word problems.

34. In Keon's homeroom class, $\frac{3}{5}$ of the students participate in sports. What percent of students participate in sports?

34.

35. The Franklins are taking a cross-country trip. They will drive 3,150 miles in all. On the first day, they drove 567 miles. What percent of their trip did they drive?

35.

36. Pete's dog weighed 30 pounds. It then lost 16% of its weight. How much did Pete's dog lose?

36.

37. Karla has read 85% of her book, which amounts to 238 pages. How long is the book?

37.

Math

Positive and Negative Integers

An integer is a number that does not contain a fractional part or a decimal. Integers include all positive and negative numbers, as well as zero. A positive integer is greater than zero and lies to the right of zero on a horizontal number line. A negative integer is less than zero and lies to the left of zero on a number line. Every positive integer has an opposite, negative number. Follow these steps to find opposite integers.

Solve: What is the opposite of 3?

First, plot the integer on a number line. 3 is a positive integer because it is to the right of zero.

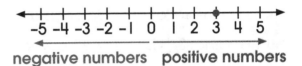

negative numbers   positive numbers

Next, find the opposite integer. The opposite integer is the same number with the opposite sign (positive or negative.) So the opposite of positive 3 is negative 3, or –3. Notice that opposite integers are the same distance from zero (3 is three units from 0 and –3 is three units from 0.)

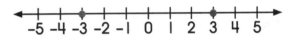

The opposite integer of 3 is –3.

Practice

Name the opposite of each number.

1. The opposite of 10 is _____.

2. The opposite of 1 is _____.

3. The opposite of 4 is _____.

4. The opposite of 13 is _____.

5. The opposite of –32 is _____.

6. The opposite of –20 is _____.

7. The opposite of –11 is _____.

8. The opposite of –3 is _____.

9. The opposite of –19 is _____.

10. The opposite of –6 is _____.

Positive and Negative Rational Numbers

A rational number is a number that can be made by dividing two integers. Rational numbers, unlike integers, include fractional parts and decimals. **Positive** rational numbers lie to the right of zero on a horizontal number line, while negative rational numbers lie to the left of zero. You can plot rational numbers and their opposites on a number line in the same way you plot integers.

Solve: Find the opposite of $3\frac{1}{2}$.

First, plot the rational number on a number line. $3\frac{1}{2}$ is halfway between positive 3 and 4 on the number line.

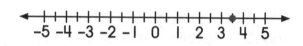

Next, plot the opposite rational number on the number line. $-3\frac{1}{2}$ is between –3 and –4 on the number line.

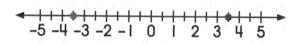

The opposite of $3\frac{1}{2}$ is $-3\frac{1}{2}$.

Practice

Plot the rational numbers and their opposite on the number line.

1. –0.75

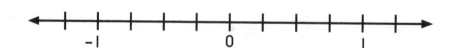

2. $\frac{4}{6}$

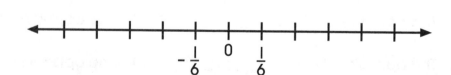

Integers can be used to describe real-life situations. Think about what the situation is describing and how it relates to positive and negative integers.

Solve: A driver is going 15 miles per hour below the speed limit. How can this be represented by an integer?

First, underline the word in the problem that tells you if this is a positive or negative integer. Here, the word "below" tells us that it is less than, or under, the speed limit.	A driver is going 15 miles per hour <u>below</u> the speed limit.
Next, write the number as a positive or negative integer. This situation can be described with a negative integer, so we will write a negative sign in front of the number.	*15 miles per hour <u>below</u> the speed limit* can be shown with the integer –15.

Practice

Use integers to represent each real-life situation.

1. 45 feet below sea level

   _____

2. a gain of 8 yards on a play

   _____

3. $528 deposit into a checking account

   _____

4. 62° above zero

   _____

5. 10 units to the left on a number line

   _____

6. withdrawal of $95 from an ATM

   _____

7. stock market decrease of 97 points

   _____

8. 34° below zero

   _____

9. 6,000 feet above sea level

   _____

Absolute Value

The absolute value of a number is its distance from zero. Therefore, the absolute value of a number is always positive. Absolute value is represented by vertical lines on either side of an integer. Find the absolute value of an integer by following these steps.

Solve: What is $|-8|$? Or, what is the absolute value of -8?

First, think of the distance from zero of the given integer on a number line.	The distance from zero of -8 on a number line is 8 units.
Next, write the number as an absolute value.	The absolute value of -8 is 8. $$|-8| = 8$$ $|-8|$ means "the absolute value of -8."

Practice

Find the absolute value of each integer.

1. $|4| =$ _____

2. $|-13| =$ _____

3. $|11| =$ _____

4. $|-2| =$ _____

5. $|-21| =$ _____

6. $|1| =$ _____

7. $-|8| =$ _____
Think: This is the opposite of the absolute value of 8.

8. $-|-15| =$ _____

9. $-|-41| =$ _____

Comparing and Ordering Integers

You can compare and order integers on a number line. A negative integer is always less than a positive integer. The farther away a negative integer is from zero, the less its value is. When comparing two negative integers, the integer that is closer to zero is greater. To compare integers, follow these steps.

Solve: Compare the following integers: 4, –4, –9, and –2. List them from *greatest* to *least*.

First, plot the integers on a number line.

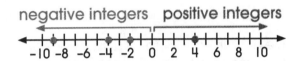

Next, compare the size of the integers based on their **distance from zero**.

4 is the greatest because it is a positive integer. –2 is only 2 units away from 0, while –4 is 4 units away, and –9 is 9 units away.

Finally, list the integers in the order the problem states.

The integers listed from greatest to least are 4, –2, –4, and –9.

Math

Practice

Use the number line to list the integers in order from least to greatest.

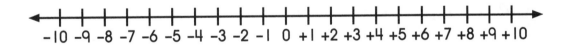

1. –3, –5, 0 _____

2. 8, –8, 2 _____

3. 0, 5, –2, –3, 2 _____

4. –6, 5, –2, –3, 2 _____

Comparing and Ordering Integers

You can compare integers using a <, >, or = sign.

Solve: Compare –4 and –6 using <, >, or =.

First, compare the size of the integers based on their **distance from zero**.

–4 is 4 units away from 0, while –6 is 6 units away from 0. Since 4 units away from 0 is closer to 0 than 6 units away, –4 is greater than –6.

Next, write a <, >, or = sign between the integers to show the comparison.

–4 is greater than –6

–4 > –6

Practice

Compare the integers using <, >, or =.

1. 66 ☐ 3

2. –24 ☐ 82

3. 88 ☐ –99

4. 99 ☐ –84

5. –37 ☐ –37

6. –33 ☐ –90

7. –27 ☐ –52

8. –49 ☐ –69

9. –8 ☐ –45

10. –1 ☐ 0

11. 8 ☐ –18

12. –4 ☐ –1

13. –7 ☐ –9

14. –83 ☐ 81

15. –11 ☐ –11

Ordered Pairs and the Coordinate Plane

Positive and negative integers can be graphed as ordered pairs on a coordinate plane. An ordered pair is two numbers written in (x, y) order. The first number in an ordered pair represents its point on the x-axis, or the horizontal axis. The second number represents the point on the y-axis, or the vertical axis.

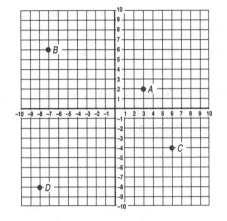

Solve: Name the ordered pairs on the coordinate plane shown here.

First, to find the x-coordinate of the ordered pair for **Point A**, count how many units the point is from zero on the x-axis.

Point A is 3 units from 0 to the right on the x-axis. That makes the x-coordinate of the ordered pair 3.

Next, find the y-coordinate of the ordered pair. Count how many units the point is from zero on the y-axis.

Point A is 2 units from 0 on the y-axis. That makes the y-coordinate of the ordered pair 2.

Finally, repeat for the other ordered pairs.

Point A: (3, 2)   Point B: (–7, 6)

Point C: (6, –4)   Point D: (–8, –8)

Remember to list the ordered pairs in (x, y) order.

Math

Practice

Use the coordinate plane to write the ordered pair for each point.

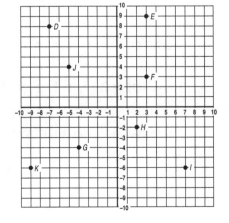

1. D _____

2. E _____

3. G _____

4. H _____

5. K _____

6. J _____

Ordered Pairs and the Coordinate Plane

You can use coordinate planes to answer questions about the distance between two points.

Solve: What is the distance between **Point F** and **Point C**? Use the coordinate plane to solve.

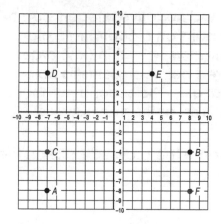

First, count along the *x*-axis between the two points. Begin at the first point in the problem (**Point F.**) Stop when you are in line with the other point (**Point C.**)

Next, count along the *y*-axis between the two points.

Finally, add the distances together to find out the total distance between two points.

Starting at **Point F**, move 15 units left along the *x*-axis to be on the same *y*-coordinate line as **Point C**.

From **Point F**, move 4 units up along the *y*-axis to get to **Point C**.

$$15 + 4 = 19$$

Point F and Point C are 19 units apart.

Practice

Use the coordinate plane above and the key shown here to answer the questions.

> A = stream
> D = school
> B = home
> E = park
> C = bookstore
> F = fire station

1. How far is it from school to the park? _____ units

2. How far is it from the fire station to the stream? _____ units

3. How far is it from the bookstore to home? _____ units

4. How far is it from the stream to the park? _____ units

5. How far is it from home to the fire station? _____ units

You can use the integer strategies you have learned so far to solve more difficult problems.

First, underline the <u>important information</u> that you will need to solve the problem.

An elevator <u>started at the first floor</u> and went <u>up 18</u> floors. It then came <u>down 11</u> floors and went <u>back up 16</u>. At what floor was it stopped?

Next, determine which operation is best for solving the problem.

This problem involves adding and subtracting, or the positive and negative integers 18, –11, and 16.

Then, write a math sentence using the information.

1 + 18 – 11 + 16 = the final floor

Finally, solve the problem.

$$1 + 18 = 19$$
$$19 - 11 = 8$$
$$8 + 16 = 24$$

The elevator stopped on the 24th floor.

Practice

Solve the problems. Show your work in the space provided.

1. At midnight, the temperature was 30°F. By 6:00 a.m., it had dropped 5° and by noon, it had increased by 11°. What was the temperature at noon?

    1.

2. During one week, the stock market did the following: Monday rose 18 points, Tuesday rose 31 points, Wednesday dropped 5 points, Thursday rose 27 points, and Friday dropped 38 points. If it started out at 1,196 on Monday, what did it end up at on Friday?

    2.

3. A submarine was located 350 feet below sea level. If it descends 125 feet, and then ascends 75 feet, what is its new location?

    3.

Chapter Review

Name the opposite of each number.

1. The opposite of 8 is _____.

2. The opposite of –1 is _____.

3. The opposite of 5 is _____.

4. The opposite of 35 is _____.

5. The opposite of –21 is _____.

6. The opposite of –16 is _____.

Find the absolute value of each integer.

7. $|-3|$ = _____

8. $|10|$ = _____

9. $|5|$ = _____

10. $|-9|$ = _____

11. $|23|$ = _____

12. $|-7|$ = _____

13. $|-13|$ = _____

14. $|-5|$ = _____

15. $|-1|$ = _____

Compare the integers using < , > , or =.

16. 82 ☐ 91

17. 31 ☐ –27

18. –44 ☐ –84

19. 23 ☐ 74

20. –10 ☐ 70

21. 51 ☐ 24

22. 74 ☐ –42

23. 99 ☐ 66

24. –23 ☐ –21

Write the numbers in order from least to greatest.

25. –89, 42, –26, 8 _____

26. –84, 91, –57, –90 _____

27. 20, –81, –5, 87 _____

28. 73, 53, 89, 55 _____

29. –91, –46, 52, 12 _____

30. 22, 41, –23, –38 _____

Use the coordinate plane to answer the questions.

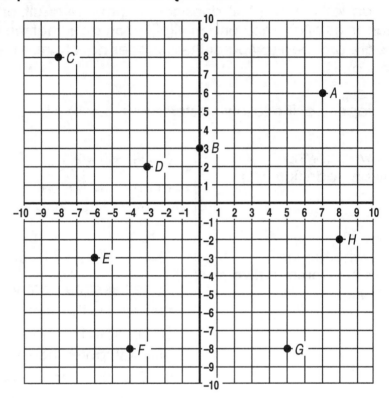

Write the ordered pair for each point.

31. A _____

32. C _____

33. E _____

34. G _____

Name the point located at each ordered pair.

35. (8, –2) _____

36. (–3, 2) _____

37. (–4, –8) _____

38. (0, 3) _____

Mark the following points on the coordinate plane.

39. *I* at (4, –3)   40. *J* at (–8, –5)   41. *K* at (–5, –5)   42. *L* at (6, 2)

Math

Properties: Commutative and Associative

The Commutative Properties of addition and multiplication state that the order in which numbers are added or multiplied does not change the result, or $a + b = b + a$. The Associative Properties of addition and multiplication state that the way in which addends or factors are grouped (by parentheses) does not change the result, or $(a \times b) \times c = a \times (b \times c)$.

Solve: Identify the property of the following statement: $(2 \times 4) \times 5 = 2 \times (4 \times 5)$

First, determine whether the statement shows an **addition** or a multiplication property.

$(2 \times 4) \times 5 = 2 \times (4 \times 5)$

This is a multiplication problem, so it shows a multiplication property.

Next, determine whether the statement shows the Commutative or Associative Property.

$(2 \times 4) \times 5 = 2 \times (4 \times 5)$

Since this statement shows the numbers in the same order but grouped in two different ways, (first with parentheses around the 2 and 4, and then with parentheses around 4 and 5) this is an Associative Property of Multiplication problem.

Practice

Name the property shown by each statement.

1. $2 \times 8 = 8 \times 2$ _____

2. $2 + (3 + 4) = (2 + 3) + 4$ _____

3. $32 + 25 = 25 + 32$ _____

4. $119 \times 120 = 120 \times 119$ _____

5. $6 \times (2 \times 3) = (6 \times 2) \times 3$ _____

6. $5 \times (5 \times 5) = (5 \times 5) \times 5$ _____

The Identity Property of Addition states that the sum of an addend and 0 is the addend, or $a + 0 = a$. The Identity Property of Multiplication states that the product of a factor and 1 is that factor, or $a \times 1 = a$. The Properties of Zero state that the product of a factor and 0 is 0, or $a \times 0 = 0$. The Properties of Zero also state that the quotient of zero and any non-zero divisor is 0, or $0 \div 5 = 0$. Numbers cannot be divided by zero.

Solve: Identify the property of the following statement: $5 + 0 = 5$

First, determine whether the statement shows an **addition** or a multiplication property.	$5 + 0 = 5$ This is an **addition** problem, so it shows an **addition** property.
Next, determine whether the statement shows the **Identity** or Zero Property.	$5 + 0 = 5$ Since this statement shows an addend (5) plus 0 this shows the Identity Property of Addition.

Practice

Name the property shown by each statement.

1. $35 \times 1 = 35$ _____

2. $0 \times 9 = 0$ _____

3. $45 + 0 = 45$ _____

4. $18 \times 0 = 0$ _____

5. $0 \div 12 = 0$ _____

6. $1 \times 1 = 1$ _____

Math

Distributive Property

The Distributive Property combines addition and multiplication operations. It states that multiplying a number by a group of numbers added together is the same as doing each multiplication step separately, or $a \times (b + c) = (a \times b) + (a \times c)$. Follow these steps to rewrite an expression using the Distributive Property.

Solve: Rewrite the following expression using the Distributive Property: $3 \times (2 + 5)$

First, **distribute** the first number to the other numbers in the expression. (An expression is a mathematical phrase that does not include an equal sign or answer). So, the 3 can be distributed to the 2 and the 5 in the expression.

$$3 \times (2 + 5)$$

$$3 \times (2 + 5) = (3 \times 2) + (3 \times 5)$$

Next, solve both sides of the equation to check your work. They should be equal!

$$3 \times (2 + 5) = (3 \times 2) + (3 \times 5)$$
$$3 \times 7 = 6 + 15$$
$$21 = 21$$

Practice

Rewrite each expression using the Distributive Property.

1. $4 \times (6 + 2) = $ _____

2. $(2 \times 5) + (2 \times 4) = $ _____

3. $(5 \times 1) + (5 \times 6) = $ _____

4. $4 \times (2 + 6) = $ _____

5. $8 \times (4 + 3) = $ _____

6. $(5 \times 0) + (5 \times 1) = $ _____

Exponents

When a number is written as an exponent, it has a base number and an exponent that tells us how many times the base is used as a factor. In 2^5, 2 is the base and 5 is the exponent. It tells us that 2 will be multiplied 5 times.

Solve: 2^5

First, determine which number is the base and which is the exponent.

Next, multiply the base by itself as many times as the exponent tells you to. 2^5 tells us to multiply 2 five times.

base ← 2^5 → exponent

$$2^5 = 2 \times 2 \times 2 \times 2 \times 2$$
$$= 4 \times 4 \times 2$$
$$= 16 \times 2$$
$$2^5 = 32$$

Practice

Calculate each exponent.

1. 3^3 _____

2. 5^5 _____

3. 1^6 _____

4. 12^2 _____

5. 8^3 _____

6. 6^3 _____

7. 7^4 _____

8. 4^4 _____

9. 11^4 _____

Math

Exponents

You can write exponents from expressions by following these steps. A number with an exponent is exponential notation.

Solve: Write $9 \times 9 \times 9 \times 9$ in exponential notation.

First, determine the base, and count the number of factors to determine the exponent.	9 is the base. It is used 4 times, so 4 will be the exponent.
Then write the expression in exponential notation.	$9 \times 9 \times 9 \times 9 = 9^4$

Practice

Use exponents to rewrite each expression in exponential notation.

1. $3 \times 3 \times 3$ _____

2. 8×8 _____

3. $7 \times 7 \times 7 \times 7 \times 7$ _____

4. 24×24 _____

5. $4 \times 4 \times 4$ _____

6. $6 \times 6 \times 6 \times 6 \times 6 \times 6$ _____

7. $2 \times 2 \times 2 \times 2$ _____

8. $38 \times 38 \times 38$ _____

9. $5 \times 5 \times 5 \times 5 \times 5$ _____

10. 8 _____

Use the order of operations to find the value of an expression with more than one operation.

Solve: $3 \times (4 + 5) + 6 \div 3$

First, perform the operation inside the parentheses.	$3 \times (4 + 5) + 6 \div 3$ $4 + 5 = 9$
Next, multiply and divide in order from left to right.	$3 \times 9 + 6 \div 3$ In this case, 3×9 is solved first, then $6 \div 3$.
Finally, add.	$27 + 2 = 29$

Practice

Circle the operation or operations that should be completed first.

1. $2 + 3 + (4 \times 6) - 7$

2. $3 \times 5 + 2 + 4$

3. $(2 \div 1) \times 4 \times 10$

4. $5 + 5 + 5 + 10 \div 5$

5. $5 \times (3 - 2) + 7$

6. $7 \times 6 \div 7 \times (5 + 5)$

Order of Operations

You can use the order of operations to help you solve expressions with exponents. An exponent of a number tells us how many times to multiply a base number.

Solve: $3 + 2^3 \times (4 - 1) \div 2$

First, perform all operations within parentheses.	$3 + 2^3 \times (4 - 1) \div 2$ $3 + 2^3 \times 3 \div 2$
Next, perform all operations with exponents. The exponent of 3 tells us we will multiply the base, 2, three times.	$3 + 2^3 \times 3 \div 2$ $2^3 = 2 \times 2 \times 2$ $3 + 8 \times 3 \div 2$
Then, multiply and divide in order from left to right.	$3 + 8 \times 3 \div 2$ $3 + 24 \div 2$ $3 + 12$
Finally, add and subtract in order from left to right.	$3 + 12 = 15$

Practice

Find the value of each expression.

1. $5 \times (5 - 3)$ _____

2. $(7 \times 8) - (4 \times 9)$ _____

3. $15 \div 3 + 16 \div 4$ _____

4. $3^2 + 5 - 1 \times 2$ _____

5. $24 \div 2 + (3 \times 4)$ _____

6. $(40 - 10) \times 10^2$ _____

7. $8 \times 8 \div 8 + 8 - 8$ _____

8. $20 + (2^4 - 8) \times 2$ _____

Scientific notation is expressed by writing a number as the product of a number between one and ten and a power of ten. The powers of ten are 10, 100, 1,000, and so on. You can refer to the chart and follow these steps to write a number in scientific notation.

10^1	10	10
10^2	10×10	100
10^3	$10 \times 10 \times 10$	$1,000$
10^4	$10 \times 10 \times 10 \times 10$	$10,000$
10^5	$10 \times 10 \times 10 \times 10 \times 10$	$100,000$

Solve: Write 3,000 in scientific notation.

First, write the base number. The base number is the number between one and ten that is in front of the zeros.	3,000 The base number is 3.
Next, count the number of zeros in the number.	3,000 There are 3 zeros.
Then, write the number of zeros as an exponent of 10.	$1,000 = 10^3$
Finally, write the base number multiplied by the exponent. This is the number in scientific notation.	3×10^3

Practice

Use the table above to help you write each number in scientific notation.

1. 30 _____

2. 4,000 _____

3. 50,000 _____

4. 600,000 _____

5. 700 _____

6. 90 _____

7. 40,000 _____

8. 100,000 _____

9. 400 _____

Math

Parts of an Expression

An algebraic expression is a combination of numbers, variables, and at least one operation. A variable is a symbol, usually a letter, that represents an unknown number or quantity. An expression does not include an equal sign or an answer. An equation is a number sentence that contains an equal sign. You can change a phrase into an expression or an equation by following these steps.

Solve: Write as an expression or an equation: 3 times the sum of 2 and n is 15.

First, determine whether the phrase is an **expression** or an equation.	This is an equation because "is 15" is an answer and "is" acts as an equal sign.
Next, underline the operation(s) in the phrase. "Times" means to multiply and "sum" means to add.	3 <u>times</u> the <u>sum</u> of 2 and n is 15
Then, circle the **numbers and variable(s)** in the phrase.	③ <u>times</u> the <u>sum</u> of ② and ⓝ is ⑮
Finally, write the equation. Write the operations as symbols and keep the variable the same.	$3 \times (2 + n) = 15$

Practice

Write each phrase as an expression or an equation.

1. five more than n

    _____

2. x added to seven

    _____

3. six times a number is 18

    _____

4. eight divided by a number is 2

    _____

5. the product of n and 11

    _____

6. seventy minus a number is 29

    _____

Math

Parts of an Expression

There are two parts of an expression— a term and a coefficient. A term is a number, variable, product, or quotient in an expression. There can be more than one term in an expression. A coefficient is a number used to multiply a variable. Use the following steps to identify the parts of an expression.

Solve: Identify the parts of the expression $3a + 5$.

First, identify the **terms**. This expression has two terms. Terms are separated by a plus or minus sign.

$$\underline{3a} + \underline{5}$$
$3a$ and 5 are both terms.

Next, identify the **coefficient**. A coefficient is the number that is used to multiply a variable.

$3a + 5$
The coefficient is 3 because it is used to multiply the variable a.

Practice

Identify the terms and the coefficient of each expression.

1. $2 + 6x$

   terms: _____ and _____

   coefficient: _____

2. $42 - 4b$

   terms: _____ and _____

   coefficient: _____

3. $12n - (4 \times 3)$

   terms: _____ and _____

   coefficient: _____

4. $5a + (2 - 1)$

   terms: _____ and _____

   coefficient: _____

5. $10y + 10$

   terms: _____ and _____

   coefficient: _____

6. $(2 + 3) + 14n$

   terms: _____ and _____

   coefficient: _____

Writing Expressions and Equations

You can write an equation or an algebraic expression in words using **variables**, **terms**, and **coefficients**.

Solve: Write an expression or equation for "four times a number, plus 2, is 6."

First, determine the **variable**. You can choose any letter you want for a variable to stand for an unknown. It's common to use the first letter of the word, so we can use *n* for "number."

Four times a **number**, plus 2, is 6.

The variable is *n*.

Next, determine the **operation(s)**. Look for key words and vocabulary that tell you which operation to use.

Four **times** a number, **plus** 2, is 6.

This statement has two operations: multiplication (times) and addition (plus).

Finally, write the expression or equation. This statement is an equation because it includes an answer, 6.

$4 \times n + 2 = 6$ OR

$4n + 2 = 6$

Practice

Translate each phrase into an expression or an equation.

1. *x* increased by 5

   _____

2. 11 decreased by a number is 7.

   _____

3. Seven times *s*

   _____

4. *c* less than 7

   _____

5. the product of 15 and *m*

   _____

6. one-fourth of *x* is 5

   _____

7. 8 times a number, plus 4, is 84.

   _____

8. a number added to 12 is 23

   _____

9. A number divided by 5 is 6.

   _____

You can use the expressions and equations strategies you have learned so far to solve more difficult problems.

First, underline the <u>important information</u> that you will need to write the equation.

Martha bought <u>I soft drink for $3.00</u> and <u>4 candy bars</u>. She spent a <u>total of $11.00</u>. Write an equation that will help you find the cost for each candy bar.

Next, determine which operation and variable is best for solving the problem.

This is an equation because there is an answer (the total of $11.00.) The unknown is the cost of candy bars. Because Martha bought 4 of them, we will multiply 4 times a variable, *c*, for candy bar. We will add $3 for the soft drink to that and have it equal the total of $11.

Finally, write an equation using the information.

$$4 \times \text{candy bars} + \$3 \text{ soft drink} = \$11$$
$$4c + 3 = 11$$

Practice

Write equations for each situation.

1. 248 students went on a trip to the zoo. All 6 buses were filled and 8 students had to travel in cars. Write an expression or equation that will help you find out how many students rode in each bus.

    1.

2. Todd sold half of his comic books and then bought 6 more. He now has 16. Write an equation that will help you find out how many comic books Todd had at the beginning.

    2.

3. A bike shop charges $12.00, plus $6.00 an hour, for renting a bike. Mike paid $48.00 to rent a bike. Write an equation that will help you find out how many hours Mike rented the bike.

    3.

Simple Steps • Sixth Grade **Expressions and Equations** 75

Use everything you have learned so far about expressions and equations to solve the problems.

Name the property shown in each statement: Associative, Commutative, or Identity.

1. $3 \times (6 \times 2) = (3 \times 6) \times 2$

    _____

2. $15 \times 1 = 1$

    _____

3. $(3 + 5) + 2 = 3 + (5 + 2)$

    _____

4. $112 \times 12 = 12 \times 112$

    _____

Rewrite each expression using the Distributive Property.

5. $3 \times (5 - 2)$ _____

6. $(5 \times 2) + (8 \times 2)$ _____

Write each problem as a product of factors.

7. 2^4 _____

8. 9^2 _____

9. 5^3 _____

10. 4^2 _____

11. 8^5 _____

12. 7^3 _____

Solve each problem using the order of operations.

13. $2^3 \times 4 + (6 \div 2)$ _____

14. $(12 \times 2) \div 2 + 4^2$ _____

15. $48 \div (12 - 8) \times (12 - 10)$ _____

16. $(3^3 + 3) \div (5 \times 2) - 3$ _____

Write the expression for each statement.

17. The product of 4 and the difference between 8 and 3 _____

18. 4 increased by the product of 5 and 3 _____

19. The difference between 16 and the product of 4 and 2 _____

20. The quotient of 25 and 5 increased by 3 _____

You can use the Distributive Property or combine like terms to simplify expressions. Follow these steps. If there is more than one variable in an expression, use the Distributive Property to simplify. If there are at least two of the same variable in an expression, combine like terms to simplify.

Simplify: $3(x + 2y)$ using the Distributive Property.

First, use the **Distributive Property** to distribute the first factor to the other factors in the next term. Both x and $2y$ can be multiplied by 3.

Then, write the **simplified** expression.

$$3x + 6y$$

$$3(x + 2y)$$

$$3x + (3 \times 2y)$$

Simplify: Simplify $6m - 4m + 3p$ by combining like terms.

First, **combine the like terms.** Like terms are terms that have the same variable. Here, $6m$ and $4m$ are like terms.

Then, write the **simplified** expression.
$$2m + 3p$$

$$6m - 4m + 3p$$
$$2m$$

Math

Practice

Use the Distributive Property to simplify.

1. $3(2a - 8b) = $ _____

2. $x(y - 4) = $ _____

3. $7(a + b) = $ _____

4. $7(5x + 8z) = $ _____

Combine like terms to simplify.

5. $9y + 6y - 2 = $ _____

6. $25x - x + 2y = $ _____

7. $4a + 18b + 11a - 10b = $ _____

8. $4a + 7 + 3a + 8 - 3a = $ _____

Simplifying Expressions

Equivalent expressions are created by simplifying values (using the Distributive Property) and combining like terms.

Simplify: $4(6x - 5)$

Use the **Distributive Property** to create an equivalent expression. Multiply each value by 4.

Combine like terms to create an equivalent expression.

Simplify: $4(r + r + r + r)$

$$4(6x - 5)$$
$$(4 \times 6x) - (4 \times 5)$$
$$24x - 20$$

$$4(r + r + r + r)$$
$$4(4r)$$
$$16r$$

Practice

Write an equivalent expression for each.

1. $7(4z + 8b)$ _____

2. $8(2x + 3^2)$ _____

3. $9(3 + 8x)$ _____

4. $\dfrac{(t + t + t)}{4}$ _____

5. $7(c + c + c)$ _____

6. $10(y + 2)$ _____

7. $5(3y + 8t + 2)$ _____

8. $6(z + 6)$ _____

9. $11(2r + 3m)$ _____

10. $\dfrac{(2x + 2x)}{8}$ _____

1-Step Addition and Subtraction Equations

You can solve one-step addition and subtraction equations by using reciprocal, or opposite, operations.

Solve: $x + 12 = 20$

First, use the reciprocal operation of subtraction to get x alone on the left side of the equation.	$x + 12 = 20$ $\underline{-12 \quad -12}$
Next, solve for the unknown.	$x = 8$
Finally, check your work. Substitute the value of the variable into the original equation and make sure the number sentence is true.	$8 + 12 = 20$

Solve: $n - 3 = 15$

First, use the reciprocal operation of addition to get n alone on the left side of the equation.	$n - 3 = 15$ $\underline{+3 \quad +3}$
Next, solve for the unknown.	$n = 18$
Finally, check your work. Substitute the value of the variable into the original equation and make sure the number sentence is true.	$18 - 3 = 15$

Practice

Solve each equation.

1. $a - 4 = 2$

2. $y + 5 = 9$

3. $x - 3 = 14$

4. $7 = x - 4$

5. $b + 7 = 19$

6. $x + 0 = 9$

Problem Solving

You can write and solve equations for addition and subtraction word problems.

First, underline the important information that you will need to solve the problem.

Kelley went to the movies. She took 20 dollars with her. When she came home, she had 6 dollars. How much money did she spend?

Next, decide what the unknown is and what variable you will use in the equation.

The unknown information is how many dollars she spent at the movies. We can use the variable d for dollars.

Then, write the equation.

$$6 + d = 20$$

Finally, solve the equation. Use the reciprocal operation of subtraction to solve an addition equation.

$$\begin{aligned} 6 + d &= 20 \\ -6 \quad &\quad -6 \\ d &= 14 \end{aligned}$$

Kelley spent $14 at the movies.
Check: $6 + 14 = 20$

Practice

Write and solve the equation for each problem.

1. Ruben read 37 pages in his history book over the weekend. He read 21 pages on Saturday. How many pages did he read on Sunday?

   1.

2. In a 25-kilometer triathlon, competitors swim 2 kilometers, run 5 kilometers, and bike the rest. How many kilometers do they bike?

   2.

You can solve one-step multiplication and division equations by using reciprocal or opposite, operations. To avoid confusion between the variable and the multiplication symbol, a variable is directly next to a number to show multiplication. For example, $2x = 2 \times x$.

Solve: $3y = 21$

First, divide the same number on each side of the equation. We divide to solve a multiplication equation because division is the reciprocal operation. This will undo the multiplication of 3 by y, and get y alone on the left side of the equation.	$\dfrac{3y}{3} = \dfrac{21}{3}$
Next, solve for the unknown.	$y = 7$
Finally, check your work. Substitute the value of the variable into the original equation.	$3(7) = 21$

Solve: $\dfrac{a}{4} = 4$

First, multiply the same number on each side of the equation. We multiply to solve a division equation because multiplication is the reciprocal operation. This will undo the division of 4 y a, and get a alone on the left side of the equation.	$\dfrac{a}{4} = 4$ $4 \times \dfrac{a}{4} = 4 \times 4$
Next, solve for the unknown.	$a = 16$
Finally, check your work. Substitute the value of the variable into the original equation.	$\dfrac{16}{4} = 4$

Math

Practice

Solve each equation.

1. $3 \times a = 9$

2. $\dfrac{n}{4} = 3$

3. $n \times 4 = 4$

Problem Solving

You can write and solve equations for multiplication and division word problems.

First, underline the <u>important information</u> that you will need to solve the problem.

Taryn practiced piano the <u>same amount of time</u> every day for <u>6 days</u>. If she practiced a <u>total of 12</u> hours, <u>how many hours did she practice each day?</u>

Next, decide what the unknown is and what variable you will use in the equation.

The unknown information is how many how many hours she practiced each day. We can use the variable h for hours.

Then, write the equation.

$$6h = 12$$

Finally, solve the equation. Use the reciprocal operation of division to solve a multiplication equation.

$$\frac{6h}{6} = \frac{12}{6}$$

$$h = 2$$

Taryn practiced piano 2 hours each day.

Check: $6(2) = 12$

Practice

Write and solve the equation for each problem.

1. A group of friends decided to equally share a package of trading cards. If there were 48 cards in the package and each person received 12, how many friends were in the group?

   1.

2. Twenty-five cars can take the ferry across the river at one time. If 150 cars took the ferry, and it was full each time, how many times did the ferry cross the river?

   2.

An inequality is a mathematical statement that compares two expressions using a <, >, ≤, ≥, or ≠ symbol. Inequalities can be solved the same way that equations are solved.

Solve: $6 + q > 14$

First, use the reciprocal operation on both sides of the inequality. Here, the reciprocal operation is subtraction.	$6 + q > 14$ $6 + q - 6 > 14 - 6$
Next, solve the inequality. This means the value of the variable q is greater than 8. Therefore, all numbers greater than 8 are in the solution set of the inequality.	$q > 8$
Finally, represent the inequality on a number line. A number line can be used to represent the possible values of the variable. An open circle shows that the values do not include 8. For inequalities that use ≤ or ≥, a closed circle indicates that the values do include that point.	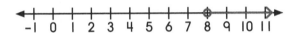

Math

Practice

Solve the inequalities and represent the possible values of the variable on a number line.

1. $6 > x - 2$

2. $d - 5 < 7$

3. $15 > k + 2$

4. $8 \le 8 + r$

5. $w + 8 \ge 11$

Dependent and Independent Variables

Sometimes word problems contain dependent and independent variables. The **dependent variable** in a problem is the value that is affected by the other values in the problem. The independent variable is the value that affects the outcome of the dependent variable.

Solve: Mackenzie can make 4 embroidered headbands in an hour. The total number of headbands (b) is equal to the number of headbands she makes per hour times the number of hours (h). Write an equation to match the situation.

First, identify the **dependent variable**.	The **dependent variable** is b, because the total number of headbands (b) that she makes depends on how many hours (h) she spends.
Next, identify the independent variable.	The independent variable is h, because the amount of hours she spends determines how many headbands she will make.
Finally, write an equation to represent the relationship between the **dependent** and independent variables.	$$b = 4h$$ The total amount of headbands she can make is equal to 4 times the number of hours she spends.

Practice

Identify the dependent and independent variables. Then, write an equation.

1. Jeremy can do 48 sit-ups, s, in one minute, m.

    _____

2. Colette buys artwork online for a total cost of c. Each picture, p, costs $12.50 and there is a shipping fee of $4.00.

    _____

3. Grapes are on sale of $2.99 a pound. Mrs. Martinez buys p pounds of grapes and a watermelon for $5.00 for a total of d dollars.

    _____

You can use the equation solving strategies you have learned so far to solve more difficult problems.

First, underline the <u>important information</u> that you will need to solve the problem.	<u>Hanna bought some peaches.</u> <u>Kevin bought 12 peaches.</u> He bought <u>2 times as many</u> as Hanna. <u>How many peaches did Hanna buy?</u>
Next, determine the **variable** and which **operation** is best for solving the problem.	The **unknown** is the number of peaches Hanna bought. We will use n for the **variable**. The words "2 **times** as many" tells us this will be a **multiplication** equation.
Then, write an **equation** using the information.	12 peaches = 2 x the number of peaches Hanna bought $$12 = 2n$$
Finally, solve the problem.	$$\frac{12}{2} = \frac{12}{2n}$$ $$6 = n$$ Hanna bought 6 peaches.

Practice

Write an equation and solve.

1. Jaden has a number of baseball cards. He has 35 more than his brother, who has 52. How many cards does Jaden have?

   1.

2. Orlando paid $71.85 for tickets to a hockey game. If he bought 3 tickets, how much did he spend on each ticket?

   2.

3. Erica's room is 1.5 times longer than it is wide. It is 18 feet long. How wide is it?

   3.

Review

Use everything you have learned so far about equations and expressions to solve the following problems.

Simplify and write an equivalent expression.

1. $9(2 + 7f)$ _____

2. $30(3x + 4)$ _____

3. $4^2(3 + 6t)$ _____

Solve the equations.

4. $12 + a = 27$ _____

5. $n + 8 = 41$ _____

6. $19 = 25 - x$ _____

7. $\dfrac{a}{5} = 3$ _____

8. $32 = b \times 2$ _____

9. $n \div 3 = 12$ _____

Solve the inequalities and represent the possible values on a number line.

10. $x - 2 < 12$

11. $f + 2 \geq 8$

12. $-10 > w - 1$

Identify the independent and dependent variable and write the equation.

13. Shayne downloads s songs for $0.99 each and spends a total cost of c.

_____

14. Large pizzas cost $10 each. Max spends d dollars on a total of p pizzas.

_____

15. Sophia has $32. She earns more money babysitting her cousins. The total amount t Sophia will have is equal to the amount m she earns babysitting plus the $32 she already has.

_____

Use exponents to rewrite each expression.

1. $2 \times 2 \times 2 \times 2 \times 2 =$ _____

2. $8 \times 8 \times 8 =$ _____

3. 25×25 _____

4. $4 \times 4 \times 4 =$ _____

5. $5 \times 5 \times 5 \times 5 \times 5 \times 5 \times 5 \times 5 =$ _____

6. $15 \times 15 \times 15 =$ _____

Find the value.

7. 3^5 _____

8. 9^3 _____

9. 6^4 _____

10. 5^4 _____

11. 7^3 _____

12. 8^5 _____

Solve each expression by following the order of operations.

13. $5 \times (5 - 3)$ _____

14. $(32 \div 8) \times 2$ _____

15. $(7 \times 8) - (4 \times 9)$ _____

16. $2^4 \times (5 + 4) \div 5$ _____

17. $15 \div 3 + 16 \div 4 \times 3^2$ _____

18. $12 + 3^3 - 12$ _____

Write each number in scientific notation.

19. 500 _____

20. 20,000 _____

21. 7,000 _____

22. 12,000 _____

23. 280,000 _____

24. 25,000,000 _____

For each term below, identify the coefficient and the variable.

25. $9y$

26. $4b$

27. m

coefficient = _____

coefficient = _____

coefficient = _____

variable = _____

variable = _____

variable = _____

Math

Chapter Review

Identify each of the following as an expression or an equation.

28. $7 + x$ _____

29. $9 + 4 = 13$ _____

30. $85 \times n$ _____

31. $10 - 6 = 4$ _____

32. $12v$ _____

33. $18 - g$ _____

Write the expression for each statement.

34. the product of 2 and the difference between 7 and 3 _____

35. 3 increased by the product of 4 and 2 _____

36. the difference between 12 and the product of 4 and 3 _____

37. the quotient of 20 and 5 increased by 16 _____

38. the product of 7 and 2 divided by 3 _____

Write an equivalent expression for each. Simplify as needed.

39. $4(a + b)$ _____

40. $6(c - f)$ _____

41. $\dfrac{(d + d)}{10}$ _____

42. $5^3(2 + 4c)$ _____

43. $3(9a + 8b)$ _____

44. $4(10b - 10c)$ _____

Solve each equation.

45. $x - 4 = 3$ _____

46. $\dfrac{m}{3} = 1$ _____

47. $3 = a - 7$ _____

48. $7 = b \div 4$ _____

49. $8 = b + 4$ _____

50. $a \div 8 = 6$ _____

51. $17 = c + 3$ _____

52. $t \div 9 = 3$ _____

53. $w - 11 = 11$ _____

54. $18 - b = 4$ _____

55. $8 \times n = 20$ _____

56. $t - 18 = 5$ _____

Solve each inequality. Circle True or False.

57. $b - 6 > 5$

   True or False:

   14 is included in the solution set of possible values of b.

58. $x + 2 < 16$

   True or False:

   15 is included in the solution set of possible values of x.

59. $2w \geq 24$

   True or False:

   12 is included in the solution set of possible values of w.

Identify the dependent and independent variable. Write an equation.

60. As a candle burns, it decreases in height by 2 inches every hour. If the candle is 12 inches tall when it is lit, how will the height change over time?

   Dependent variable: _____

   Independent variable: _____

   Equation: _____

61. Students have been assigned to read a book that is 150 pages. Every student reads at a different speed. Depending on reading speed, how many days will it take different students to read the assigned book?

   Dependent variable: _____

   Independent variable: _____

   Equation: _____

62. As a daffodil grows, it increases in height by 3 inches every 2 days. If the daffodil plant starts at 1 inch on day 1, how will the height change over time?

   Dependent variable: _____

   Independent variable: _____

   Equation: _____

63. The temperature in an oven increases by 8° every minute. If the starting temperature of the oven is 250°, how will the temperature change over time?

   Dependent variable: _____

   Independent variable: _____

   Equation: _____

Area: Rectangles

Area is the number of square units it takes to cover a figure. Area is expressed in square units, or units². To find the area of a rectangle, **multiply the length by the width,** using this formula:

7 units

2 units

$$A = l \times w$$

Solve: Find the area of this rectangle.

First, determine the **length** and the **width** of the rectangle. Here, the **length** is **7 units** and the **width** is **2 units.**

7 units

2 units

Next, use the formula to **multiply** the **length** and the **width** to find the area. Write your answer in square units.

$$A = l \times w$$
$$7 \times 2 = 14 \text{ units}^2$$

Practice

Find the area of each rectangle.

1.

3 yd.

6 yd.

A = _____ yd.²

2.

18 m

A = _____ m²

3.

12 cm

23 cm

A = _____ cm²

4.

9 km

24 km

A = _____ km²

5.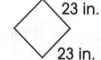

23 in.

23 in.

A = _____ in.²

6.

8 ft.

6 ft.

A = _____ ft.²

The area of a triangle equals $\frac{1}{2}$ of the base times the height. It is expressed in square units, or units², and can be solved using this formula:

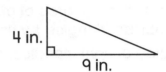

$$A = \frac{1}{2} \times b \times h, \text{ or } A = \frac{1}{2}bh$$

Solve: Find the area of this right triangle.

First, determine the **base** and the **height** of the triangle. Here, the **base** is 9 inches and the **height** is 4 inches.

Next, use the formula to **multiply** $\frac{1}{2}$ of the **base** and the **height** to find the area. Write your answer in square units.

$$A = \frac{1}{2} \times b \times h$$

$$A = \frac{1}{2} \times 9 \times 4$$

$$A = \frac{1}{2} \times 36$$

$$A = 18 \text{ in.}^2$$

Math

Practice

Find the area of each right triangle.

1.
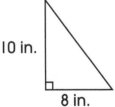

10 in.

8 in.

$A =$ _____ in.²

2.
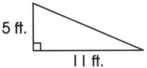

5 ft.

11 ft.

$A =$ _____ ft.²

3.

5 ft.

5 ft.

$A =$ _____ ft.²

Area: Triangles

The area of a triangle is related to the area of a rectangle. You can find the area of other triangles, such as acute and obtuse triangles, by using the same formula used for the area of right triangles, $A = \frac{1}{2}bh$.

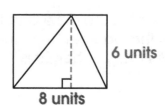
6 units
8 units

Solve: Find the area of this acute triangle.

First, determine the **base** and the **height** of the triangle. Here, the **base** is **8 units** and the **height** is **6 units**. The dashed line indicates the **height** of the triangle. The height of a triangle is the distance from the base to the highest point on the triangle, creating a perpendicular line to the base.

6 units
8 units

Next, use the formula to **multiply** $\frac{1}{2}$ of the **base** and the **height** to find the area. Write your answer in square units.

$A = \frac{1}{2}bh$

$A = \frac{1}{2} \times 8 \times 6$

$A = \frac{1}{2} \times 48$

$A = 24 \text{ units}^2$

Practice

Find the area of each triangle.

1.
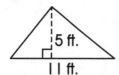
5 ft.
11 ft.

2.
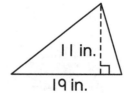
11 in.
19 in.

3.
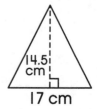
14.5 cm
17 cm

$A = \underline{\hspace{2cm}} \text{ ft.}^2$

$A = \underline{\hspace{2cm}} \text{ in.}^2$

$A = \underline{\hspace{2cm}} \text{ cm}^2$

Math

A parallelogram is a quadrilateral polygon with 2 sets of parallel sides. To find the area of a parallelogram, multiply the measure of its base by the measure of its height:

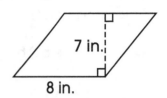

$A = b \times h$, or $A = bh$.

Solve: Find the area of the parallelogram.

First, determine the base and the height of the parallelogram. The height is the perpendicular dotted line from one base to the other. Here, the base is 8 inches and the height is 7 inches.

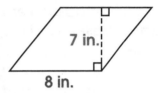

Finally, use the formula to multiply the length and the height to find the area. Write your answer in square units.

$A = b \times h$

$A = 8 \times 7$

$A = 56$ in.^{2}

Practice

Find the area of each parallelogram.

1.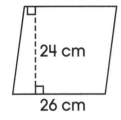

24 cm

26 cm

$A =$ _____ sq. cm

2.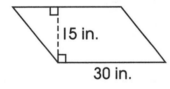

15 in.

30 in.

$A =$ _____ sq. in.

3.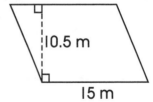

10.5 m

15 m

$A =$ _____ sq. m

Math

Area: Trapezoids

A trapezoid is a quadrilateral with exactly one pair of parallel sides. To find the area of a trapezoid, use this formula:

$$A = \frac{1}{2}(b_1 + b_2)h$$

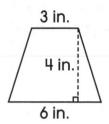

Solve: Find the area of the trapezoid.

First, determine the **bases** of the trapezoid. The parallel sides of a trapezoid are the bases. Let's call the top base "**base₁**" and the bottom base "**base₂**."

Next, determine the **height** of the trapezoid. The **height** is represented by the **dotted line** between **base₁** and **base₂**.

Finally, use the formula to find the area of the trapezoid. Why do we use this formula? Parallelograms can be divided into two equal trapezoids. The area of each trapezoid is half the area of the parallelogram, so the area of the trapezoid is half the product of its **height** and the sum of its **bases**.

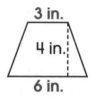

$$A = \frac{1}{2}(b_1 + b_2)h$$

$$= \frac{1}{2}(3 + 6)4$$

$$= \frac{1}{2}(9)4$$

$$= \frac{1}{2}\,36$$

Area = 18 in.²

Practice

Find the area of the trapezoids.

1.

   $A =$ _____ cm²

2.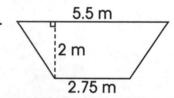

   $A =$ _____ m²

3.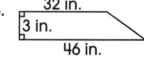

   $A =$ _____ in.²

You know how to find the area of a trapezoid by using the formula $A = \frac{1}{2}($base$_1$ + base$_2) \times$ height. **But why does this work?** Think of placing two of the same-sized trapezoids together to form a rectangle. The area of the trapezoid is half of the area of the rectangle.

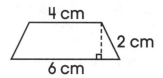

Solve: Find the area of the trapezoid.

First, imagine two same-sized trapezoids. Flip one over and put them together to make a parallelogram or a rectangle.

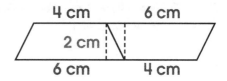

Next, find the area of the parallelogram. Use the formula $A =$ base $\times$ height.

Base = 6 + 4 = 10 cm
Height = 2 cm
A = 10 × 2 = 20 cm²

Finally, find the area of the original trapezoid. Check to see that it is equal to half the area of the parallelogram.

$$A = \frac{1}{2}(\text{base}_1 + \text{base}_2) \times \text{height}$$

$$= \frac{1}{2}(6 + 4) \times 2$$

$$= \frac{1}{2}(10) \times 2$$

$$= 10 \text{ cm}^2$$

10 cm² is half of 20 cm². The area of the trapezoid is half of the parallelogram.

Math

Practice

Find the area of the trapezoids.

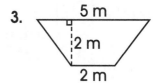

1. 12 in. / 10 in. / 15 in.

$A =$ _____ in.²

2. 5 ft. / 3 ft. / 9 ft.

$A =$ _____ ft.²

3. 5 m / 2 m / 2 m

$A =$ _____ m²

Area: Irregular Shapes

To find the area of an irregular shape, or a composite figure, separate the shape into its component figures and find the area of each one.

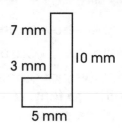

Solve: Find the area of this irregular shape.

First, divide the figure into two or more figures. Here, we can split this figure into two rectangles, **Figure A** and Figure B, as shown by the dotted line.

Next, find the area of **Figure A**. To find the missing side measurement of Figure A, look at the vertical measurements you already know: 10 mm and 7 mm. The missing side is the difference between 10 and 7, or 3 mm.

Then, find the area of Figure B. Follow the same steps to find the missing side measurement.

Finally, add the two areas together to get the area of the original irregular shape.

Area = $l \times w$

$= 3 \times 3$

$= 9$ mm²

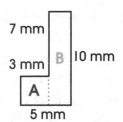

Area = $l \times w$

$= 10 \times 2$

$= 20$ mm²

$9 + 20 = 29$ mm²

The area of the irregular shape is 29 mm².

Practice

Find the area of each figure.

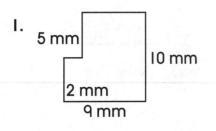

1.

5 mm
10 mm
2 mm
9 mm

$A = \underline{\hspace{2cm}}$ mm²

2.

10 yd.
8 yd.
8 yd.
3 yd.

$A = \underline{\hspace{2cm}}$ yd.²

3.

8 cm
4 cm
3 cm
2 cm

$A = \underline{\hspace{2cm}}$ cm²

Some irregular shapes are made up of more than one type of figure.

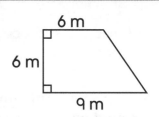

Solve: Find the area of this irregular figure.

First, divide the figure into two or more shapes. This figure can be divided into a **square** and a triangle.

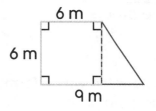

Next, find the area of the **first figure**. This figure is a **square**. Use the formula to find the area of this square.

$$Area = l \times w$$
$$= 6 \times 6$$
Area of square
$$= 36 \text{ m}^2$$

Then, find the area of the second figure. This figure is a triangle. Because the triangle was lined up with the square, we know that it is a right triangle. The side that is 6 m is the height because it is is where the right angle is. The 3 m side is the base.

$$A = \frac{1}{2}bh$$
$$A = \frac{1}{2}3(6)$$
$$A = \frac{1}{2}(18)$$

Area of triangle = 9 m²

Finally, add the two areas together to get the area of the original irregular shape.

$$36 + 9 = 45 \text{ m}^2$$

The area of the irregular shape is 45 m².

Practice

Find the area of each figure.

1.
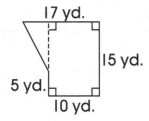

$A =$ _____ yd.²

2.
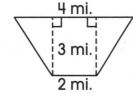

$A =$ _____ mi.²

3.
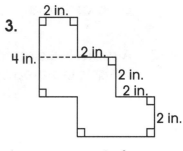

$A =$ _____ in.²

Problem Solving

You can use the strategies you have learned so far about finding area to solve more difficult problems.

First, underline the important information that you will need to solve the problem.

A city park is shaped like a right triangle. Its base is 20 yards and its height is 48 yards. What is the area of the park?

Next, determine which formula is best for solving the problem.

Since the park is shaped like a right triangle, we can use the formula for finding the area of triangles: $A = \frac{1}{2}bh$

Then, write an equation using the information.

$$A = \frac{1}{2}20 \times 48$$

Finally, solve the problem.

$$A = \frac{1}{2}960$$

Area of the park = 480 yards^2

Practice

Solve the problems. Show your work in the space provided.

1. Craig's backyard is a rectangle 25 meters long and 20 meters wide. What is the area of Craig's yard?

    1.

2. A flag is shaped like a right triangle with a base of 25 inches and a height of 30 inches. What is the area of the flag?

    2.

3. A room is 8.6 meters wide and 10.2 meters long. What is the area of the room?

    3.

Use everything you have learned so far about area to solve the problems.

Find the area of the triangles.

1. 8 in. ⌐‾‾‾‾‾‾‾‾‾‾‾‾

   60 in.

   A = _____ in.²

2.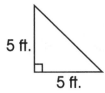
   5 ft.

   5 ft.

   A = _____ ft.²

3.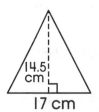
   14.5 cm

   17 cm

   A = _____ cm²

Find the area of the parallelograms.

4.
   1.7 m

   3.6 m

   A = _____ m²

5.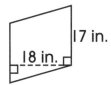
   17 in.

   18 in.

   A = _____ in.²

6.
   21 mm

   31 mm

   A = _____ mm²

Find the area of the trapezoids.

7. 8 cm

   7 cm

   10 cm

   A = _____ cm²

8.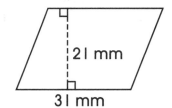
   4.6 ft.

   3 ft.

   7.2 ft

   A = _____ ft.²

Find the area of the irregular shapes.

9.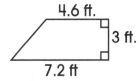
   3 in.

   9 in.

   5 in.

   8 in.

   A = _____ ft.²

10.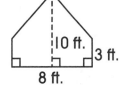
   10 ft.

   3 ft.

   8 ft.

   A = _____ ft.²

Simple Steps • Sixth Grade

Math

Volume of Rectangular Prisms

Volume is the amount of space something takes up. The volume of a rectangular prism is the product of the measure of its length times its width, then times its height. Since volume measures three dimensions, it is measured in cubic units, or units^3. Use the formula $V = l \times w \times h$

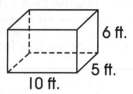

Solve: Find the volume of the rectangular solid.

First, determine which measurement is the length, width, and height of the solid.

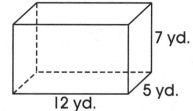

Next, find the volume by using the formula: $V = l \times w \times h$.

$V = l \times w \times h$

$= 10 \times 5 \times 6$

$= 50 \times 6$

Volume = 300 cubic feet, or 300 ft^3

Practice

Find the volume of each rectangular solid.

1.

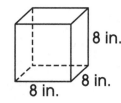

8 in.
8 in.
8 in.

$V =$ _____ in.^{3}

2.

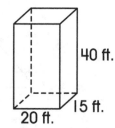

40 ft.
15 ft.
20 ft.

$V =$ _____ ft.^{3}

3.

7 yd.
5 yd.
12 yd.

$V =$ _____ yd.^{3}

Volume of Rectangular Prisms

The volume of a rectangular prism with fractional edge lengths can be measured by packing the solid with cubes that share a common denominator with the edge lengths.

Solve: Find the volume of this rectangular solid.

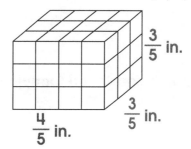

In this rectangular solid, each side length has a denominator of 5, so the solid can be packed with $\frac{1}{5}$ inch cubes to determine its volume. First, calculate the volume of the $\frac{1}{5}$ inch cube.

$$\frac{1}{5} \times \frac{1}{5} \times \frac{1}{5} = \frac{1}{125} \text{ in.}^3$$

Then, add up the cubes in the solid.

Finally, multiply the number of cubes times the volume of 1 cube.
You get the same answer when you use the formula $V = l \times w \times h$.

You can see from the top layer that there are 12 cubes per layer, and
$$12 \times 3 = 36.$$
$$36 \times \frac{1}{125} = \frac{36}{125} \text{ in.}^3$$
$$\frac{4}{5} \times \frac{3}{5} \times \frac{3}{5} = \frac{36}{125}$$
$$\text{Volume} = \frac{36}{125} \text{ cubic inches, or in.}^3$$

Practice

Find the volume of each rectangular solid.

1.

$\frac{3}{7}$ in.
$\frac{2}{7}$ in.
$\frac{5}{7}$ in.

$V =$ _____ cu. in.

2.

$\frac{5}{9}$ cm
$\frac{8}{9}$ cm
$\frac{4}{9}$ cm

$V =$ _____ cu. cm

Math

Problem Solving

You can use the area strategies you have learned so far to solve more difficult problems.

First, underline the <u>important information</u> that you will need to solve the problem.

A shipping crate is <u>0.85 meters long, 0.4 meters wide</u>, and <u>0.3 meters high</u>. <u>What is the volume of the crate?</u>

Next, determine which formula is best for solving the problem.

Since the question is asking us to find the volume of a crate, which is a rectangular prism, we can use the formula $V = l \times w \times h$ to solve the problem.

Then, write an equation using the information.

$$V = 0.85 \times 0.4 \times 0.3$$

Finally, the problem.

$$V = 0.102 \text{ m}^3$$

The volume of the crate is 0.102 m³.

Practice

Solve the problems. Show your work in the space provided.

1. Andrew has an aquarium that is 16 inches long, 10 inches wide, and 9 inches deep. What is the volume of Andrew's aquarium?

   1.

2. Megan's jewelry box is 25 centimeters long, 12 centimeters wide, and 10 centimeters high. What is the volume of Megan's jewelry box?

   2.

3. A cereal box is 13 inches high, 3 inches wide, and 9 inches long. What is the volume of the box?

   3.

A net is a pattern that can be folded to cover a solid figure. The area of the net equals the surface area of the solid.

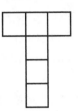

Solve: Which solid figure would this net cover?

First, visualize folding the net along each line to determine which solid figure it would cover.

This is a net for a cube. If you folded it on each edge, or line, it would create a cube.

Practice

Draw a line to match the figure with each net.

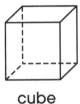

cube

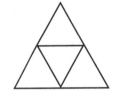

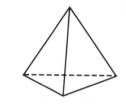

triangular pyramid

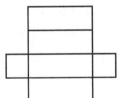

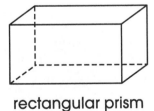

rectangular prism

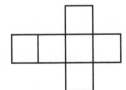

Math

Surface Area of Rectangular Prisms

You can use nets to find the surface area of a solid figure. The surface area of a solid is the sum of the areas of all faces of the solid. A rectangular solid, or a rectangular prism, has 6 faces.

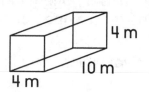

Solve: Find the surface area of this rectangular prism.

First, create a net for the figure. Imagine cutting open the solid figure along the lines and laying out the flat net. Notice there are two square faces and four rectangles.

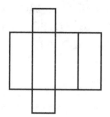

Next, label the measurements for each of the faces. You can determine the measurement of each side by using what you know about shapes. Every side of the square faces is 4 m, and each of the rectangle faces measure 4 by 10 m.

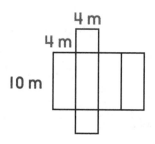

Then, find the area of each face. Label the area of each face inside the net. The squares are each 4 m × 4 m, or 16 m² and the rectangles are each 10 m x 4 m, or 40 m².

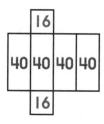

Finally, find the total surface area of the rectangular prism by adding the areas of the faces.

$16 + 16 + 40 + 40 + 40 + 40 = 192$ m²

Practice

Find the surface area of each figure.

1. 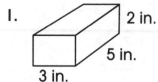 2 in.
   5 in.
   3 in. $SA =$ _____ yd.²

2. 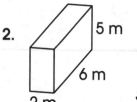 5 m
   6 m
   2 m $SA =$ _____ m²

Practice

Find the surface area of each rectangular solid.

1.

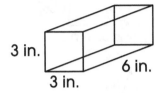

3 in.

3 in.

6 in.

SA = _____ in.²

2.

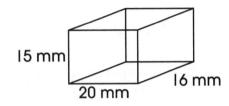

15 mm

20 mm

16 mm

SA = _____ mm²

3.

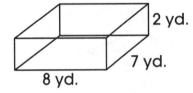

2 yd.

7 yd.

8 yd.

SA = _____ sq. yd.

4.

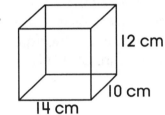

12 cm

10 cm

14 cm

SA = _____ sq. cm

5. Find the surface area of the figure for this net.

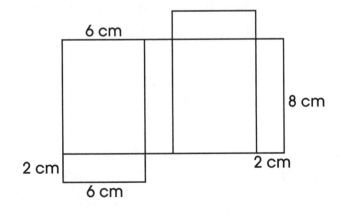

6 cm

8 cm

2 cm

2 cm

6 cm

SA = _____ sq. cm

Math

Surface Area of Pyramids

The surface area of a solid is the sum of the areas of all faces of the solid. You can use nets to find the surface area of a square pyramid.

$h = 11$ in.

$b = 8$ in.

Solve: Find the surface area of this pyramid using a net.

First, create a net for the pyramid. Imagine cutting the solid open to lay it flat. There are 4 triangle faces, one for each side of the square base.

Next, label the length of the sides. The square base has a measurement of 8 in. on each side. Each triangle face has a base of 8 in. and a height of 11 in.

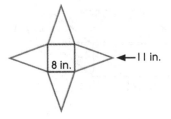

8 in.   ← 11 in.

Then, find the area of each face. Remember, there are 4 triangles in the net.

Area of square = $l \times w =$
$8 \times 8 = 64$ in²

Area of triangle = $\frac{1}{2} \times b \times h =$
$\frac{1}{2}(8 \times 11) = 44$ in²

Finally, add the areas of all of the faces to find the surface area of the pyramid.

$64 + 44 + 44 + 44 + 44 = 240$ in²
The surface area of the square pyramid is 240 in²

Practice

Find the surface area of each square pyramid.

1.
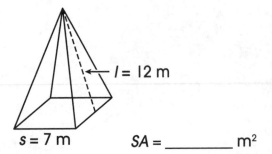

$l = 12$ m

$s = 7$ m $SA =$ _____ m²

2.
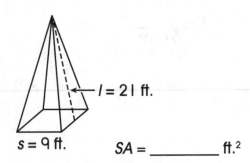

$l = 21$ ft.

$s = 9$ ft. $SA =$ _____ ft.²

Math

Find the surface area of each pyramid.

1.

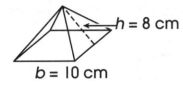

$h = 8$ cm

$b = 10$ cm

$SA =$ _____ cm²

2.

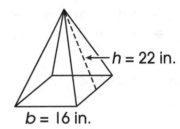

$h = 22$ in.

$b = 16$ in.

$SA =$ _____ in.²

3.

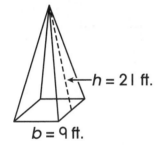

$h = 21$ ft.

$b = 9$ ft.

$SA =$ _____ ft.²

4.

$h = 17.5$ in.

$b = 22$ in.

$SA =$ _____ in.²

5. Find the surface area of this figure using the net.

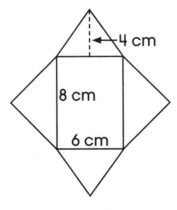

4 cm

8 cm

6 cm

$SA =$ _____ cm²

Graphing Rectangles

Coordinate planes can help you solve problems with rectangles.

Solve: Use the coordinate plane. If points $A(5, 2)$, $B(5, -7)$ and $C(-5, -7)$ are vertices of a rectangle, where is vertex D located?

First, **connect the points**, or vertices, A, B, and C.

Next, **visualize** where lines from Point A and Point C would meet to complete the rectangle. This is Point D.

Finally, **plot** Point D on the coordinate plane. Point D is located at point $(5, 2)$. You have plotted rectangle $ABCD$.

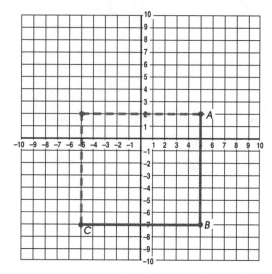

Math

Practice

Use the grids to graph the rectangles. Find the missing vertex of each one.

1. a rectangle with points at $(0, 2)$, $(-6, 2)$, and $(-6, 4)$

   The missing point is at

   _____.

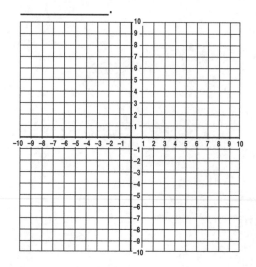

2. a rectangle with points at $(3, -4)$, $(3, 5)$, and $(-2, 5)$

   The missing point is at

   _____.

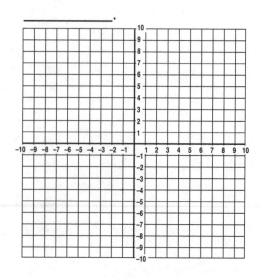

Right triangles can also be graphed on a coordinate plane. Use everything you have learned so far about geometry to solve the problems.

Solve: If points $A(4, 8)$ and $B(-8, -3)$ are vertices of the longest side of a right triangle, where is vertex C located?

First, plot the known points on the coordinate plane. Here, we will plot points A and B.

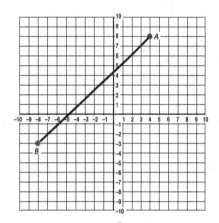

Next, connect the points A and B.

Then, draw lines straight from points A and B parallel with the x- and y-axes to find where vertex C will fall. Since this is a right triangle, Point C could be at $(-8, 8)$ or $(4, -3)$.

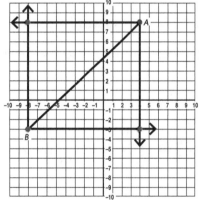

Math

Practice

Use the coordinate grid to find the missing vertex.

1. a right triangle with points at $(3, 2)$ and $(-5, 6)$

   The missing point is at

   _____ or _____.

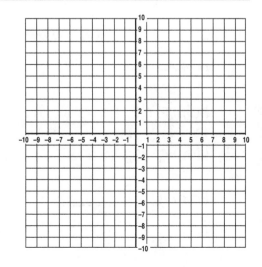

Find the volume of the rectangular prisms.

1.

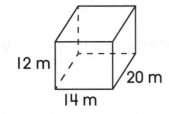

12 m   20 m
14 m

$V =$ _____ m³

2.

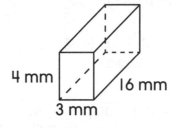

4 mm   16 mm
3 mm

$V =$ _____ mm³

Find the surface area of the rectangular prism. Draw a net to solve.

3.

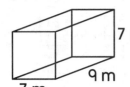

7 m
9 m
7 m

$SA =$ _____ sq. m

Find the surface area of the pyramid. Draw a net to solve.

4.

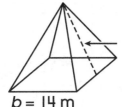

$h = 16$ m

$b = 14$ m

$SA =$ _____ sq. m

Plot the points to graph a rectangle.

5. Point E: (5, 2)

Point F: (–2, 2)

Point G: (5, –4)

Point H: _____

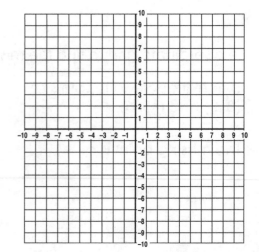

Solve the problems about rectangle area.

1. 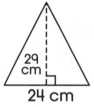 6 in.

A = 54 sq. in.

l = _____ in.

2. 4.5 ft.

A = 58.5 sq. ft.

l = _____ ft.

___

Find the area of the triangles.

3.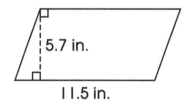

29 cm

24 cm

A = _____ sq. cm

4.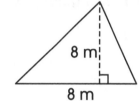

8 m

8 m

A = _____ sq. m

___

Find the area of the parallelograms.

5.

5.7 in.

11.5 in.

A = _____ sq. in.

6.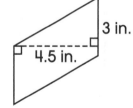

3 in.

4.5 in.

A = _____ in.²

___

Find the area of the trapezoids.

7.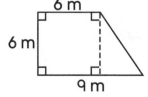

6 m

6 m

9 m

A = _____ sq. m

8.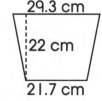

29.3 cm

22 cm

21.7 cm

A = _____ sq. cm

Find the area of the irregular shapes.

9.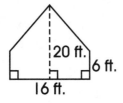

20 ft.
6 ft.
16 ft.

A = _____ sq. ft.

10.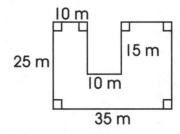

10 m
25 m
15 m
10 m
35 m

A = _____ m²

Find the volume of the rectangular prisms.

11.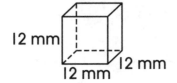

12 mm
12 mm
12 mm

A = _____ cu. mm

12.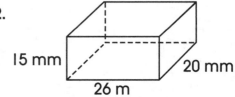

15 mm
26 m
20 mm

A = _____ cu. mm

Draw a net for the rectangular prism and find the surface area.

13.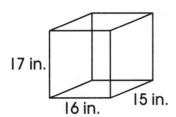

17 in.
16 in.
15 in.

SA = _____ in.²

Draw a net for the pyramid and find the surface area.

14.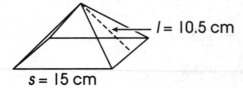

l = 10.5 cm
s = 15 cm

SA = _____ cm²

Use the grids to graph the polygons. Find the missing vertex of each one.

15. a rectangle with points
at (4, –3), (4, –6) and (–3, –6)

The missing point is at _____.

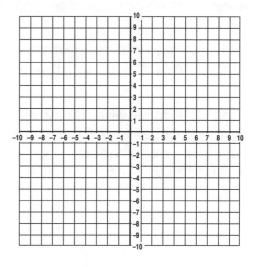

16. a right triangle with points
at (–4, –6) and (5, 2)

The missing point is at

_____ or _____.

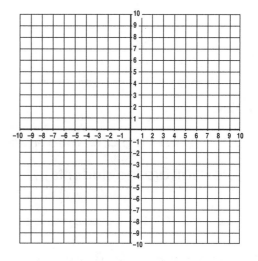

Asking Statistical Questions

A statistical question has answers that vary, instead of a single answer. A statistical question must be answered by collecting data.

Solve: Determine which question is a statistical question: "What are the ages of the students at my school?" or "How old am I?"

First, determine whether the answers to each question will vary, and whether you will need to collect data to find the answers.

"What are the ages of the students at my school?" has answers that will vary. You will need to collect data on the students in your school to find those answers.

"How old am I?" has only one answer. You will not need to collect data to find the answer.

Next, determine which question is statistical.

"What are the ages of the students at my school?" is a statistical question because the answers will vary and must be found by collecting data.

Practice

Read each question and write *statistical* or *not statistical*.

1. How tall are the students in my class?

   _____

2. What grades did students score on the test?

   _____

3. How many marbles are in the jar?

   _____

4. What was the difference in rainfall between March and April?

   _____

You can **collect data** or design a study by following these steps.

Solve: Collect data to find out which brand of granola bar provides the most protein with the least fat.

First, choose a **question** to ask. This should be a specific question based on what you want to learn from your study.

Which brand of granola bar provides the most protein with the least fat?

Next, identify your **sample**. A sample is a part of a population. A population is the set of all items of interest to your study. It is easier to work with a sample versus the whole population because you probably cannot collect data from every member of the population. The sample must accurately represent the whole population, and not be biased. You want to be able to draw conclusions about the population based on the sample.

The entire population would be every brand of granola bar for sale in your town. Since it is unlikely you could collect data from every member of the population, use a sample. The **sample** for this study may be **all brands of granola bars for sale at** *three* **stores** in your community.

Then, **collect data.** Data are items of information, such as facts or statistics. In this study, we want data on protein and fat.

To gather the data, for your chosen sample you would go to three stores. You would **record all brands of granola bars and the amounts of protein and fat in each.**

Continued on page 116.

Continued from page 115.

Then, organize your **data** in a meaningful way, such as in a table.

Nutrition Facts about Granola Bars in Grams (g)		
Brand	**Protein**	**Total Fat**
X	5 g	2 g
Y	6 g	4 g
Z	2 g	1 g

Next, **analyze** the data and interpret the results to determine the answer to your question.

You can find out which granola bar provides the most protein with the least amount of fat by using fractions to find the total fat per gram of protein in each brand. Then, convert the fractions to decimals to make them easier to compare.

From your analysis, you could conclude that Brand X is the most nutritious granola bar because it contains the least fat per gram of protein.

Brand X: $\dfrac{(2\ g\ fat)}{(5\ g\ protein)}$
= 0.4 g fat per gram of protein

Brand Y: $\dfrac{(4\ g\ fat)}{(6\ g\ protein)}$
= 0.66 g fat per gram of protein

Brand Z: $\dfrac{(1\ g\ fat)}{(2\ g\ protein)}$
= 0.5 g fat per gram of protein

Collecting Data and Designing a Study

You can design your own study by following these steps.

Solve: Design a study and collect data for the question: What is the most popular _____ among males and females? Choose a category to fill in the blank, such as pet, sport, or music genre.

First, identify your sample.	Choose a sample of 20 people: 10 males and 10 females. You can include family, friends, and classmates.
Next, collect the data.	List 4 choices within the category. If your category is "pet," you might list cat, dog, snake, and bird. Design a survey form that lists the choices and asks people to choose their favorite. Include a way for people to identify themselves as male or female. Collect the completed forms.
Then, analyze the data.	List your four choices in the first column of the table below. Divide the surveys into those submitted by males and those by females. Add the scores for the first choice of males and record in the table. Repeat for the other three choices. Do the same for the females' choices. Complete the Total Score column by totaling across the rows.

Which choice received the most votes?

_____

What fraction of the votes came from males?

_____

What fraction of the votes came from females?

_____

Popularity of _____

Choices	Males	Females	Total Score

Finally, interpret the results.	Write a one-sentence answer to your study question.

_____

_____

_____

Describing Data

Data can be described by how the values relate to each other and how they are spread out.

Solve: Describe the following set of data: 10, 7, 8, 8, 23, 45, 77, 90, and 90.

First, look for ways to describe the numbers in the data set.	Think of ways the data can be described, such as what the highest and the least value are, how far apart the values are spread, any values that are repeated, and what the middle value is when the data is listed in order.
Next, write at least three descriptions of the data set.	The lowest value in the data is 7. The highest value in the data is 90. The data is spread over 83 points. (90 − 7) The middle value of the data is 23. 8 and 90 each appear twice in the data. All of the values are greater than 0.

Practice

Write three descriptions of each data set.

1. 62, 68, 63, 67, 69, 63, 67

    A. _____

    B. _____

    C. _____

2. 0, 0, 2, 8, 6, 10, 100

    A. _____

    B. _____

    C. _____

Math

The mean of a data set is found by adding all of the numbers in the data together and dividing by the total number of values in the data set. Another word for mean is "average."

Solve: Find the mean for the data set: 84, 66, 102, 114, 78, and 90.

First, add all of the values in the data set together.	$84 + 66 + 102 + 114 + 78 + 90 = 534$
Next, divide the sum by the number of values in the data set to find the mean. There are 6 numbers in this data set.	$$\begin{array}{r} 89 \\ 6\overline{)534} \end{array}$$ The mean of the data set is 89.

Practice

Find the mean of each data set.

1. 48, 64, 80, 48

   _____

2. 84, 140, 105, 119, 105, 84, 105

   _____

3. 119, 140, 119, 91, 91, 126, 91

   _____

4. 52, 52, 64, 80

   _____

Math

Median

The median of a data set is the middle number when the values are placed in order from least to greatest. If there are an even number of values in the data set, the median is the average of the two middle terms.

Solve: Find the median of the data set: 35, 29, 26, 37, 21, 38, 38, and 36.

First, put the data in order from least to greatest.	21, 26, 29, 35, 36, 37, 38, 38
Finally, count in from the outside to find the middle value to find the median. Notice that there are 2 values in the middle. To find the median, we need to find the mean of these two numbers.	21, 26, 29, 35, 36, 37, 38, 38 → 35, 36 ← $35 + 36 = 71$ $71 \div 2 = 35.5$

The median of this data set is **35.5**.

Practice

Find the median of each data set.

1. 3, 9, 6, 2, 1, 10, 1, 2, 1 _____

2. 10, 3, 5, 1, 7, 8, 5, 1, 5 _____

3. 12, 8, 7, 8, 10, 12 _____

4. 23, 32, 38, 40, 30, 34, 23 _____

5. 78, 35, 85, 93, 62, 95, 88, 51, 45 _____

6. 97, 64, 25, 26, 8, 24, 36, 72, 56 _____

The mode of a data set is the value that occurs the most often. Sometimes a data set has more than one mode.

Solve: Find the mode in the data set: 2, 6, 1, 8, 10, 3, 10, 1, 10

First, put the data in order from **least** to greatest.	1, 1, 2, 3, 6, 8, 10, 10, 10
Next, look for the value that occurs most often. This is the mode.	1, 1, 2, 3, 6, 8, (10, 10, 10)
	There are three 10s in this set of data.
	The mode of the data set is 10.

Practice

Find the mode for each set of data.

1. 3, 2, 8, 5, 1, 4, 4, 3, 4

   _____

2. 24, 16, 26, 12, 28, 23, 28, 26, 28

   _____

3. 16, 18, 12, 15, 21, 26, 26

   _____

4. 253, 295, 204, 151, 118, 277, 277

   _____

5. 95, 73, 55, 69, 72, 65, 73, 72, 73

   _____

Math

Using Measures of Center to Analyze Data

Measures of center can be used to describe a data set. Each measure of center allows for different observations about the set. The mean is the most popular measure of center. It is the average, so it provides the clearest picture of the center of the data, but only if there are no outliers. Outliers are values that are far away from the majority of the numbers in the set. If there are outliers in the set, the median is the most useful measure of center. The mode is the most useful measure when the values in the data set are non-numerical.

Determine the best measure of center for this data set: 3, 4, 5, 5, 7, 6, 21

First, determine if the data in the set are numerical or non-numerical.	The data in this set are numerical. So the mode may not be the most useful measure of center.
Next, determine if there are any outliers in the data set.	21 is an outlier in the data set, so the mean may not be the most useful measure of center.
Finally, choose the best measure of center to describe the data set.	The best measure of center for this data set is the median, because it will provide the clearest picture of the center of the data.

Practice

Tell which measure of center would be best for describing each data set.

1. 62, 65, 72, 68, 66 _____

2. 0, 1, 3, 5, 5, 5, 7, 9, 9, 11, 15, 99 _____

3. red, blue, green, red, blue, yellow, blue _____

4. 8, 25, 19, 19, 25, 9, 9, 18, 25, 9, 8, 7, 10 _____

5. $14.60, $7.25, $15.70, $15.25, $14.90 _____

6. 54, 72, 85, 67, 93, 85, 61, 89 _____

Using Measures of Center to Analyze Data

Find the measures of center for each data set and decide which would be best to describe the data set. Remember to look for any outliers that can affect the mean!

1. Cesar's Test Scores: 84, 80, 78, 90, 76, 88, 86, 80, 94

    Which is the best measure of center?

    _____

    Mean: _____

    Median: _____

    Mode: _____

2. Basketball Team Scores: 78, 77, 81, 84, 67, 78, 75, 42

    Which is the best measure of center?

    _____

    Mean: _____

    Median: _____

    Mode: _____

3. Daily Theater Attendance: 124, 127, 111, 119, 107, 99, 115

    Which is the best measure of center?

    _____

    Mean: _____

    Median: _____

    Mode: _____

4. Marisa's Daily Tips: $15, $21, $18, $13, $52, $21, $25

    Which is the best measure of center?

    _____

    Mean: _____

    Median: _____

    Mode: _____

Range

Range is one way to describe a measure of variation, rather than a measure of center. A measure of variation describes how spread out a set of data is. The range of a data set is the difference between the largest and smallest values contained in the data set.

Solve: Find the range of the set of data: 11, 12, 15, 15, 13, and 12

First, put the values in the data set in order from least to greatest.	11, 12, 12, 13, 15, 15
Next, subtract to find the difference between the largest and the smallest value. This is the range.	$15 - 11 = 4$ The range of this set of data is 4.

Practice

Find the range of each data set.

1. 11, 10, 12, 9

   _____

2. 79, 79, 79, 84

   _____

3. 25, 30, 32, 23, 27, 22

   _____

4. 96, 94, 101, 96, 91, 92

   _____

5. 36, 33, 37, 37, 41, 33

   _____

6. 506, 508, 510, 509

   _____

7. 277, 280, 287, 276

   _____

8. 10, 8, 9, 12, 6, 8

   _____

Quartiles are numbers that divide data into 4 equal parts. The median quartile divides the data in half. The lower quartile is the median of the lower half of the data. The upper quartile is the median of the upper half of the data. The interquartile range (IQR) of a data set is the difference between the lower quartile and the upper quartile. IQR is used to measure the variability of a data set.

Solve: Find the interquartile range (IQR) for the data set: 13, 15, 9, 35, 25, 17, and 19

First, put the data set in order from least to greatest and split the data into three parts: lower half, median, and upper half.	9, 13, 15, 17, 19, 25, 35
Then, find the medians of the lower half (Q1) and upper half (Q3). Q1 is the first quartile and Q3 is the third quartile.	Median of Q1 = 13 Median of Q3 = 25
Finally, subtract the medians to find interquartile range (the IQR) of the data set.	Median of Q3 – Median of Q1 = IQR 25 – 13 = 12 The IQR of the data set is 12.

Math

Practice

Find the interquartile range for each set of data.

1. 6, 1, 3, 8, 5, 11, 1, 5

   median: _____

   Q1 median: _____

   Q3 median: _____

   IQR: _____

2. 80, 90, 95, 85, 70

   median: _____

   Q1 median: _____

   Q3 median: _____

   IQR: _____

3. 70, 75, 90, 100, 95

   median: _____

   Q1 median: _____

   Q3 median: _____

   IQR: _____

4. 45, 43, 13, 11, 5, 2

   median: _____

   Q median 1: _____

   Q3 median: _____

   IQR: _____

Mean Absolute Deviation

The **mean absolute deviation (MAD)** of a data set is a value that shows if the data set is consistent. The closer the mean absolute deviation of a data set is to zero, the more consistent it is. MAD tells how far away each value in the set is from the middle.

Solve: Find the mean absolute deviation of the data set: 17, 19, 8, 32, 21, 24, 19.

First, put the data set in order from least to greatest.	8, 17, 19, 19, 21, 24, 32
Next, find the **mean** of the data set.	$8 + 17 + 19 + 19 + 21 + 24 + 32 = 140$ $140 - 7 = 20$ Mean = 20
Then, find the **absolute value** of the difference between the mean and each value in the set.	$20 - 8 = 12$; $\|12\| = 12$ $20 - 17 = 3$; $\|3\| = 3$ $20 - 19 = 1$; $\|1\| = 1$ $20 - 19 = 1$; $\|1\| = 1$ $20 - 21 = -1$; $\|-1\| = 1$ $20 - 24 = -4$; $\|-4\| = 4$ $20 - 32 = -12$; $\|-12\| = 12$
Then, find the mean of those absolute values. This number is the mean absolute deviation.	$12 + 3 + 1 + 1 + 1 + 4 + 12 = 34$ $34 \div 7 = 4.86$ Mean absolute deviation = 4.86

Practice

Find the mean absolute deviation of each data set. Round each answer to two decimal places.

1. 10, 16, 18, 15, 15, 10, 23

   mean: _____

   value differences: _____

   MAD: _____

2. 41, 56, 38, 45, 55, 51, 52

   mean: _____

   value differences: _____

   MAD: _____

A measure of center for a data set summarizes all of its values with a single number. A measure of variation describes how a data set's values vary with a single number. The range of a data set is a measure of variability.

Solve: Complete the table by listing the measures of variability for each data set. Round answers to two decimal places.

Data	Range	IQR	MAD
1. 43, 48, 80, 53, 59, 65, 58, 66, 70, 50, 76, 62	_____	_____	_____
2. 12, 47, 26, 25, 38, 45, 35, 35, 41, 39, 32, 25, 18, 30	_____	_____	_____
3. 99, 45, 23, 67, 45, 91, 82, 78, 62, 51	_____	_____	_____
4. 10, 2, 5, 6, 7, 3, 4	_____	_____	_____
5. 23, 56, 45, 65, 59, 55, 61, 54, 85, 25	_____	_____	_____
6. 55, 63, 88, 97, 58, 90, 88, 71, 65, 77, 75, 88, 95, 86	_____	_____	_____

Math

Using Measures of Variability

Use measures of center and variability to summarize this data set. Round answers to two decimal places.

A school keeps track of how many students are buying notebooks each month from the school store. They collected this information.

Month	Notebooks Sold
Jan.	25
Feb.	30
Mar.	15
Apr.	20
May	15
June	5
July	0
Aug.	35
Sept.	20
Oct.	15
Nov.	20
Dec.	30

mode: _____

median: _____

mean: _____

range: _____

IQR: _____

MAD: _____

Write 2 to 3 sentences that describe the data set.

_____

_____

_____

_____

Which would be a better measure of center for this data: mean or median? Why?

_____

_____

_____

_____

Use everything you have learned so far about probability and statistics to solve the problems.

Your class just took a science test. These are the scores: 97, 99, 81, 78, 34, 96, 63, 100, 85, 88, 79, 82, 94, 85, 83, and 72.

1. Find the following using this data set:

    mode: _____

    median: _____

    mean: _____

    range: _____

    IQR: _____

    MAD: _____

2. Write 2 to 3 sentences that describe this data set.

    _____

    _____

    _____

    _____

    _____

3. Which measure of central tendency would be more useful to analyze this data: mean or median? Explain why.

    _____

    _____

    _____

Math

Box Plots

A box plot displays data along a number line, using quartiles. Quartiles are numbers that divide the data into quarters, or 4 equal parts. The median, or middle quartile, divides the data in half. The lower quartile is the median of the lower half of the data. The upper quartile is the median of the upper half of the data.

Solve: The results of a test include these 15 scores: 66, 56, 75, 77, 98, 72, 48, 83, 73, 89, 65, 74, 87, 85, and 81. Create a box plot to display the data.

First, list the data in order from least to greatest. 48 is the lower extreme (lowest value) and 98 is the upper extreme (highest value).

48, 56, 65, 66, 72, 73, 74, 75, 77, 81, 83, 85, 87, 89, 98

Next, find the median, lower quartile, and upper quartile of the data.

The median is 75. The lower quartile is 66, or the median of the data between 48 and 75. The upper quartile is 85, or the median of the data between 75 and 98.

Then, draw a number line and plot the extremes, quartiles, and median. Draw a line through the extremes, quartiles, and medians. Draw a box around the median from the lower quartile to the upper quartile. This box encloses 50% of the data. 25% of the data lies between the lower extreme and the lower quartile. 25% of the data lies between the upper quartile and the upper extreme.

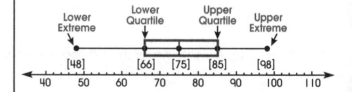

Practice

Answer the questions using the box plot above.

1. Half of the students scored higher than _____ on the test.

2. _____ scores are represented in the box part of the plot.

3. The range of the scores on the test is _____.

Use what you have learned about box plots to create your own.

Solve: The following miles were ridden in a bike-a-thon at school: 12, 21, 14, 13, 18, 16, 19, 21, 19, 16, and 15. Create a box plot to display the data.

First, write the data in order from least to greatest.	12, 13, 14, 15, 16, 16, 18, 19, 19, 21, 21

Then, find the **median** and plot the point on the number line. Here, the median is 16.

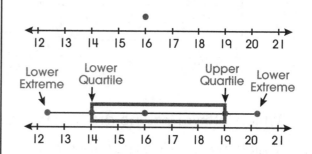

Then, find and plot the **lower quartile** and extreme, and the **upper quartile** and extreme. Draw a box around the median and quartiles, and draw a line through the quartiles and extremes.

Practice

The scores on a quiz were 10, 40, 5, 15, 25, 35, 30.

1. What is the median of these scores? _____

2. What is the lower quartile? _____

3. What is the upper quartile? _____

4. Using the number line below, draw a box plot for these scores.

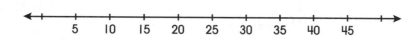

Histograms

A histogram is a type of bar graph. In a histogram, the categories are consecutive and the intervals are equal. Each bar shows a range of data. There is no space between the bars. A histogram is created from a frequency table.

Solve: Read the frequency table and histogram below to answer the questions.

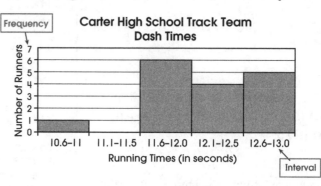

Dash	
Running Times	Number of Runners
10.6–11	1
11.1–11.5	0
11.6–12.0	6
12.1–12.5	4
12.6–13.0	5

1. Which interval has the greatest number of runners?

2. Which interval does not have a frequency?

First, look at the relationship between the intervals in the frequency table and the histogram. Answer the first question.

The interval 11.6–12.0 has a frequency of 6, or 6 runners. That is the greatest number of runners.

Next, answer the second question.

The interval 11.1–11.5 has a 0 frequency in the table, so that means there are 0 runners in that interval. The histogram matches.

Practice

Refer to the histogram to answer the following questions.

1. What information is shown on the frequency axis?

   _____

2. What do the intervals show? _____

3. How many employees drive 15 miles or less to work? _____

4. How many employees drive more than 15 miles to work? _____

Histograms

You can analyze data from a frequency table and display the information in a histogram. Histograms allow you to see the measure of center more clearly.

Solve: The frequency table displays data on the height of trees in a forest. Use the information to display the data in a histogram.

Height of Trees in a Forest

Height (ft.)	Number of Trees
0–5	50
6–10	125
11–15	150
16–20	300
21–25	250

Height of Trees in a Forest

Number of Trees

Height (ft.)

First, label the x- and y-axes and the title of the histogram.

The x-axis is the height of the trees, in feet. The y-axis is the frequency, or the number of trees. The title of the histogram should match the title of the frequency table.

Next, label the intervals on the x- and y-axes to match the intervals in the table.

The frequency axis, or y-axis, can be labeled in intervals of 25. The x-axis should be labeled in ranges to match the table (0–5, 6–10, 11–15, and so on).

Finally, color in the data to match each range interval on the x-axis.

Think of this like drawing or shading in data on a bar graph. Do not leave any spaces between the bars.

Practice

Use the histogram you created above to answer the following questions.

1. How many trees were measured in all? _____

2. In what range did the fewest trees fall? _____

3. In what range did the least trees fall? _____

4. How many more trees were 16–20 feet tall than 11–15 feet tall? _____

Dot Plots

Dot plots are another way to display data. A dot plot is a graph that shows frequency of data on a number line. Dot plots make it easy to identify any measures of center, such as the mode or range, as well as any outliers.

Solve: The Eagles baseball team scored these numbers of runs per game: 4, 2, 6, 3, 1, 0, 2, 0, 4, 5, 0, 7, 6, 4, 3, 2, 6, 8, 1, 3, 11, 7, and 3. Make a dot plot. Then, answer the questions.

First draw a number line from the least to the greatest value in the set. Label the title of the dot plot to match the problem.

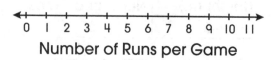

Number of Runs per Game

Next, plot a **dot** above each number every time it appears in the set. The number of **dots** above each number shows how many times that number appears, or its frequency.

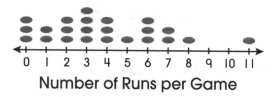

Number of Runs per Game

Finally, answer the questions:

1. How many games did the Eagles play?
2. What is the mode? The range?
3. What is the median?
4. Are there any outliers in the data?

1. The Eagles played a total of 23 games because there are 23 dots.
2. The mode is 3, because it appears most frequently on the dot plot. The range is 11 (11 – 0).
3. The median is 3.
4. The outlier is 11 because it is much farther away from the other numbers.

Practice

Answer the questions based on the dot plot below.

1. How many students' height were measured? _____

2. What is the mode? The median? _____

3. What is the range of heights in the class? _____

Height of My Classmates

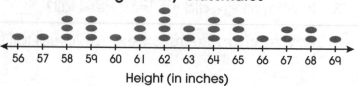

Height (in inches)

Dot plots can also help you see clusters and gaps in the data. Clusters are groups of points separated from other points. Gaps are large spaces between points.

Solve: Create a dot plot for the number of cans recycled each week: 21, 12, 13, 10, 14, 20, 16, 22, 22, 25, 14, 15, 24, 15, 21, 13, 16, 15, 15, and 14. Use the dot plot to answer the questions.

First, create a dot plots using the data. Draw, label, and title a number line, then draw a dot over the number each time it appears in the data set.

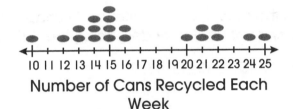

Number of Cans Recycled Each Week

Next, answer the questions.

1. Where are the largest clusters of data?
2. Where is the largest gap of data?
3. What is the mode?
4. What is the range of data?

1. The largest clusters of data in the plot lie in the 12–16 range and the 20–22 range.
2. The largest gap is in the 17–19 range.
3. The mode is 15.
4. The range is 15.

Practice

1. Create a dot plot for the average number of transactions that each sales clerk handled in a day: 51, 57, 56, 45, 54, 55, 60, 59, 58, 57, 55, 56, 54, 70, 59, 58, 57, 56, 51, 55, 58, and 56.

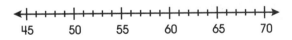

2. What is the mode? _____

3. What is the data range? _____

4. Where is the largest cluster of data? _____

5. Where is the largest gap of data? _____

Write a statistical question for each category.

1. age _____

2. saving money _____

Find the measures of center and variability for each set of data. Circle the best measure of center for describing the data set.

3. 9, 15, 7, 13, 13, 13, 21

   mean: _____   range: _____

   median: _____   IQR: _____

   mode: _____   MAD: _____

4. 45, 38, 52, 47, 33, 54, 47, 39, 41

   mean: _____   range: _____

   median: _____   IQR: _____

   mode: _____   MAD: _____

---

5. Use the set of data below to create a box plot.

   38, 25, 22, 18, 12, 36, 31, 22, 34

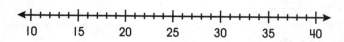

6. A teacher decides to collect information on how long students spend doing homework each evening. She talks to 15 students and receives this data (in minutes): 30, 15, 60, 45, 15, 45, 45, 60, 75, 30, 45, 30, 50, 15, and 55. Find the measures of center and measures of variability for the data. Then, use the data to draw a box plot.

mean: _____   range: _____   Box Plot

median: _____   IQR: _____

mode: _____   MAD: _____

Use the data below to complete the following.

Renee's parents are going to buy a new car. To help them choose an environmentally friendly car, Renee recorded the gas mileage of their top 10 choices. She used letters for the cars so her parents wouldn't be biased. Use her data to complete a histogram showing the range of gas mileages.

7.

Car	Gas Mileage (mpg)
A	19
B	14
C	21
D	38
E	8
F	36
G	26
H	18
I	16
J	28

8. How many cars are they considering that get fewer than 20 miles per gallon?

_____

9. How many cars are they considering that get more than 20 miles per gallon?

_____

Math

Use the data set in the problem below to create a dot plot and answer the questions.

10. The height of 18 6th graders is collected in inches. Their heights are 50, 53, 56, 54, 64, 56, 48, 54, 58, 60, 56, 54, 57, 52, 56, 53, 58, and 52 inches. Create a dot plot to display the data.

11. What is the mode of the data set? _____

12. What is the range of the data set? _____

13. What is the median of the data set? _____

14. Where are the largest clusters of data? _____

15. Are there any outliers? _____

16. Where is the largest gap in the data? _____

17. Write 2 to 3 sentences that describe this data set.

_____

_____

_____

_____

Multiply or divide.

1.
$$\begin{array}{r} 248 \\ \times\ 32 \\ \hline \end{array}$$

2.
$$\begin{array}{r} 432 \\ \times\ 218 \\ \hline \end{array}$$

3.
$$\begin{array}{r} 0.68 \\ \times\ 8.9 \\ \hline \end{array}$$

4.
$$\begin{array}{r} 10.65 \\ \times\ 2.31 \\ \hline \end{array}$$

5. $24\overline{)5482}$

6. $17\overline{)45820}$

7. $0.8\overline{)3.84}$

8. $3.5\overline{)9.52}$

9. $\dfrac{1}{8} \times \dfrac{3}{5}$

10. $\dfrac{2}{3} \times \dfrac{3}{7}$

11. $3\dfrac{1}{7} \times \dfrac{5}{8}$

12. $2\dfrac{1}{3} \times \dfrac{13}{8}$

13. $\dfrac{6}{7} \div \dfrac{1}{2}$

14. $\dfrac{3}{5} \div \dfrac{7}{10}$

15. $\dfrac{5}{8} \div \dfrac{1}{3}$

16. $1\dfrac{2}{3} \div \dfrac{3}{5}$

Complete the chart with the equivalent decimals, percents, and simplified fractions.

	Percent	Decimal	Fraction		Percent	Decimal	Fraction
17.	25%	_____	_____	20.	____%	0.44	_____
18.	110%	_____	_____	21.	____%	0.98	_____
19.	73%	_____	_____	22.	____%	0.65	_____

Solve each ratio.

23. $\dfrac{3}{5} = \dfrac{\boxed{}}{20}$

24. $\dfrac{\boxed{}}{6} = \dfrac{12}{18}$

25. $\dfrac{4}{\boxed{}} = \dfrac{10}{20}$

26. $\dfrac{5}{8} = \dfrac{15}{\boxed{}}$

Compare the integers using >, <, or =.

27. $-12\ \boxed{}\ -30$

28. $82\ \boxed{}\ 17$

29. $-21\ \boxed{}\ -57$

30. $-29\ \boxed{}\ -45$

Write each power as a product of factors.

31. 4^2 _____

32. 15^3 _____

33. 2^6 _____

Use exponents to rewrite each expression.

34. $5 \times 5 \times 5$ _____

35. $6 \times 6 \times 6 \times 6 \times 6$ _____

36. $12 \times 12 \times 12 \times 12$ _____

Math Review

Plot the given coordinates on the grid. Then, answer the questions.

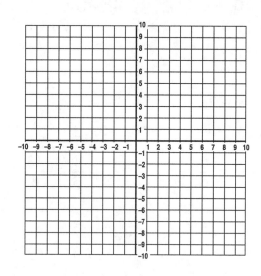

37. A (–3, 7)

38. B (3, –3)

39. C (–8, –6)

40. D (4, –6)

41. E (–10, 5)

42. How many units is it from Point A to Point E? _____ units

43. How many units is it from Point B to Point C? _____ units

44. How many units is it from Point D to Point E? _____ units

Use the coordinate grid to find the missing vertex of each polygon.

45. a rectangle with points at (4, 6), (–2, 6), and (–2, 1)

   The missing point is at _____.

46. a right triangle with points at (4, 0) and (10, –4)

   The missing point is at

   _____ or _____.

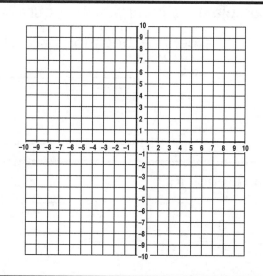

Write an equivalent expression for each.

47. $3 \times (4 + 2) =$ _____

48. $(5 \times 2) - (3 \times 2) =$ _____

49. $(6 \times 8) + (6 \times 4) =$ _____

50. $8 \times (7 - 4) =$ _____

Solve each inequality or equation.

51. $c - 23 < 6$ _____

52. $d + 11 > 15$ _____

53. $28 = a + 9$ _____

54. $8 \times b = 48$ _____

55. $p - 13 = 5$ _____

56. $n \div 8 = 5$ _____

Find the area, surface area, or volume of each figure.

57.

14 cm

18 cm

$A =$ _____ cm²

58.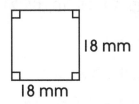

18 mm

18 mm

$A =$ _____ mm²

59.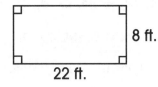

8 ft.

22 ft.

$A =$ _____ ft.²

60.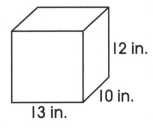

12 in.

10 in.

13 in.

$SA =$ _____ in.²

61.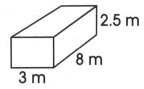

2.5 m

8 m

3 m

$V =$ _____ m³

62.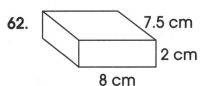

7.5 cm

2 cm

8 cm

$SA =$ _____ cm²

63.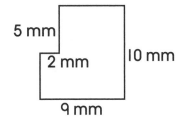

5 mm

2 mm   10 mm

9 mm

$A =$ _____ mm²

64.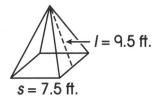

$l = 9.5$ ft.

$s = 7.5$ ft.

$SA =$ _____ ft.²

65.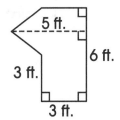

5 ft.

6 ft.

3 ft.

3 ft.

$A =$ _____ ft.²

Find the area of the trapezoids.

66.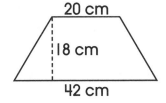

20 cm

18 cm

42 cm

$A =$ _____ cm²

67.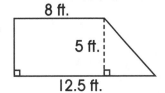

8 ft.

5 ft.

12.5 ft.

$A =$ _____ ft.²

68. A trapezoid has a base of 22 meters, a base of 36 meters, and a height of 14 meters. What is the area of the trapezoid?

Math

Mrs. Alvarez gave a quiz that was worth a total of 23 points. Her students' scores were: 9, 18, 12, 9, 13, 22, 8, 23, 16, 17, 22, 20, 22, 15, 10, 17, 21, 23, 14, and 11.

Use the data set to complete the following:

69. Complete the histogram using the data set.

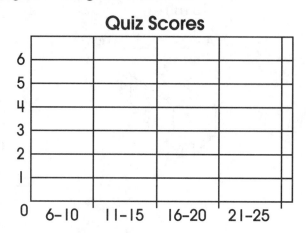

70. Create a dot plot using the data set.

71. Create a box plot using the data set.

72. Find the measures of center and variability for the data.

mean: _____   range: _____

median: _____   IQR: _____

mode: _____   MAD: _____

LANGUAGE ARTS

Language Arts Introduction

Simple Steps for Sixth Grade uses a combination of sentence examples and color coding designed to build students' language arts skills and deepen their understanding of language arts concepts.

Instructions

The instructional sections of this book are organized around examples. In these sections, key language arts concepts and terms are assigned colors. This can help students visualize a connection between the skill they are learning and the way that it is applied.

1. The left side of the page explains a language arts concept.

2. The right side of the page show how the concept is applied at the sentence level.

3. On the left, the words items, words, phrases, and adjectives are colored purple, and the word commas is colored blue.

4. On the right, each item separated by a comma is colored purple, and each comma is colored blue.

Commas: Series, Multiple Adjectives

A comma is used to separate items in a sentence. It can be used in different ways.

Series or serial commas are used when there are at least three items listed in a sentence in a row. The items can be words or phrases. Commas are used to separate them.

Commas are also used with multiple adjectives. This occurs when more than one adjective describes a noun.

Make sure the adjectives equally modify the noun, and that one item is not actually an adverb modifying the adjective. In that case, do not include a comma.

My favorite foods are pizza, pasta salad, and vegetable burritos.

I bought pens, pencils, paper, and envelopes at the office supply store.

To make a pizza you have to roll the crust, spread the sauce, and add the toppings.

It was a warm, breezy day.

That was one wild, crazy roller coaster ride!

Sheila bought a pretty, purple dress to wear to the dance.

Calvin read a hilariously funny book.
(There is no comma in this sentence because hilariously is an adverb modifying the adjective funny, not book.)

The ending of the love story was sadly bittersweet.
(There is no comma in this sentence because sadly is an adverb modifying bittersweet, not love story.)

Practice

Practice questions, proofreading exercises, and writing activities follow the concepts after they are explained, giving students an opportunity to work with what they have just learned.

Review

Review sections are included throughout each chapter, along with a chapter review section at the end of each chapter and an overall language arts review at the end of the language arts section.

Common and Proper Nouns

Common nouns name people, places, and things. They are general nouns. They do not name specific people, places, or things. Common nouns usually begin with lowercase letters.

a person: teacher	I like my teacher.
a place: country	I will visit another country.
a thing: book	What is your favorite book?
pilot	The pilot told us to fasten our seatbelts.
uncle	My uncle is taking me to a baseball game tonight.
restaurant	This is the best restaurant in town.
school	He just enrolled at a new school.
gum	May I please have a stick of gum?
today	We're taking our reading test later today.

Practice

Circle all of the common nouns in this paragraph.

I took my cat to see the veterinarian when she got sick. I had to put her in a special container to take her on a bus to the doctor's office on State Street. After we arrived, we sat in the waiting room for about a half hour. In the exam room, the doctor put Princess on a table to take a look at her. Dr. Chen looked inside her mouth, nose, and ears. He told me Princess had a cold. Then, he gave me a prescription for medicine to help her get well. I took Princess back to my house and made sure to give her a pill every day. Soon, my cat was feeling much better!

Common and Proper Nouns

Proper nouns also name people, places, and things. However, they are not general like common nouns. **Proper nouns** name specific people, places, or things. They usually begin with capital letters.

a specific person: Ms. Crane	Ms. Crane is our new math teacher.
a specific place: Peru	We're going to visit the country of Peru.
a specific thing: *Animal Farm*	*Animal Farm* is one of my favorite books.
Miranda	Miranda wants to be a pilot when she grows up.
Uncle Gary	Uncle Gary is taking me to a baseball game tonight.
Midtown Grill	Midtown Grill is my favorite restaurant.
Central Elementary School	He just enrolled at Central Elementary School.
Mr. Popper's Bubble Gum	May I please have a stick of Mr. Popper's Bubble Gum?
Friday	We're taking our reading test on Friday.

Practice

Circle all of the proper nouns in this paragraph.

Sydney is the capital of New South Wales, Australia. It is the nation's largest city. Sydney was founded in 1788. At the time, less than 1,000 people lived there. The discovery of gold in 1851 helped the population increase. Today, almost five million people live there. Manufacturing is a major industry in the city. Sydney is also the headquarters of many large companies. Some of the city's most famous sites include the Sydney Opera House, the Sydney Harbour Bridge, and the Australia Square Tower.

Regular and Irregular Plural Nouns

A plural noun names more than one person, place, or thing. To form a regular plural noun, add the letter s to the end of a word.

baskets   cars   footballs   houses

Irregular plural nouns **can be made in different ways.**

Use the letters es for irregular plural nouns that end with **s, x, z, ch,** or **sh**.	dresses taxes benches
If a noun ends in the letters **f** or **fe**, and the final sound of the plural form is **v**, it is an irregular plural noun. Change the **f** to a **v** and add es.	knives thieves calves
If a noun ends in the letters **f** or **fe**, and the final sound of the plural form is **f**, it is a regular plural noun. Just add an s.	roofs cliffs surfs

Practice

Write each noun in the correct plural form.

1. match _____

2. wolf _____

3. eyebrow _____

4. street _____

5. wife _____

6. trophy _____

7. sheriff _____

8. toothbrush _____

9. fox _____

10. leaf _____

11. banana _____

12. cuff _____

Regular and Irregular Plural Nouns

A plural noun names more than one person, place, or thing. Some words that end in a y are regular plural nouns, and some nouns that end in a y are irregular plural nouns.

If a noun ends with a vowel and a y, it is a regular noun. Just add the letter s to form a regular plural noun.	boys keys plays
If a noun ends with a consonant and a y, it is an irregular noun. To form an irregular plural noun, change the y to an i and add the letters es.	cities countries flies

Practice

Write each noun in the correct plural form.

1. story _____

2. monkey _____

3. toy _____

4. day _____

5. butterfly _____

6. puppy _____

7. lady _____

8. guy _____

9. flurry _____

10. ray _____

11. turkey _____

12. biography _____

Subject and Object Pronouns

A pronoun **is a word used in place of a** noun. **A subject pronoun** replaces a noun **that is the subject of a sentence.** I, you, he, she, **and** it **are subject pronouns.**

James found the ball.
(James is the subject of the sentence.)

He found the ball.
(He is the subject pronoun.)

Baseball is my favorite sport.
(Baseball is the subject of the sentence.)

It is my favorite sport.
(It is the subject pronoun.)

An object pronoun **replaces a** noun **that is the object of a sentence.** Me, you, him, her, **and** it **are object pronouns.**

Give the book to Keisha.
(Keisha is the object of the sentence.)

Give the book to her.
(her is the object pronoun.)

James put the book away.
(book is the object of the sentence.)

James put it away.
(it is the object pronoun.)

Practice

Identify the bolded word in each sentence as a subject pronoun or an object pronoun.

1. Jessica, please put **it** over there. _____

2. **I** have practice after school today. _____

3. **He** doesn't like string beans. _____

4. Tommy gave his old jacket to **me**. _____

Language Arts

Possessive and Intensive Pronouns

A **possessive pronoun** demonstrates possession. It shows that something belongs to someone or something else. My, mine, yours, his, hers, ours, its, and theirs are examples of possessive pronouns.

Anna gave my ball to Matt.	The possessive pronoun my shows who owns the ball.
Those suitcases are theirs.	The possessive pronoun theirs shows who owns the suitcases.

An **intensive pronoun** ends in –self or –selves. Myself, yourself, himself, and herself are examples of intensive pronouns. This kind of pronoun usually appears right after the subject of a sentence and emphasizes it.

I myself am too tired to go to the movies.	The possessive pronoun myself emphasizes the subject I.
You yourselves are responsible for cleaning up the mess.	The possessive pronoun yourselves emphasizes the subject you.

Practice

Identify the bolded word in each sentence as a possessive pronoun or an intensive pronoun.

1. That new purple hoodie is **mine**. _____

2. What do you want to do on **your** birthday? _____

3. She **herself** does not like foreign films. _____

4. I **myself** prefer to watch scary movies. _____

Language Arts

A **demonstrative pronoun** replaces a **noun** **without naming it.** This, that, these, **and** those **are demonstrative pronouns.**

This **and** that **are singular.** These **and** those **are plural.**

This **and** these usually identify someone or something close. That **and** those usually identify someone or something farther away.

This was a fun time.	The demonstrative pronoun this refers to an event or an experience.
That took too long to do.	The demonstrative pronoun that refers to an event or an experience.
Can you put these on the table?	The demonstrative pronoun these refers to a group of things.
Those are ripe and will taste better.	The demonstrative pronoun those refers to a group of things.

Practice

Draw a line to match a demonstrative pronoun from Column A to a noun it could replace from Column B.

Column A	Column B
this	one pen on the other side of the room
that	several pencils in your pocket
these	one magazine on a nearby table
those	many newspapers at a distant store

Language Arts

Relative Pronouns

Language Arts

Relative pronouns **are related to** nouns **that have already been stated. Who, whose, that, and** which **are relative pronouns. They are used to combine two sentences that share a common noun.**

Carmen is a doctor.
Carmen lives next door to me.

Carmen is the doctor who lives next door to me.

(who refers to Carmen)

Miguel is a barber.
Miguel's shop is on Elm Street.

Miguel is the barber whose shop is on Elm Street.

(whose refers to Miguel)

You just read a report.
The report is incorrect.

The report that you just read is correct.

(that refers to the report)

The magazine articles are too long.
The magazine articles must be cut.

The magazine articles, which are too long, must be cut.

(which refers to the magazine articles)

Practice

Complete the sentences by circling the correct relative pronoun in parentheses.

1. Someone (who, which) likes bananas might like kiwi too.

2. She likes movies (which, that) have a lot of action.

3. Racers (whose, which) cars are ready can drive to the starting line.

4. The bananas, (who, which) are the ripest fruits we have in the house, should be used in the recipe.

An **indefinite pronoun** does not specifically name the noun that it replaces. Here are some examples of indefinite pronouns.

all	everybody	one
another	everyone	several
any	everything	some
anybody	few	somebody
anyone	many	something
anything	nobody	
each	none	

Many were invited to the party, but only a few came.	The indefinite pronoun **many** does not identify who or what came to the party.
We donated **everything** from the attic to the charity event.	The indefinite pronoun **everything** does not identify what was donated.
They let us buy **anything** we wanted.	The indefinite pronoun **anything** does not identify what was bought.

Practice

Underline all of the indefinite pronouns in this paragraph.

Each of the cooks in town made ice cream cones for the fair. The cooks were put in pairs. One made the ice cream while another made the cones. You wouldn't think there would be any problems. However, there were some. Different customers wanted different things. One wanted cherry, while another wanted chocolate. Several wanted two scoops with different flavors. But the cooks were ready for anything. They also made snow cones. They even made milkshakes that were a big hit. By the end of the day, everything had been eaten.

Pronoun-Antecedent Agreement

The noun that a pronoun refers to is called the antecedent.

If the noun is singular, the pronoun must be singular, too. If the noun is plural, the pronoun must be plural too. This is known as pronoun-antecedent agreement.

Here are examples of singular nouns and the pronouns that replace them.

noun: student
pronouns: his, her

Every student opened his or her book.

noun: Marco
pronoun: he

Marco found a lost wallet as he was walking home.

noun: cat
pronoun: its

The cat licked its paws clean.

Here are examples of plural nouns and the pronouns that replace them.

noun: students
pronoun: their

All of the students turned in their papers.

nouns: Jeni and I
pronoun: our

Jeni and I treated our mother to lunch.

noun: children
pronoun: they

The children decided they wanted to play hide and seek.

Practice

Rewrite the sentences so the nouns and pronouns agree.

1. Some students forgot to bring his and her notes to class.

   _____

2. My friend Leo left their jacket behind in class.

   _____

3. When she missed the bus home, Ling had to walk to their house.

   _____

4. The teachers held a meeting in his lounge yesterday afternoon.

   _____

5. Jennifer wished they had not come to the party alone.

   _____

6. Michael tried to find the book that they had misplaced earlier.

   _____

7. The players put all of the gear away in her lockers after the game.

   _____

8. The dogs pulled free of its owners and ran down the path.

   _____

9. My two best friends lend me its toys whenever I ask.

   _____

Language Arts

Pronoun Shifts

A pronoun shift happens when a writer changes a pronoun in the middle of a sentence or a paragraph. This can confuse readers. Here are examples of pronoun shifts and how to correct them.

As a photographer, he has an interesting career because they meet all kinds of people.	He is a singular pronoun. They is a plural pronoun. This is an example of a pronoun shift.
As a photographer, he has an interesting career because he meets all kinds of people.	This sentence is now written correctly.
After the choir concert, we singers gathered backstage to celebrate their success.	We is a first-person pronoun. Their is a third-person pronoun. This is an example of a pronoun shift.
After the choir concert, we singers gathered backstage to celebrate our success.	This sentence is now written correctly.

Practice

Rewrite the sentences to correct the pronoun shifts.

1. If you want to ride this roller coaster, they need to be at least 48 inches tall.

   _____

2. Mrs. Lee said she gave all of their students the instructions before giving the test.

   _____

3. As a magician, she must work hard to safeguard their secrets.

   _____

Language Arts

Use everything you have learned so far about nouns and pronouns to answer the questions.

1. Correct the mistakes in the use of common nouns and proper nouns. Use the proofreading marks explained in the box to the right.

/ lowercase letter
≡ capital letter

John muir was born in 1838 in dunbar, scotland. From a very young age, he had a love of Nature. He traveled all over the world. He came to the united states to observe nature and take notes on what he saw. He wrote many nature Books. John Muir was concerned for the welfare of the land. He wanted to protect it, so he asked president theodore roosevelt for help. The National park System was founded by John Muir to set aside land for Parks. The first was yellowstone national park. John Muir also founded the sierra club to teach others about nature and how to protect it. John Muir is known as one of the world's greatest conservation leaders.

2. Use the lines to explain how the nouns were made into their plural forms. The first one is done for you.

Column A	Column B	
match	matches	If the noun ends in **ch**, add an **es**.
sheriff	sheriffs	_____
knife	knives	_____
eyebrow	eyebrows	_____
brush	brushes	_____
automobile	automobiles	_____
butterfly	butterflies	_____

Language Arts

Language Arts

Identify the bolded word in each sentence as a subject pronoun or an object pronoun.

3. **We** only rented the practice room for an hour. _____

4. **She** guessed there would be a surprise party. _____

5. Pilar gave **us** some advice that really helped. _____

6. Lee looked all over but wasn't able to find **it**. _____

Complete each of the following sentences with an intensive pronoun.

7. Jessa _____ baked all of these muffins.

8. The Boy Scouts _____ set up all of these tents.

9. The smoke _____ did all of this damage to the house.

10. We _____ created the website in just a couple of days.

11. Oliver _____ wrote that poem.

12. You _____ must clean up all of these dominoes.

13. Draw a line to match a demonstrative pronoun from Column A to a noun it could replace from Column B.

Column A	Column B
this	many ants on the ground
that	one book on the shelf
these	a number of bananas at a market
those	one experience at a soccer match

Complete each sentence by choosing the correct relative pronoun in parentheses. Circle the correct answer.

14. Bicyclers (which, whose) bikes are ready can follow the path.

15. He likes novels (who, that) are set in other countries.

16. The man (who, whose) lives across the street is an actor.

17. The car (who, that) you drove is blocking the driveway.

18. **Rewrite the following school news report. Replace the underlined words with indefinite pronouns. More than one answer is acceptable in many sentences.**

The whole community attended the fundraiser for the school. The bake sale was a big success. Not a single item was left at the end of the evening. Chris and his friends looked for more brownies. Most of the students enjoyed the food, music, and art. Six or seven of the attendees promised to help with next year's fundraiser.

_____

_____

_____

_____

_____

Complete each sentence below by writing the correct pronoun on the line. In some cases, there may be more than one acceptable answer.

19. They did not go to the Girl Scouts meeting, so _____ didn't hear the news.

20. Since he is leaving for college this fall, _____ is getting a car.

21. I met with the soccer coach, and _____ said I could to join the team.

22. When they got home, _____ wanted to have a snack.

23. I need to get my permission slip signed if _____ want to go to the art museum.

24. Is Jorge going to join you and me at the pool, or will he call _____ first?

Regular Present-Tense and Past-Tense Verbs

A **verb** is a word that tells an action or a state of being.

I **walked** home.	**Walking** is an action.
I **feel** sick.	**Feeling** is a state of being.

A present-tense verb names an action or state of being that is happening now. A past-tense verb names an action or state that has happened already.

To change regular present-tense verbs to past-tense verbs, add the letters **-ed** to the end of the word. Here are some common regular verbs.

Present-tense verb	Past-tense verb
The students play touch football.	The students played touch football yesterday.
We open the packages.	We opened the packages earlier.
I turn on the light.	I turned on the light already.

Practice

On the first line, write a sentence using a present-tense verb. On the second line, rewrite the sentence using the past-tense form of the verb.

1. _____

2. _____

Regular Present-Tense and Past-Tense Verbs

Practice

Write each verb in present tense in the first sentence. Then, write it in past tense in the second sentence.

1. mend   Today, I _____   Yesterday, I _____

2. cook   Today, I _____   Yesterday, I _____

3. bake   Today, I _____   Yesterday, I _____

4. answer   Today, I _____   Yesterday, I _____

5. wave   Today, I _____   Yesterday, I _____

6. scream   Today, I _____   Yesterday, I _____

7. bike   Today, I _____   Yesterday, I _____

8. jump   Today, I _____   Yesterday, I _____

9. whisper   Today, I _____   Yesterday, I _____

10. divide   Today, I _____   Yesterday, I _____

11. act   Today, I _____   Yesterday, I _____

12. cycle   Today, I _____   Yesterday, I _____

13. mow   Today, I _____   Yesterday, I _____

15. yell   Today, I _____   Yesterday, I _____

16. rake   Today, I _____   Yesterday, I _____

Language Arts

Irregular Present-Tense and Past-Tense Verbs

Irregular verbs do not follow the same rules as regular verbs when switching from the present tense to the past tense.

Here are some common irregular verbs.

Present-tense verb	Past-tense verb
I am happy.	I was happy yesterday.
I begin the book.	I began the book this morning.
We choose a new president.	We chose a new president last month.
I come home.	I came home an hour ago.
We eat lunch.	We ate lunch earlier.
We make dinner.	We made dinner already.
I sit in the chair.	I sat in the chair a minute ago.
I throw the ball.	I threw the ball already.
We fly through the air.	We flew through the air.
We wake at dawn.	We woke at dawn.
I see what you did there.	I saw what you did there.
I know all the answers to the test.	I knew all the answers to the test.

Language Arts

Irregular Present-Tense and Past-Tense Verbs

Practice

Write each verb in present tense in the first sentence. Then, write it in past tense in the second sentence. If you need help, you can look up the verb in a dictionary.

1. catch   Today, I _____   Yesterday, I _____

2. tell   Today, I _____   Yesterday, I _____

3. are   Today, I _____   Yesterday, I _____

4. dig   Today, I _____   Yesterday, I _____

5. feel   Today, I _____   Yesterday, I _____

6. ring   Today, I _____   Yesterday, I _____

7. build   Today, I _____   Yesterday, I _____

8. has   Today, I _____   Yesterday, I _____

9. write   Today, I _____   Yesterday, I _____

10. speak   Today, I _____   Yesterday, I _____

Write a paragraph about one of your hobbies. Use at least three present-tense irregular verbs and three past-tense irregular verbs.

_____

_____

_____

_____

_____

_____

_____

Language Arts

Subject-Verb Agreement

A **verb** is a word that tells an action or a state of being.

A verb must agree in number with the subject of a sentence.
- If the subject is singular, the verb must be singular.
- If the subject is plural, the verb must be plural.

This is known as subject-verb agreement.

The apples tastes good.	Apples is a plural subject. Tastes is a singular verb. The subject and the verb do not agree.
The apples taste good.	This sentence is now written correctly.
The flower are beautiful.	Flower is a singular subject. Are is a plural verb. The subject and the verb do not agree.
The flower is beautiful.	This sentence is now written correctly.
The flower and apple sits on the table.	Flower and apple is a compound subject. Sits is a singular verb. The subject and the verb do not agree.
The flower and apple sit on the table.	This sentence is now written correctly.

Here are some rules to remember for subject-verb agreement.

If the subject is a compound subject and includes the word **and**, a **plural** verb is needed.	Tyler **and** Inez bake a pie together.
If the subject is a compound subject and includes the words **nor** or **or**, then the verb must agree with the subject closest to it.	Neither Tyler **nor** Inez likes blueberry pie.
If the subject and the verb are separated by **a number of words**, the subject and the verb still must agree with each other.	Inez, **along with her sisters**, works at the bakery.

Practice

Circle the correct verb for each sentence.

1. Jill (jump, jumps) rope after school.

2. Jill and Katie (jump, jumps) rope after school.

3. Jill and her friends (jump, jumps) rope after school.

4. Jill, as well as her friends, (jump, jumps) rope after school.

5. Michael (practice, practices) the violin after school.

6. Michael and Mia (practice, practices) the violin after school.

7. Neither Michael nor Mia (practice, practices) the violin on weekends.

Action Verbs

An action verb is a word that tells an action. Action verbs come in regular and irregular forms. They have present-tense, past-tense, and future-tense forms, too.

Here are the different forms of the regular action verb **visit**.

Present-tense form	Sam and Christine visit every summer.
Past-tense form	Sam and Christine visited last summer.
Future-tense form	Sam and Christine will visit next summer.

Here are the different forms of the irregular action verb **eat**.

Present-tense form	I bet Marco and Jim eat the whole pie.
Past-tense form	Marco and Jim ate the whole pie at lunch.
Future-tense form	Marco and Jim will eat the whole pie.

Practice

Write a note to a friend or family member. Tell him or her about a recent event in school or another activity in which you participated. Use at least 10 action verbs. Underline all of the action verbs in your note.

_____

_____

_____

_____

A helping verb is not a main verb. It helps form some of the tenses of a main verb. The verb to be is one kind of helping verb. Here are the different forms.

is	are	was	were	am	been

Helping verbs often help express time or mood. Here are some examples.

shall	had	do
will	would	can
could	should	did
may	must	
have	has	

Main verbs that end in **ing** can be a clue that there is a helping verb in the sentence.	The athlete was training for hours. The dancer had been practicing for days.

Practice

Underline the helping verb or verbs in each sentence.

1. I have been following her music career for years.

2. It has been days since we've seen each other.

3. We could ride this train to get home faster.

4. It will take a long time to finish all of these chores.

5. This assignment was given to us yesterday morning.

Language Arts

Linking Verbs

A linking verb does not name an action. It connects a subject to a noun or adjective. The most common linking verbs are the forms of the verb to be.

is   are   was   were   am   been

Here are other kinds of linking verbs.

Some linking verbs are those of the five senses.

The pencil feels sharp.

You look pretty in that outfit.

These roses smell the best.

I sound weird when I have a cold.

His soup tastes delicious.

Some linking verbs reflect a state of being.

I appear different than I once did.

The man becomes angry when he has to wait.

She grows tired of doing this assignment.

I remain determined to finish.

We seem upset, but we're not.

Practice

Circle the linking verb and underline the noun or adjective it links to in each sentence.

1. The crowd at the baseball game appears excited.

2. The audience thought the play was good.

3. The lettuce in this salad tastes bitter.

4. The line to get into the restaurant seems long.

5. Syd, Mitzi, and Deb were the top runners in the race.

Language Arts

A **transitive verb** transfers an action to the **object** in a sentence.

The hail storm **broke** the **car windows**.	**Broke** is the **transitive verb**.
	Car windows is the **object**.

The **object** of a **transitive verb** can be a **direct object** or an **indirect object**.

They **sent** a **claim**.	**Sent** is the **transitive verb**.
	Claim is the **direct object**.
They **sent** the **insurance agency** a **claim**.	**Sent** is the **transitive verb**.
	Insurance agency is the **indirect object**.
	Claim is the **direct object**.

Practice

Column A contains the subjects of sentences and the transitive verbs. Column B contains the direct and indirect objects. Draw a line from Column A to the sentence ending that makes the most sense in Column B.

Column A	Column B
The outfielder caught	several laps.
Marie froze	her fans a new story.
The swimmers swam	the ice cubes for later.
The author wrote	the baseball.

Language Arts

Gerunds, Participles, and Infinitives

Gerunds, participles, and infinitives are verbs that take on the role of other parts of speech in a sentence.

A gerund is a verb that is used as a noun. This type of verb ends in the letters ing.

Cooking is one of my favorite activities.	The gerund cooking acts as a noun in this sentence.

A participle is a verb that can also act as an adjective. This type of verb ends in ed or ing.

Those falling snowflakes are very pretty.	The participle falling acts as an adjective in this sentence.
The ordered parts should arrive soon.	The participle ordered acts as an adjective in this sentence.

An infinitive is a verb that can be used as a noun, adjective, or adverb. This type of verb includes the word to.

It is important to listen during math class.	The infinitive to listen acts as a noun in this sentence.
The last student to report on the topic led the research team.	The infinitive to report acts as an adjective in this sentence.
Roger watched the movie to write about it for the school paper.	The infinitive to write acts an adverb in this sentence.

Language Arts

Gerunds, Participles, and Infinitives

Practice

The following sentences contain verbs that act as gerunds, participles, or infinitives. Identify which is which by placing a **G** for gerund, **P** for participle, or **I** for infinitive after each sentence. Underline the gerund, participle, or infinitive. Then, on the line below, write a new sentence which includes that verb.

1. Acting is all Sally wants to do. _____

   _____

2. Logs burned in this fireplace are small. _____

   _____

3. To jump for the shot would be the best thing to do. _____

   _____

4. Matthew brought a sandwich to eat in case the meeting ran long. _____

   _____

5. Ann watched the special on television to learn about habitats. _____

   _____

6. The students singing on stage are from our school. _____

   _____

7. Running is an excellent exercise. _____

   _____

8. The polished car sparkled in the sunlight. _____

   _____

Language Arts

Use everything you have learned so far about verbs to answer the questions.

1. Correct the mistakes in the use of present and past tense verbs. Use the proofreading marks explained in the box to the right.

| ℓ delete a word |
| ∧ insert a word |

Hello from Northland Auditorium, home of the Riverdale Cook-Off and Bake-Off. The chefs are ready for the bake-off. The chefs cook meals last night. The judges award prizes for the best meals last night. The chefs baked today. Early this morning, the judges call the chefs over. They talk with them about their recipes. The judges will now observed the baking. Two cooks answered a question for the judges. They act nervous. The judges tasted all of the baked goods. What will win the blue ribbon? Will cookies, cakes, brownies, or candy captured the top prize? We will find out the results soon.

---

2. Underline the irregular present and past tense verbs in this paragraph.

They jump. They fall. They fly through the air. Who are they? They are students of Aikido. Aikido means *the way of harmony*. It is a Japanese form of self-defense. Partners work together. They use wrists, joints, and elbows to block, pin, and throw each other. They learn the moves together and work in harmony with each other. Aikido is an art that tests both mind and body. The founder of Aikido was born in 1883. He wrote hundreds of techniques. Aikido grew throughout Japan and throughout the world. Thousands of students take Aikido today.

Circle the correct verb for each sentence. Make sure the subject and verb agree.

3. Ross and Regina (like, likes) veggie lasagna.

4. Ross and his brothers (enjoy, enjoys) Italian bread.

5. Ross, as well as his parents, (eat, eats) dinner at 6 every night.

6. Does Jill or her friends (want, wants) to ride with me?

Identify the bolded word in each sentence as an action verb, helping verb, linking verb, or transitive verb.

7. Pilar **danced** from the start of the party to the end. _____

8. Bambi **had been** waiting in line for hours for tickets. _____

9. Karen's father **bought** soybeans and pumpkins at the fair. _____

10. The dog barked and **barked** all night long. _____

11. Mr. Thomas **became** successful after much hard work. _____

12. The coach **sent** the team to the locker room after practice. _____

13. The little kids **should** stay with their older siblings. _____

14. This singer's voice **sounds** weak compared to the others. _____

Choose a verb from the box to fill in the blanks in the sentences. Then, on the line below, explain if the verb is a gerund, participle, or infinitive and which part of speech it is within the sentence.

to catch	joking
to drink	swimming

15. _____ is Jed's favorite activity on the weekends.

_____

16. She jumped high _____ the ball.

_____

17. The _____ comedians performed at school.

_____

18. Jim takes plenty of water _____ on long runs.

_____

Language Arts

Appositives

An **appositive** is a **noun or pronoun** **that follows** another noun or pronoun. **It further identifies the other noun or pronoun or provides more information about it.**

Mrs. Glover is the appositive in this sentence. It provides more information about **Angela's mother**.

Angela's mother, Mrs. Glover, plans to visit our school.

Use **commas** to set off an appositive if it renames the **noun or pronoun**.

My hometown, Cincinnati, is my favorite place in the world.

Do not use commas if the appositive tells **which one** out of different options.

A major city like San Francisco can be a fun place to visit.

Practice

Write the appositive in each sentence on the blank line.

1. _____ My friend Tina wants a horse.

2. _____ We rode in his new car, a convertible.

3. _____ Have you met our new senator, Ms. Abbot?

4. _____ My cousin Carl is outgoing and has a lot of friends

5. _____ Do you often eat the cereal Oaties for breakfast?

6. _____ Kiki's cat, Samantha, will only eat tuna fish.

7. _____ Their teacher, Mr. Lopez, shows them how to solve math problems.

8. _____ My dog, a Siberian Husky, loves snow and cold weather.

9. _____ Your sister Ella is the best soccer player on the team.

Language Arts

Adjectives

An adjective is a word that describes a noun or pronoun. There are two types of adjectives: common adjectives and proper adjectives.

Most adjectives are common adjectives. They are not capitalized.	The cold water felt good on the hot day.
Proper adjectives are formed from proper nouns. They are always capitalized.	The children wanted to order French fries to eat.

Practice

The common adjectives in the box relate to the five senses. Use them to complete the sentences below.

minty	smoky	rough	smooth	spicy
sharp	woodsy	loud	sweet	bright

1. That dress has so many _____ colors!

2. You can get a splinter from a piece of _____ wood.

3. Could you please turn down that _____ music?

4. He got a bottle of _____ cologne for his birthday.

5. My stomach can't handle too much _____ food.

6. This beach is covered with _____ stones.

7. My favorite summer food is _____ blueberries.

8. When I chew gum, it gives me _____ breath.

9. The _____ crack of thunder filled the air.

10. I coughed as _____ fumes poured from the car.

Adverbs

An adverb is a word that modifies a verb, an adjective, or another adverb. Adverbs often, but not always, end in the letters ly.

Adverbs can tell how or why.	The soldier fought courageously. Jamie closed the door softly because her sister was sleeping.
Adverbs can tell when or how often.	We went to the movies yesterday with a big group of friends. I always order a salad for lunch.
Adverbs can tell where.	Please place the letter inside the envelope and mail it.
Adverbs can tell how much.	I can barely hear the television

Practice

Write the words from the box in the correct categories below.

scarcely	today	cleverly	outside	joyfully
entirely	there	tomorrow	never	luckily

How or Why	When or How Often	Where	How Much

Language Arts

A **conjunction** is a word that connects words or phrases in a sentence. There are three types of conjunctions.

Coordinating conjunctions connect words, phrases, or independent clauses that are equal or of the same type. The coordinating conjunctions are and, but, or, nor, for, yet, and so.

The coordinating conjunction and connects the adjective soft to the adjective shiny.	The horse's mane is soft and shiny.

Subordinating conjunctions connect two clauses that are not equal. They connect dependent clauses to independent clauses. After, as long as, since, and while are examples of subordinating conjunctions.

The subordinating conjunction until connects a dependent clause to an independent clause to complete the meaning of this sentence.	We can't save for our spring vacation until we get part-time jobs.

Correlative conjunctions are used with pairs and are used together. Both/and, either/or, and neither/nor are examples of correlative conjunctions.

The correlative conjunctions neither and nor connect the nouns pizza and pasta.	Neither pizza nor pasta was listed on the menu.

Practice

Underline the conjunctions in the sentences. Then, identify them as coordinating conjunctions, subordinating conjunctions, or correlative conjunctions.

1. Both Marta and her sister are attending dance camp. _____

2. The cold and fluffy snow covered the ground. _____

3. You can hang out with your friends after you clean your room. _____

Language Arts

Interjections

An interjection is a word or phrase used to express surprise or strong emotion. Common interjections include: ah, aw, hey, hi, oh, no, ouch, uh, wow, and yeah.

Exclamation marks are usually used after an interjection to separate it from the rest of the sentence.	Hooray! We are the champions.
A comma is used if the feeling expressed by the interjection is not as strong.	Uh-huh, the Oakdale Grizzlies had a great basketball season.
Sometimes, question marks are used to punctuate an interjection.	Well? How does the team look for next year?

Practice

Choose an interjection from the box to place before each sentence below. Decide whether an exclamation point, comma, or question mark is the best punctuation.

Ouch	Hey	Okay	Hooray!
Oh	Wow	Yay	Uh

1. _____ It's so good to see you.

2. _____ We've made it to the top.

3. _____ I really scraped up my knee!

4. _____ Tonight we celebrate!

5. _____ Dessert is served.

6. _____ I hope I do better on the next test.

7. _____ Dessert is served.

8. _____ I hope I do better on the next test.

A **preposition** is a word or a group of words that shows the relationship between an object and another word in the sentence.

In this sentence, **upon** is the preposition, and **dock** is the object of the preposition.

They sat **upon** the **dock**.

Here is a list of common prepositions.

above	beside	off
across	between	on
after	by	outside
along	down	over
around	during	to
at	except	toward
away	for	under
because	from	until
before	in	up
behind	inside	with
below	into	within
beneath	near	without

Practice

Complete the following sentences by circling the preposition that works best.

1. Look to see what's (behind, down from) your car when you back out.

2. I really like the little café right (across, away from) the street.

3. My kid sister likes watching the birds (outside, toward) the window.

4. Our cats are only allowed to go (around, inside) certain rooms.

5. Let's climb (over, between) this fallen tree that's blocking our path.

Prepositional Phrases

A prepositional phrase includes a preposition and the object that follows. It can also include adjectives or adverbs that modify the object. Prepositional phrases often tell when or where something is happening.

The prepositional phrase in this sentence includes the preposition upon and the object dock.	They sat upon the dock.
The prepositional phrase in this sentence includes the preposition upon, the object the dock, and the modifiers high and wooden.	They sat upon the high, wooden dock.

Practice

Match the beginnings of sentences in Column A with the prepositional phrases that match them best in Column B.

Column A	Column B
1. The clouds are moving	in the shallow end.
2. We can leave	outside this window.
3. The stadium was built	within the town limits.
4. You can see the garden	across the sky.
5. Swimming is permitted only	after the next speech.

Write two sentences that include prepositional phrases. Underline the prepositional phrases in your sentences.

1. _____

2. _____

An article is a specific word that serves as an adjective before a noun. There are two types of articles: definite and indefinite articles.

The word the is a definite article. That means it names a specific noun.	I bought bread from the bakery near me.
	This sentence tells about a specific bakery.
A and an are indefinite articles. That means they name nouns that are not specific.	I want to go to a bakery to buy bread.
	This sentence does not tell about a specific bakery.

Here is how to use a and an.

Use the word a before a noun that begins with a consonant or a consonant sound.	a cat a school a one-way street
Use the word an before a noun that begins with a vowel or a vowel sound.	an olive an envelope an honest person

Practice

Complete the following sentences by circling the correct answer in parentheses.

1. Mike and Jen rented the apartment above (a, an, the) bookstore.

2. Henry wants to get (a, an, the) car with four doors.

3. An amoeba is (a, an, the) one-celled animal.

4. Coordinating the play turned out to be quite (a, an, the) ordeal.

5. Todd wants to rent (a, an, the) canoe for the weekend.

Language Arts

Review

Use everything you have learned so far about appositives, adjectives, conjunctions, interjections, and prepositions to answer the questions.

Rewrite each sentence on the line below to include the appositive in parentheses.

1. Jamie subscribes to that magazine. (*Horses*)

   _____

2. Mario's father just opened a bakery. (Mr. Rodriguez)

   _____

3. My last name is very common. (Jackson)

   _____

4. Carmen's neighbor runs a day care center. (Ms. Mitchell)

   _____

5. Have you ever eaten that frozen treat? (Ice Pops)

   _____

6. **Circle the common adjectives and underline the proper adjectives in this paragraph.**

   Lighthouses are tall towers with bright lights that guide ships at night or in the fog. One famous lighthouse is located in Marblehead, Ohio. Marblehead Lighthouse is the oldest lighthouse and has been in operation since 1822. The 65-foot high tower is made of limestone. Throughout the years, it has been operated by lighthouse keepers. They lighted the projection lamps, kept logs of passing ships, recorded the weather, and organized rescue efforts. As technology changed with time, the type of light used also changed. Electric light replaced lanterns in 1923. Today, a 300mm lens flashes green signals every six seconds. It can be seen for up to 11 nautical miles. The United States Coast Guard now operates the Marblehead Lighthouse. Its beacon warns sailors and keeps those on the lake waters safe.

7. Match the words in Column A with their relationship in Column B.

Column A	Column B
both mushrooms and olives	equal (coordinate)
before it gets dark	pairs (correlative)
after the race	dependent (subordinate)
neither pennies nor nickels	equal (coordinate)
music and dance	pairs (correlative)
purple or blue shirt	dependent (subordinate)

Write a sentence for each interjection in the box. Decide whether an exclamation point, comma, or question mark is the best punctuation.

Aw	Eeek	Okay	Ouch	Wow

8. _____

9. _____

10. _____

11. _____

12. _____

Circle the preposition and underline the entire prepositional phrase in each sentence.

13. A gray squirrel sat on the roof.

14. A jogger ran down the street.

15. The tree sat behind the white fence.

16. Lauren will be coming to my house later.

17. The clouds floated through the bright sky.

Language Arts

Chapter Review

Complete the following sentences by circling the best answer in parentheses.

1. I like to visit the (museum, Museum) on Sundays.

2. The New York (museum, Museum) of Art is one famous museum.

3. Paul Klee was a famous artist who loved and painted many (cats, cat).

4. (Women, Womans) were the subject of many of the paintings of Henri Matisse.

5. Claude Monet's parents did not want (he, him) to become an artist.

6. Marc Chagall liked to paint violins in memory of his uncle (which, who) played.

7. Pierre-Auguste Renoir believed (anyone, everyone) should work with his or her hands.

8. Karen (herself, yourself) has only visited this one art museum.

9. I (myself, ourselves) have visited more than a dozen.

10. An artist should always follow (their, his/her) heart.

Circle the regular past-tense verb and underline the irregular past-tense verb.

11. Last weekend we played ball and we built sand castles.

Circle the action verb and underline the helping verb phrase.

12. The golfer hit the ball to the left; he should have hit it straight ahead.

Circle the transitive verb and underline its object.

13. The artists drew many paintings.

Circle the infinitive.

14. The author is going to write at the beach.

Identify the part of speech underlined in each sentence as an adjective (**ADJ**), adverbs (**ADV**), conjunction (**CON**), or interjection (**INJ**).

15. _____ Kay brought a <u>huge</u> orange to go with her lunch.

16. _____ <u>Really</u>? Do you think the project will be ready in time?

17. _____ Lynn wants to buy the blue <u>or</u> red bracelet.

18. _____ Annie can't babysit <u>tomorrow</u> because she's busy.

19. _____ The <u>heavy</u> rain made it difficult to see the road.

20. _____ <u>Awesome</u>! We biked all the way to the top of the mountain.

21. _____ Bobcats hunt both during the night <u>and</u> during the day.

22. _____ The kids wanted to ride the <u>newest</u> roller coaster.

23. _____ This assignment needs to be finished by this <u>afternoon</u>.

24. _____ <u>Oh no</u>, I hope I do better on the next test.

25. **Circle the prepositions and underline the objects of the prepositions in the paragraph.**

The West Wing is located in the White House. The President of the United States has his office in the West Wing. It is called the Oval Office. The West Wing houses the executive staff's offices, in addition to the president's office. The chief of staff's office is across from the Oval Office. The vice president works beside the chief of staff. The press secretary and the communication director's offices are along the main corridor. The Roosevelt Room (a conference room), the Cabinet Room (the cabinet is a group of advisers who are heads of government departments), and the President's secretary's office are a little farther down the corridor. Outside of the press secretary's window is the Rose Garden. The West Colonnade runs alongside the Rose Garden. The Press Room is inside the West Colonnade. The Press Room sits on top of an old swimming pool. The swimming pool is a remnant of Franklin D. Roosevelt's administration. That completes the tour of the West Wing.

26. **Some of the sentences in the paragraph need helping verbs to make them complete. Insert helping verbs when needed. Use the proofreader mark from the box to the right.**

∧ insert a word

Glacier National Park located in Montana. Glacier National Park aptly named. Glaciers left from the ice age remain in the park. Grizzly bears said to be the mascot of the park. Rangers said that they observed the bears' almost human-like behavior. The mountain goats of Glacier National Park live high in the mountains. The visitors go high up to find them. Glacier National Park known as one of the top night spots of the national parks. Because it is located far away from cities, the skies are dark and millions of stars seen at night. You visit Glacier National Park any time of year.

27. **What is your favorite play, movie, or television show? Write a paragraph to describe it. Underline the articles you used.**

_____

_____

_____

_____

_____

_____

_____

Language Arts

A declarative sentence **makes a statement. Use a** period **at the end to punctuate a** declarative sentence.

A declarative sentence can make a statement about a person.	Louise just won a scholarship to attend college.
A declarative sentence can make a statement about a place.	A new restaurant opened on Roosevelt Street this summer.
A declarative sentence can make a statement about a thing.	My necklace fell to the floor when the clasp broke.

Declarative sentences **can be written in different tenses.**

A declarative sentence can make a statement about the past.	Steve parked the car near the entrance to the park earlier.
A declarative sentence can make a statement about the present.	I am finishing up my homework right now.
A declarative sentence can make a statement about the future.	We will be visiting my grandmother in a month.

Practice

Write three declarative sentences about a subject of your choosing. Don't forget to use periods at the end of your sentences.

1. _____

2. _____

3. _____

Language Arts

Declarative Sentences

Practice

Identify the declarative sentences by placing a ✓ on the line provided. Leave the other sentences blank.

1. _____ Have you ever heard of a red-eyed tree frog?

2. _____ Red-eyed tree frogs are small, colorful, musical frogs with big red eyes.

3. _____ Where do red-eyed tree frogs live?

4. _____ They primarily live in South America, Central America, and parts of Mexico.

5. _____ They like lowland rain forests close to rivers and hills.

6. _____ How small are red-eyed tree frogs?

7. _____ Female red-eyed tree frogs grow to be 3 inches long.

8. _____ Males grow to be only 2 inches long.

9. _____ Do they have any color other than red eyes?

10. _____ Their bodies are neon green with dashes of yellow and blue.

11. _____ Their upper legs are bright blue and their feet are orange or red.

12. _____ How are these tree frogs musical?

13. _____ Red-eyed tree frogs are nocturnal and can be heard in their trees at night.

14. _____ Why are these frogs called *tree frogs*?

15. _____ They live mostly in trees.

An **interrogative sentence** asks a question. Use a question mark at the end to punctuate an interrogative sentence.

An interrogative sentence can ask a question about a person.	Can Raj play on our team?
An interrogative sentence can ask a question about a place.	Is your hometown big or small?
An interrogative sentence can ask a question about a thing.	Do these pants come in blue?

Interrogative sentences **can be written in different tenses.**

An interrogative sentence can ask a question about the past.	Did you see that new superhero movie last night?
An interrogative sentence can ask a question about the present.	Can you help me carry these packages into the house?
An interrogative sentence can ask a question about the future.	Will dinner be at seven o'clock tonight?

Practice

Write three interrogative sentences about a subject of your choosing. Don't forget to use question marks at the end of your sentences.

1. _____

2. _____

3. _____

Language Arts

Interrogative Sentences

Practice

Complete the following sentences by circling the correct punctuation at the end of each.

1. Who is your hero (? .)

2. Do you have Mr. Bell for history this year (? .)

3. What is your favorite food (? .)

4. Can we leave first thing in the morning (? .)

5. When does the bus leave (? .)

6. Green is my favorite color (? .)

7. Where are we going on the field trip next week (? .)

8. I'm going to have Mr. Stubbert for history next year (? .)

9. Why don't we go out for dinner (? .)

10. Can Charlie come over for dinner (? .)

11. How many stars are in the sky (? .)

12. I'm going to take the bus downtown (? .)

13. What's your favorite color (? .)

14. How many sisters and brothers do you have (? .)

15. That building looks very unusual (? .)

16. Have you ever seen the Grand Canyon (? .)

17. Are you going to take swimming lessons this summer (? .)

18. I am so clumsy, I dropped my tray at lunch (? .)

19. How do you want to decorate the gym for the dance (? .)

20. I like broccoli on my salad (? .)

An **exclamatory sentence** expresses urgency, surprise, or strong emotion. Use an **exclamation mark** at the end to punctuate an exclamatory sentence.

An exclamatory sentence can make a bold statement about a person.	I just won concert tickets on the radio!
An exclamatory sentence can make a bold statement about a place.	The mountain is hundreds of feet high!
An exclamatory sentence can make a bold statement about a thing.	Only one more test before summer break!
An exclamatory sentence can also be used in dialogue.	"I did it!" Kelly shouted when she learned she got an A on her exam.

Exclamatory sentence can be written in different tenses.

An exclamatory sentence can make a bold statement about the past.	I won first prize at the fair this afternoon!
An exclamatory sentence can make a bold statement about the present.	This is the best birthday party ever!
An exclamatory sentence can make a bold statement about the future.	I will be flying on an airplane for the first time next week!

Practice

Write two interrogative sentences about a subject of your choosing. Don't forget to use exclamation marks at the end of your sentences.

1. _____

2. _____

Exclamatory Sentences

Practice

Proofread the following skit. Punctuate the sentences by adding periods, question marks, or exclamation marks on the spaces.

"Karen and Dave," shouted Sandra, "we're going to a planetarium___"

"What is a planetarium___" asked Karen.

"A planetarium," answered Sandra, "is a room with a large dome ceiling___ Images of the sky are projected onto the ceiling with a star projector. Planetariums are amazing ___"

Dave continued, "You can see the movements of the sun, moon, planets, and stars___ I've always wanted to go to a planetarium___"

Sandra said, "They shorten the time so you can see in just minutes what it takes the objects years to complete___"

"Will we be able to see the constellations of the zodiac___" asked Karen.

"Yes, I believe so," answered Dave. "We will even be able to see how the objects in the sky will look thousands of years from now___"

"We'll sit in seats like we're at the movie theater, but it will really look like we're outside," said Sandra.

Karen exclaimed, "I can't wait to go to the planetarium___"

Write two sentence pairs. Write two declarative sentences using periods as the end punctuation. Then, write two similar sentences that show stronger emotion or surprise. You can add interjections if you like. Be sure to change the end punctuation to an exclamation mark.

1. _____

2. _____

An imperative sentence **makes a demand. It is often written in the present tense.**

The **subject** of an imperative sentence is often not expressed. It is usually the understood subject **you**.

Get on Bus #610.
(**You** get on Bus #610.)

Pick up that piece of paper.
(**You** pick up that piece of paper.)

Hand me your completed essays.
(**You** hand me your completed essays.)

Imperative sentences **can use different kinds of punctuation.**

An imperative sentence can end with a period.

Help me move the sofa to the other side of the room.

An imperative sentence can end with an exclamation mark.

Answer the phone before it stops ringing!

Practice

Write a paragraph that gives instructions on how to make or do something. Use at least three imperative sentences.

_____

_____

_____

_____

_____

_____

_____

Language Arts

Imperative Sentences

Practice

Identify the following sentences by writing **D** for declarative, **IN** for interrogative, **E** for exclamatory, or **IM** for imperative after each sentence.

1. Hop over that puddle! _____

2. How many more days until spring break? _____

3. I won the contest! _____

4. I don't want anchovies on my pizza. _____

5. Visit my lemonade stand this summer. _____

6. What is the distance of a century bicycle ride? _____

7. Announce the winners as they come across the finish line. _____

8. The firefighter saved everyone in the house! _____

9. Think about what you want to serve at the party. _____

10. My favorite appetizer is vegetable stuffed mushrooms. _____

11. Whom do you admire most? _____

12. The fundraiser was a huge success! _____

13. Hand me the wrench. _____

14. Can you meet us at the zoo? _____

15. Wash the dishes after you clear off the table. _____

16. I can't wait to see this movie!. _____

17. Her parents said she could come over for dinner. _____

Use everything you have learned so far about sentences to answer the questions.

The sentences in Column A are missing their punctuation. Add the correct punctuation. Then, draw a line to match them with their type of sentence in Column B.

Column A	Column B
1. I will be thirteen on my next birthday	declarative
2. Hurry up and open your presents	interrogative
3. How old are you	imperative
4. Oh no, the wind just blew my hat away	exclamatory
5. Is it supposed to snow all weekend	interrogative
6. Autumn is my favorite season	exclamatory
7. Where are my shoes	declarative
8. We just won the state championship	interrogative
9. Watch where you're going	declarative
10. Basketball is my favorite sport	imperative

Use periods, question marks, and exclamation marks to complete the following sentences.

11. What are the largest trees in the world

12. Redwood trees are the largest trees in the world

13. Redwoods can grow to be 240 feet tall

14. Find out how long redwoods live

15. Redwoods can live more than 2000 years

16. Redwood trees are located along the Pacific Coast in the United States

17. Redwood fossils have been found all over the world

18. Fossils from redwood trees have been found from as long ago as 160 million years

19. Wow those are the tallest redwood trees I have ever seen

Simple Sentences

A simple sentence has one independent clause. It expresses one complete thought.

An independent clause expresses a complete thought and can stand alone.	The city zoo recently closed.
A dependent clause expresses an incomplete thought and cannot stand alone.	because there haven't been many visitors

Simple sentences can take different forms.

A simple sentence can have one or more simple subjects.	Goats live at the sanctuary. Goats and turkeys live at the sanctuary.
A simple sentence can have one or more simple predicates (verbs).	The goats played with the other animals. The turkeys played and talked with the other animals.
A simple sentence can have more than one simple subject and more than one simple predicate (verb).	The goats and the turkeys played and talked with the other animals.

Practice

Write S next to the sentences. Write DC next to the dependent clauses.

1. while I read a book _____

2. She's playing basketball with her friends. _____

3. Baked fish tastes delicious. _____

4. especially with roasted vegetables _____

Simple Sentences

Practice

Match the simple sentences in Column A to the correct description of sentence parts in Column B.

Column A	Column B
1. Farm Sanctuary rescues and protects farm animals.	one subject
2. Farm Sanctuary members have helped to pass farm animal protection laws.	two subjects
3. The New York sanctuary and the California sanctuary are home to hundreds of rescued farm animals.	one predicate
4. Farm Sanctuary offers a humane education program to schools.	two predicates
5. At Farm Sanctuary, people and animals work and play together.	two subjects/ two predicates

Write simple sentences as described below.

1. one subject

_____

2. more than one subject

_____

3. one predicate

_____

4. more than one predicate

_____

5. more than one subject and more than one predicate

_____

Simple Steps • Sixth Grade

Sentences 197

Language Arts

Compound Sentences

A compound sentence has two or more independent clauses joined together. It expresses more than one complete thought.

This compound sentence contains two independent clauses.	He didn't think he was a fan of Shakespeare, yet he enjoyed the play.
Each independent clause could be written as a separate sentence.	He didn't think he was a fan of Shakespeare. He enjoyed the play.

There are two ways to form a compound sentence.

A compound sentence can be two independent clauses joined by a semicolon.	Joan wanted to watch the basketball game; her roommate wanted to watch a baking show.
A compound sentence can be two independent clauses joined by a comma and a coordinate conjunction.	Joan wanted to watch the basketball game, but her roommate wanted to watch a baking show.

Practice

Identify whether each sentence is a compound sentence or a simple sentence. Write CS for compound sentence and SS for simple sentence.

1. I'd like to visit Yellowstone National Park. _____

2. Jamie tries to clean her room, but her brother keeps interrupting her. _____

3. I helped my dad mow the grass today; I also pulled weeds in the garden. _____

4. It's too hot to play outside _____

Practice

Match the independent clauses in Column A with the independent clauses in Column B to create compound sentences. Write the compound sentences on the lines below. Remember to punctuate the sentence correctly and to include coordinate conjunctions if needed.

Column A	Column B
1. The football game was exciting.	They have a good record this year.
2. My favorite team is playing.	I'm going to get pizza after the game.
3. My school's colors are blue and white.	The score was close.
4. I'm going to get a pretzel at halftime.	The season isn't over yet.
5. My team won the game.	The opposing team's colors are green and gold.

1. _____

_____

2. _____

_____

3. _____

_____

4. _____

_____

5. _____

_____

Complex Sentences

A complex sentence has one independent clause and one or more dependent clauses joined together. It expresses more than one complete thought. The dependent clause can be placed before the independent clause or after.

This complex sentence contains one independent clause and one dependent clause.	You can go to the movies if you finish your homework.
The independent clause could be written as a separate sentence, but the dependent clause could not.	You can go to the movies. if you finish your homework

Here are two ways to form a complex sentence.

A complex sentence can be formed using a **relative pronoun**.	My mother asked me to drop off these flowers for Mrs. Hastings, **whose** house is on our way to school.
	Mrs. Hastings, **who** loves to garden, will plant the flowers as soon as she can.
A complex sentence can be formed using a **subordinate conjunction**.	We planted tomatoes and lettuce in the community garden **because** we wanted to use them to make salads.
	We will also donate vegetables to the food bank **so** other people can enjoy eating them, too.

Practice

Put a check mark ✓ on the line in front of any complex sentences below.

1. _____ I like biking because it is good exercise.

2. _____ Tony is going to order pasta with mushrooms, which is his favorite dish.

3. _____ History is my favorite subject.

4. _____ Mr. Baum, who is also the baseball coach, is my favorite teacher.

5. _____ While Kim is a good speller, Jerry is better.

6. _____ I would like a salad for lunch, yet soup sounds good too.

7. _____ Erin made the basketball team after two weeks of tryouts.

8. _____ Although it's going to snow, I think we should still hike the trails.

9. _____ Unless it rains, we'll walk, not ride.

10. _____ We can continue hiking until it gets icy.

___

Write four complex sentences on the lines below. Remember to include either a relative pronoun or a subordinate conjunction.

11. _____

_____

12. _____

_____

13. _____

_____

14. _____

_____

Sentence Fragments

A sentence fragment is not a complete sentence. It is a group of words that is missing a subject, a predicate, or both. A sentence fragment is also a group of words that does not express a complete thought, as in a dependent clause.

This sentence fragment has no subject.	Doesn't have good insulation.
This is a complete sentence with a subject.	The window doesn't have good insulation.
This sentence fragment has no predicate.	The flowers in the spring.
This is a complete sentence with a predicate.	The flowers will bloom in the spring.
This sentence fragment has no subject or predicate. It is a dependent clause because it does not express a complete thought.	Since the lemonade was too sour.
This is a complete sentence with a subject and a predicate.	We drank water since the lemonade was too sour.

Practice

Write **CS** next to the complete sentences. Write **SF** next to the sentence fragments.

1. into the woods _____

2. The meadow was swarming with birds and insects. _____

3. don't know how to swim _____

4. Tell me how to solve this puzzle. _____

Practice

Complete the following sentence fragments by choosing a phrase from the box.

> It was presented
> The statue's height
> Construction began
> is "Liberty Enlightening the World."
> stands on Liberty Island in the New York Harbor.

1. The Statue of Liberty _____
   (look for a verb phrase)

2. _____ in France in 1875. (look for
   a subject and a verb)

3. _____ to the United States on July 4,
   1884. (look for a subject and verb)

4. The official name of the Statue of Liberty _____.
   (look for a verb phrase)

5. _____ from base to torch is 152 feet,
   2 inches. (look for a subject)

Create your own sentences from these sentence fragments.

1. In the summer, I like

   _____

2. Is one of my favorite winter activities

   _____

3. During the fall

   _____

4. When the weather turns warm in the spring

   _____

Combining Sentences and Sentence Variety

Combining sentences that are short and choppy makes text easier to read. It also creates sentence variety, which makes writing much more interesting. Sentences can be combined in different ways.

You can create a sentence with compound subjects.

The lightning is coming.
The thunder is coming

The lightning and the thunder are coming.

You can create a sentence with compound predicates.

The president of our class is honest.
The president of our class is loyal.

The president of our class is honest and loyal.

You can combine adjectives with nouns.

I went to a party.
It was a costume party.

I went to a costume party.

You can combine adverbs with verbs.

Timothy ran quickly.
Timothy ran in the race.

Timothy ran quickly in the race.

You can create a complex sentence using a **subordinate conjunction**.

Donna wanted to go to the reunion.
Donna wanted to go if her best friend Diane went.

Donna wanted to go to the reunion if her best friend Diane went.

Combining Sentences and Sentence Variety

Practice

Rewrite the following paragraphs by combining sentences. Turn simple sentences into compound or complex sentences to create sentence variety.

Charles Schulz was one of America's most famous cartoonists. He created the most popular comic strip ever. He wrote the most popular comic strip ever: *Peanuts*. The *Peanuts* characters are some of the most popular characters ever seen in comic strips. The characters are also popular in books. The characters are popular on television too. The *Peanuts* comic strip made its debut in seven newspapers in 1950.

Charles Schulz based much of *Peanuts* on his own life. He actually had a black and white dog named Spike. Spike was the inspiration for Snoopy. Snoopy is the world's most famous beagle. The *Peanuts* characters teach us all lessons about ourselves. They teach us about the world around us. That is one reason why the characters have remained popular for so many years.

_____

_____

_____

_____

_____

_____

_____

_____

_____

_____

_____

_____

Language Arts

Use everything you have learned so far about sentences to answer the questions.

Write one simple sentence, two compound sentences, and two complex sentences on the lines below.

1. Simple Sentence:

   _____

2. Compound Sentence:

   _____

3. Compound Sentence:

   _____

4. Complex Sentence:

   _____

5. Complex Sentence:

   _____

Identify the following sentences as either sentence fragments or complete sentences. Write **F** for fragment and **CS** for complete sentence. Then, for the sentences that are fragments, tell why they are fragments (for example, missing a subject). Write your answer on the line below each sentence.

6. _____ The satellite is orbiting Mars.

   _____

7. _____ As though the sun were shining.

   _____

8. _____ Since the whole class is going on the field trip.

   _____

1. Rewrite the exclamatory sentence as an imperative sentence.
   You should drink the hot tea slowly!

   _____

2. Rewrite the interrogative sentence as a declarative sentence.
   Are you going to the game on Saturday?

   _____

3. Rewrite the imperative sentence as an interrogative sentence.
   Hit the ball far!

   _____

4. Rewrite the declarative sentence as an imperative sentence.
   We all should recycle the papers instead of putting them in the trash.

   _____

Write whether the following sentences are simple, compound, complex, or a sentence fragment. If they are simple sentences or sentence fragments, rewrite them.

5. She jogged through the mist. She jogged slowly.

   _____

6. The chefs cooked and baked in the competition.

   _____

7. After dinner, I'm going for a walk.

   _____

8. Although I studied hard,

   _____

Language Arts

Follow the directions below to write different kinds of sentences. Then, identify the type of sentence you wrote in parentheses.

9. Write a sentence with a simple subject.

_____

10. Write a sentence with compound subjects.

_____

11. Write a sentence with compound verbs.

_____

12. Write a sentence with combined adjectives.

_____

13. Write a sentence with combined adverbs.

_____

14. Write a sentence that uses a subordinate conjunction.

_____

15. Write a sentence that uses a coordinate conjunction.

_____

16. Write a sentence that uses a relative pronoun.

_____

17. Write a sentence that has a dependent clause and an independent clause.

_____

18. Write a sentence that has two independent clauses.

_____

19. Write a dialogue with four characters. They are attending an exciting activity at school, such as a game, a fair, or a dance. Have them interact and discuss what they see and do. In your skit, use declarative, interrogative, exclamatory, and imperative sentences. Remember to include the proper punctuation.

_____

_____

_____

_____

_____

_____

_____

_____

_____

_____

_____

_____

_____

_____

_____

_____

_____

_____

_____

Language Arts

Capitalizing Proper Nouns

Proper nouns are specific people, places, and things. They include the days of the week and the months of the year. They always begin with a capital letter.

Capitalize days of the week.	Monday Tuesday Wednesday Thursday Friday Saturday Sunday
Capitalize months of the year.	January February March April May June July August September October November December
Also, capitalize months of the year when they serve as adjectives.	They ran the marathon on a sunny June morning. October days when the air is crisp are my favorites.

Practice

Rewrite the following sentences after unscrambling the names of days of the week or months of the year.

1. The month of jeun is Adopt a Shelter Cat Month.

   _____

2. Earth Day, a day for environmental awareness, is celebrated in Ipari.

   _____

3. Do you want to go to the movies on ywdeadesn?

   _____

4. This year, Valentine's Day falls on the second naydom of barufrey.

   _____

5. The state of Colorado has its own day, and it's celebrated in stuagu.

   _____

6. Shogatsu is the name for New Year in Japan; it is celebrated in najruay.

   _____

Write a paragraph about your favorite day of the week or month of the year.

_____

_____

_____

_____

_____

_____

_____

Capitalizing Proper Nouns

Proper nouns **include the** names of historical events, nations, **and** languages. **They always begin with a capital letter.**

Capitalize historical events, periods of time, **and** documents from history.	Cold War Renaissance Period Treaty of Paris
Capitalize the names of nations **and** nationalities.	United States; American Great Britain; British Nigeria; Nigerian Brazil; Brazilian
Capitalize the names of languages.	Mandarin English Spanish Japanese
Also, capitalize the names of nationalities or languages when they serve as adjectives.	Have you ever eaten a Dutch apple pie? I am studying for a test tomorrow in French class.

Write a paragraph about an historical event that interests you or a nation you would like to visit. "Don't forget to use capitals when needed."

_____

_____

_____

_____

_____

Practice

Complete the following sentences by circling the correct answer in parentheses.
Hint: Not all choices need to be capitalized.

1. The war lasting from 1939 to 1945 was (world war II, World War II).

2. The (italian, Italian) language is one of the romance languages.

3. An (era, Era) is considered to be any important period of time.

4. The season begins for (baseball teams, Baseball Teams) in April.

5. Mikhail Baryshnikov is of (russian, Russian) descent.

6. The (boston red sox, Boston Red Sox) won the World Series in 2004.

7. The (magna carta, Magna Carta) was written in 1215.

8. The (english, English) cocker spaniel was the number one dog in popularity in Britain from the 1930s through the 1950s.

9. The (victorian era, Victorian Era) lasted from 1839 to 1901, during the reign of Queen Victoria in England.

10. The (french, French) soufflé is a dessert served warm.

11. The first ten amendments to the Constitution of the United States is the (bill of rights, Bill of Rights).

12. The (battle of waterloo, Battle of Waterloo) took place in Belgium in 1815.

13. The (cuban missile crisis, Cuban Missile Crisis) took place in October 1962.

14. Paella is a traditional (spanish, Spanish) dish made with rice.

15. We saw a signed copy of the (declaration of independence, Declaration of Independence) on display at the National Archives in Washington, D.C..

Capitalizing Proper Nouns

Proper nouns **include the** names of sports teams **and** organizations. **They always begin with a capital letter.**

Capitalize the names of sports teams.	Detroit Tigers New York Giants Houston Rockets
Capitalize the names of organizations.	The Humane Society Mitchell Animal Shelter Red Rose Nature Society

Practice

Circle the name of the sports team or organization in each sentence.

1. I volunteer for the American Red Cross.

2. I just got tickets to the Los Angeles Sunrays game.

3. While walking to school, we pass the Smithson Art Association.

4. Have you ever watched the New England Eagles play?

5. You're invited to join the Weston Board Game Club.

6. We've decided to name our baseball team the Foster Park Falcons.

7. Next week, she's going on a class trip to the Art Institute of Chicago.

8. The New York Yankees won their first World Series in 1923.

Capitalizing Proper Nouns

Proper nouns **include the** names of government departments **and regions** of the country. **They always begin with a capital letter.**

Capitalize the names of government departments.	Department of Energy Department of Homeland Security Department of Health and Human Services
Capitalize the names of regions of the country.	East Coast Midwest Pacific Northwest
Words that give directions are **not** capitalized.	I live on the north side of town.

Practice

Circle the name of the government department or region of the country in each sentence.

1. My mom and dad work for the Department of Transportation.

2. Tina and her family are moving to the Midwest this summer.

3. San Francisco is a city on the West Coast.

4. Tasha's aunt works for the State Department.

5. The Southwest gets lots of sun, but not much rain.

6. My mom stopped at the Bureau of Motor Vehicles to renew her driver's license.

Language Arts

Capitalizing Proper Nouns

Proper nouns **include** titles **and** geographic names. **They always begin with a capital letter.**

Capitalize the titles of books, songs, movies, plays, newspapers, and magazines. Most titles are also underlined or italicized in text.	*Charlotte's Web* *The Raven* *Time* *West Side Story*
Place quotes around the titles of short works, such as songs, poems, short stories, and articles.	Song: "Stay with Me" Story: "The Tortoise and the Hare"
Capitalize titles when directly followed by a name.	Mayor Franklin Senator Santos Professor Gupta
Capitalize geographic names, such as countries, states, cities, counties, bodies of water, public areas, roads, highways, and buildings.	Columbia Hawaii Athens Queens County Chesapeake Bay Sierra Nevada Range Main Street Route 66 Globe Theatre

Practice

Complete the following sentences by circling the best answer in parentheses.

1. My favorite song is ("Firework", "firework") by Katy Perry.

2. The (President, president) of the organization is visiting on Tuesday.

3. At 2:00 pm, (Governor, governor) Spencer is making a speech.

4. Valerie and Gerald watched the sunset from the (Eiffel Tower, eiffel tower).

Follow this capitalization rule for sentences.

Capitalize the **first word** of a sentence.	The wind blew through the trees. Please clean your room today. Watch out! Can I borrow that pen?

Practice

Complete the following sentences by circling the best answer in parentheses.

1. (The, the) girls' team beat the boys' team by three seconds.

2. (The, the) airplane was going to be delayed.

3. (My, my) cousin is visiting us for the summer from England.

4. (Do, do) you know what time the (Movie, movie) is supposed to start?

5. Are you going to the (Mountains, mountains) or the beach for vacation?

6. (Be, be) careful because the sidewalk is very slippery!

7. (Monday, monday) is my least favorite day of the week.

8. (Help, help)! I can't lift this box by myself.

9. (Let's, let's) pack a picnic and take it to the park.

Language Arts

Capitalizing Direct Quotations

Follow these capitalization rules for direct quotations.

Capitalize the first word of a direct quotation.	My father said, "Finish your homework and then we'll go for a ride." "I'm almost finished now," I happily answered.
If a continuous sentence in a direct quotation is split and the second half is not a new sentence, do not capitalize it.	"Keep your hands and arms inside the car," said the attendant, "and stay seated."
If a new sentence begins after the split in a direct quotation, then capitalize it as you would with any sentence.	"Roller coasters are my favorite rides," I said. "I can ride them all day."
Indirect quotations are not capitalized.	My father said he had been working on his car for weeks.

Practice

Complete the following sentences by circling the best answer in parentheses.

1. T.C. said, "(Baseball, baseball) is my favorite sport."

2. The technician said (The, the) car would be ready in a few hours.

3. "Don't rush through your homework," said the teacher, "(And, and) stay focused."

4. Mrs. Wilson told her husband that (He, he) should be careful shoveling the snow.

A personal letter has five parts: the heading, salutation, body, closing, **and signature.**

The heading is the address of the person writing the letter and the date it is written. The name of the street, city, state, and month are all capitalized.

1245 Hollow Dr.
Phoenix, AZ 85044

March 31, 2016

The salutation is the greeting. It should be capitalized. It ends with a comma.

Dear Karen,

The body is the main part of the letter. It contains sentences that are capitalized in the standard way.

It was nice meeting you at the concert. Thanks again for helping me and my friend get VIP seats. It was so much fun! Let's definitely keep in touch.

The closing can be written in many ways. Only the first word is capitalized. It ends with a comma.

Thanks,
Sincerely,
All the best,

The signature is usually only your first name in a personal letter. It is always capitalized.

Pia

Language Arts

Capitalizing Personal Letters

Practice

Name the parts of the personal letter below by writing the names on the lines provided. Identify each section as the heading, salutation, body, closing, or signature. Then, circle the capital letters.

_____

_____

_____

_____
_____

7511 Hibernia Rd.
Seattle, WA 40000

February 31, 2014

Dear Uncle Josh,

How are you? My ski trip has been great. I even learned how to snowboard. I think I'll be really sore tomorrow. All of the fundraising was worth it. Thanks for helping us out. I'm glad our class got to take this trip. I hope I'll get to come back someday.

Thank you,

Lucy

A business letter has six parts: the heading, inside address, salutation, body, closing, and signature.

The heading is the address of the person writing the letter and the date it is written. The name of the street, city, state, and month are all capitalized.

4003 Fourteenth St.
Amlin, NH 20000

September 6, 2016

The inside address includes the name and complete address of the person to whom the letter is going.

Mark Dillon, Director
S.A.S. Productions
100 Otterbein Ave.
Rochester, NY 20000

The salutation is the greeting. It should be capitalized. It ends with a colon.

Dear Mr. Dillon:
To Whom It May Concern:

The body is the main part of the letter. It contains sentences that are capitalized in the standard way.

Thank you for interviewing me for the job opening. I hope you will strongly consider me for the position. I look forward to hearing from you soon.

The closing can be written in many ways. Only the first word is capitalized. It ends with a comma.

Yours truly,
Sincerely,
Very truly,

The signature includes both your first name and last name. Both names should be capitalized. Add your handwritten signature between the closing and the typed signature.

Leigh Greenburg

Language Arts

Capitalizing Business Letters

Practice

Write the heading, inside address, salutation, body, closing, and signature of a business letter. Make up the names and other information if needed, but be sure you capitalize correctly.

_____

_____

_____

_____

_____

_____

_____

_____

_____

_____

_____

_____

_____

_____

_____

_____

Use everything you have learned so far about capitalization to answer the questions.

Complete the following sentences by circling the best answer in parentheses.

1. "Riley," called Gillian, "(Let's, let's) use carrots and raisins on our snowman."

2. Our teacher said the test will be on (Wednesday, wednesday).

3. (Winters, winters) in the north are cold and blustery.

4. The summer solstice occurs in the month of (June, june).

5. Drive (North, north) on Route 3 and then you'll be close to the community center.

6. The hostess said, "(Your, your) table will be ready in 10 minutes."

7. The U.S. (Constitution, constitution) was written in Philadelphia in 1787.

8. The (Peace Corps, peace corps) is a federal agency that reports to Congress and the Executive Branch.

9. "(My, my) shift starts at 3:00, so let's study when I'm finished," said Celia.

10. The high school offers (Italian, italian) as one of its languages.

11. The (Aveda Corporation, aveda corporation) is located in Minnesota.

12. North America is located in the (Northern, northern) hemisphere.

13. In the fairy tale, the princess said (She, she) was waiting for her prince.

14. The (Danish, danish) pastry is baked fresh every day.

15. My favorite baseball team is the (San Francisco Giants, San Francisco giants).

16. The pep rally will be held in the gym on (Friday, friday) afternoon.

17. The (Sierra Club, sierra club) is an environmental organization for people of all ages.

18. Doug said, "(My, my) Aunt Clara makes the best blueberry muffins."

19. The winter solstice occurs in the month of (December, december).

Language Arts

Language Arts

20. Write a personal letter or a business letter on the lines below. Be sure to include the required sections and follow the rules for capitalization.

_____

_____

_____

_____

_____

_____

_____

_____

_____

_____

_____

_____

_____

_____

_____

_____

_____

_____

_____

_____

_____

A **period** is used at the end of different kinds of sentences.

A **period** appears at the end of a declarative sentence.	Louise just won a scholarship to attend college.
A **period** appears at the end of an imperative sentence when the statement is not urgent.	Please pick your clothes up off the floor.
A **period** can be used in dialogue. It appears inside the **quotation mark**.	Terrance said, "It seems like a great day for a picnic."
If the quote comes at the beginning of the sentence, use a **comma** at the end of the direct quotation and before the **quotation mark**. Place a **period** at the end of the sentence.	"If it gets cold, put on your jacket," said Robyn.

Practice

Rewrite the following sentences by adding periods where necessary.

1. Check out at the far counter

   _____

2. Janet said, "Let's take a long walk"

   _____

3. "Hiking is my favorite hobby," said Charlie

   _____

4. Reach a little farther, and you will have touched the top

   _____

Language Arts

Periods: Abbreviations and Initials

A **period** is also used for abbreviations or initials.

Use a **period** after each part of an abbreviation. An abbreviation is a shortened form of a word or phrase.	M.A. (Master of Arts)
Use a **period** after each letter of an initial. An initial is the first letter of a name.	Samuel L. Jackson

---

Practice

Rewrite the following sentences by adding periods where necessary.

1. Kathryn received her MA from the University of Arizona.

   _____

2. My favorite actress is Vivica A Fox.

   _____

3. JRR Tolkien is my favorite author.

   _____

4. My younger sister's favorite book is *Junie B Jones Smells Something Fishy*.

   _____

5. Franklin D Roosevelt was first elected president in 1932.

   _____

6. Mrs Obrador is the principal at my school.

   _____

A question mark **is used in different ways.**

A question mark appears at the end of an interrogative sentence, or a sentence that asks a question.	How was your trip?

In quotations, a question mark **can be placed either inside or outside of the closing quotation mark depending on the meaning of the sentence.**

The question mark is placed inside the **quotation mark** when it is part of the quotation.	The coach asked, "How many push-ups can you do?"
The question mark is placed outside the **quotation mark** when it punctuates the whole sentence.	Did the coach say, "Try to do twice as many as you did last week"?
A question mark is not used in sentences with indirect quotations. Instead, use other punctuation, such as a **period.**	Suhad said he asked the librarian for help finding the book.

Practice

Write one interrogative sentence. Then, write one sentence where a question mark punctuates a quotation.

1. _____

2. _____

Question Marks

Practice

Draw a line to match the sentences in Column A with their descriptions in Column B.

Column A

1. Bill asked the guide how long the museum would be open.

2. Could you tell that funny joke again?

3. Sylvia's mother asked, "What time is your track meet on Saturday?"

4. Did the weather reporter say, "Expect six inches of snow tonight"?

5. Where did you park the car?

6. Did you say, "Read page four"?

7. Sam asked for a quarter to make a wish in the well.

8. The teacher asked, "What is the square root of 64?"

9. We asked for directions after getting lost on the way to the restaurant.

10. "Why are you wearing that funny hat?" I asked.

11. What is the recipe for this delicious stir fry?

12. Can you remember if I said, "Meet us here at 4 p.m."?

Column B

interrogative sentence

question mark punctuating quotation

question mark punctuating entire sentence

indirect quotation

question mark punctuating entire sentence

indirect quotation

interrogative sentence

question mark punctuating quotation

question mark punctuating entire sentence

interrogative sentence

indirect quotation

question mark punctuating quotation

An **exclamation mark** is used in different ways.

An **exclamation mark** is used at the end of an exclamatory sentence. This type of sentence expresses surprise.	We have to read all three chapters for homework tonight!
An exclamatory sentence can also express a strong emotion, such as anger or fear. It also requires an **exclamation mark**.	I think I just saw a ghost!
Interjections sometimes require **exclamation marks**.	Aha! I've come up with the answer!
It's important not to overuse exclamation marks. If a sentence does not expresses surprise, urgency, or strong emotion, use a **period** or other punctuation instead.	I don't feel like going to the park today.

Language Arts

Practice

Choose a word from the box to complete the following sentences to express strong emotion or surprise. Not all of the words will be used.

warm	far	fast
loud	hot	soft

1. Don't touch the stove; it is _____!

2. Look how _____ that race car driver took the curve!

3. Please turn down that _____ music!

4. The trapeze performer is so _____ from the ground!

Commas: Series and Multiple Adjectives

A comma is used to separate items in a sentence. It can be used in different ways.

Series or serial commas are used when there are at least three items listed in a sentence in a row. The items can be words or phrases. Commas are used to separate them.

My favorite foods are pizza, pasta salad, and vegetable burritos.

I bought pens, pencils, paper, and envelopes at the office supply store.

To make a pizza you have to roll the crust, spread the sauce, and add the toppings.

Commas are also used with multiple adjectives. This occurs when more than one adjective describes a noun.

It was a warm, breezy day.

That was one wild, crazy roller coaster ride!

Sheila bought a pretty, purple dress to wear to the dance.

Make sure the adjectives equally modify the noun, and that one item is not actually an adverb modifying the adjective. In that case, do not include a comma.

Calvin read a hilariously funny book.
(There is no comma in this sentence because hilariously is an adverb modifying the adjective funny, not book.)

The ending of the love story was sadly bittersweet.
(There is no comma in this sentence because sadly is an adverb modifying bittersweet, not love story.)

Language Arts

Commas: Series and Multiple Adjectives

Practice

Rewrite the sentences on the lines below to add the correct punctuation. If the sentence is already correct, leave the line blank.

1. Before you leave, eat your breakfast brush your teeth and grab your backpack.

    _____

2. I like cool breezy springtime days the best.

    _____

3. This skateboard moves ridiculously fast.

    _____

4. I'm bringing fruit cheese crackers and juice for our picnic.

    _____

5. Be careful with that soup because it's unbelievably hot.

    _____

6. Next time, bring a sketchbook markers and colored pencils to art class.

    _____

7. Look at that shiny new red convertible!

    _____

8. This afternoon, we need to get groceries fix dinner and take the dogs for a walk.

    _____

Commas: Direct Address and Set-off Dialogue

A comma is used to separate items in a sentence. It can be used in different ways.

Commas are used to separate the name of a person spoken to from the rest of the sentence. This is called a direct address.	Ken, please help me get dinner on the table.
	Your grocery store delivery has arrived, Adam.
	Mrs. Washington, will you be attending the parent-teacher conference?
In a direct address, if the name appears in the middle of a sentence, two commas are needed.	Wake up, Andrew, you're going to be late.
	How did you do, Karen, in the tennis match?
	Have you heard, Dad, about our plans for the weekend?
Commas are also used to set off dialogue from the rest of the sentence.	The salesperson said, "Our gym has classes in aerobics and kickboxing."
	"Let's go to the movies this weekend," Sarah said.
	She heard her mother yell, "Hurry up or you'll be late for school!"

Practice

Write one sentence with a series, one with direct address, and one with multiple adjectives.

1. _____

2. _____

3. _____

Commas: Direct Address and Set-off Dialogue

Practice

Rewrite the sentences on the lines below to add the correct punctuation.

1. "Reese guess what I'm doing this weekend" said Dani.

   _____

2. Carmen please answer the door.

   _____

3. Patricia smiled and said "I've got a nice surprise for you."

   _____

4. I yelled to my sister up the stairs "Don't forget to bring down my sneakers!"

   _____

5. Mr. Kwan I hope you'll come to our garage sale on Saturday.

   _____

6. Can you help me Dennis with cleanup after the school fair?

   _____

7. "That is the craziest thing I have ever heard" she answered with a laugh.

   _____

8. Did your team win Maria in the football game?

   _____

Commas: Combining Sentences

Simple sentences may become more interesting when they are combined into compound sentences or complex sentences. Sometimes, this means using commas.

Use a comma to combine two independent clauses with a coordinate conjunction and create a compound sentence.

The students read three chapters, and they answered the questions at the end of each chapter.

When combining an independent clause with a dependent clause (a complex sentence), use a comma. The clauses are connected with a comma and subordinate conjunction. Together, they create a complex sentence.

Even though the skies were sunny now, clouds were rolling in.

Practice

Identify each type of sentence below. Write **Compound** or **Complex** on the lines.

1. Lisa plays trombone in the band, and her sister Lee plays trumpet.

   _____

2. The distance is long, but the runner is strong.

   _____

3. Unless the movie is a comedy, I don't think I want to see it.

   _____

4. Although the forecast called for rain, they decided to have the picnic anyway.

   _____

5. As long as the designs are good, the clothes will sell well.

   _____

6. The portrait is modern, but it has an antique look.

   _____

Commas **are also used in personal letters and business letters.**

Commas appear in four of the five parts of a personal letter.

Heading: 2633 Lane Road
Meridian, OH 30000
June 3, 2015

Salutation: Dear Kelly,

Body: Happy birthday! You're the best, and I miss seeing you every day.

Closing: Your friend,

Commas appear in four of the six parts of the business letter.

Heading: 2200 Meridian Drive
Riverside, CA 10000
October 10, 2015

Inside Address: Ms. Corrine Fifelski
Lakeview Sound Design
907 Effington Boulevard
Boulder, CO 20000

Body: Thank you for bringing me in for an interview. I enjoyed learning more about your company, and I look forward to hearing from you.

Closing: Sincerely,

Practice

Read each line from a personal letter or a business letter. If it is missing a comma, write an X on the line. If not, leave the line blank.

1. _____ 1473 Oliver Drive

2. _____ Dear Tiffany

3. _____ I went to the grocery store bookstore and shoe store.

4. _____ Your sister,

5. _____ April 17 2004

6. _____ Portland ME

Language Arts

Quotation Marks

Quotation marks **are used in a sentence with dialogue or other kinds of quotations.**

Quotation marks show the exact words of a speaker. They are placed before and after all of the words in the direct quotation.

"Let's go to the movies tonight," said Janice. "That new animated film was just released."

Quotation marks are also used when a direct quotation is made within a direct quotation. In this case, single quotation marks are used to set off the inside quotation.

John said, "Miss Robinson clearly said, 'The project is due tomorrow.'"

Quotation marks are used with some titles. Quotation marks are used with the titles of short works, including stories, poems, songs, and articles in magazines and newspapers.

"North Carolina Wins the Championship"

"Just Another Love Song"

Quotation marks are not used with the titles of long works, such as books or plays.

The Wizard of Oz

Romeo and Juliet

If a title is quoted within a direct quotation, then single quotation marks are used.

Melissa said, "Did you read the article 'Saving Our Oceans' in this magazine?"

Practice

Write one sentence of dialogue that includes a direct quotation by a character. Write one sentence that includes a title in quotation marks. Write one direct quotation of your own.

1. _____

2. _____

3. _____

Practice

On the lines, write a **DQ** for a direct quotation, **IQ** for an inside quotation, **T** for a title of a short work, and **TQ** for a title within a quotation. Then, rewrite the sentence to include the quotation marks.

1. _____ Sandra shouted, Our team won the game!

_____

2. _____ Suzie responded, I heard the coach say, This was my best team ever!

_____

3. _____ The magazine *Sports Today* had an article called A Winning Season.

_____

4. _____ What did the article A Winning Season say about our team? Sandra asked.

_____

5. _____ The writer of the article thinks we could win the championship, Suzie said.

_____

6. _____ He said, The team is strong offensively and defensively and could go all the way, continued Suzie.

_____

_____

7. _____ This is so exciting! yelled Sandra.

_____

8. _____ Suzie said, Let's go check out our newspaper *Community Times* and see what they had to say!

_____

_____

Apostrophes

An apostrophe can be used in two ways.

Apostrophes are used in contractions, which are shortened forms of words. The words are shortened by leaving out letters. Apostrophes take the place of the omitted letters.

he is = he's

can not = can't

Apostrophes are also used to form possessives, which show possession, or ownership. To form a singular possessive, or the possessive of a singular noun, add an apostrophe and an s.

I'll carry Harry's notebook.

There are two ways to form a plural possessive, or the possessive of a plural noun.

For plural nouns ending in s, simply add the apostrophe.

The puppies' guardians are very happy.

If the plural noun does not end in an s, add both the apostrophe and an s.

The women's team has won every game.

Practice

The sentences in Column A contain words with apostrophes. Match these sentences to the types of apostrophes used in Column B. Draw a line to make your match.

Column A	Column B
1. Felicia's jacket is in my car.	contraction
2. He's my best friend.	singular possessive
3. The men's shirts are on the second floor.	plural possessive ending in s
4. The girls' tickets are at the box office.	plural possessive not ending in s

A colon is used to introduce a series, to set off a clause, for emphasis, in time, or in a business letter.

Colons are used to introduce a series in a sentence.	My favorite vegetables include the following: broccoli, red peppers, and spinach.
Colons are sometimes used instead of a comma (in more formal cases) to set off a clause.	The radio announcer said: "The game is postponed due to torrential rains."
Colons are used to set off a word or phrase for emphasis.	The skiers got off of the mountain as they expected the worst: an avalanche.
Colons are used when writing the time.	Is your appointment at 9:00 or 10:00?
Business letters use colons in the salutation.	Dear Ms. Massey:

Practice

Identify why the colon is used in each sentence. Write **S** for series, **C** for clause, **E** for emphasis, **T** for time, or **L** for business letter.

1. _____ The teacher said to do the following: read two chapters, answer the questions, and write a paragraph.

2. _____ My alarm goes off at 6:15 a.m.

3. _____ The coach gave us some tips: eat right and train hard.

4. _____ All of my hard training paid off when I saw the sign ahead: Finish.

5. _____ Dear Dr. Brooks:

6. _____ The host said: "Let's eat!"

Language Arts

Semicolons

A semicolon is a cross between a period and a comma. Semicolons can be used to join two independent clauses, to separate clauses containing commas, and to separate groups which contain commas.

Semicolons are used to join two independent clauses when a coordinate conjunction is not used.	The city's sounds are loud; I love the excitement.
Semicolons are used to separate clauses that already contain commas.	After the sun sets, the lights come on; the city is beautiful at night.
When words or phrases already contain commas, semicolons are used to separate them instead of series commas.	Billie's new apartment has a bedroom for her, her sister, and her brother; a laundry room; an exercise room; and a game room.

Practice

Rewrite the following sentences, adding semicolons where needed.

1. The insulation in the room wasn't very effective it was freezing.

   _____

2. Although we were relieved it didn't rain, we needed it a drought was upon us.

   _____

3. They needed equipment to start a business computer monitor printer and furniture, such as desks, chairs, and lamps.

   _____

   _____

4. Riana has a talent for art it is her favorite subject.

   _____

Hyphens **are used to divide words at the end of a line and to create new words. They are also used between numbers.**

Use a hyphen to divide a word into syllables.	beau-ti-ful per-form
Do not divide one-syllable words with fewer than six letters.	through piece
Do not divide one letter from the rest of the word.	event-ful not: e-ventful
Divide syllables after the vowel if the vowel is a syllable on its own.	come-dy not: com-edy
Divide words with double consonants between the consonants.	swim-ming mir-ror
Hyphens can be used to create new words when combined with words and word parts such as *self*, *ex*, and *great*.	The pianist was self-taught. My great-grandmother is 105 years old. I just saw our ex-mayor at the store.
Hyphens are used between numbers.	twenty-one

Language Arts

Practice

Circle the word that includes the correct use of punctuation from the two choices for each item.

1. instru-ment   instr-ument   2. o-ceanographer   ocean-ographer

3. thirty two   thirty-two   4. char-ity   chari-ty

5. ch-air   chair   6. run-ning   runn-ing

7. great aunt   great-aunt   8. sixty-four   sixty four

Parentheses

Parentheses are used to show supplementary material, to set off phrases in a stronger way than commas, and to enclose numbers.

Parentheses show supplementary material. Supplementary material is a word or phrase that gives additional information.	Theresa's mother (a dentist) will speak to our class next week.
Sometimes, words or phrases that might be set off with commas are set off with parentheses instead. It gives the information more emphasis.	Leo's apartment building, the one with the nice window boxes, was voted prettiest in the neighborhood.
	Leo's apartment building (the one with the nice window boxes) was voted prettiest in the neighborhood.
Parentheses are also used to enclose numbers.	Jacklyn wants to join the track team because (1) it is good exercise, (2) she can travel to other schools and cities, and (3) she can meet new friends.

Practice

Match the sentences in Column A with the reason why parentheses are used in Column B. Draw a line to make your match.

Column A

1. When cooking rice, don't forget to (1) rinse the rice, (2) steam the rice, and (3) eat the rice!

2. The preliminary findings (announced yesterday) are important to the study.

3. The dinosaur bones (a huge discovery) can be seen in the museum.

Column B

supplementary material

set off with emphasis

enclose numbers

Use everything you have learned so far about punctuation to answer the questions.

Complete the following sentences by circling the best end punctuation in parentheses.

1. Bees are fascinating creatures (. !)

2. Can bees talk (. ?)

3. Scientists have discovered that bees talk to each other (. !)

4. How do they talk (? !)

5. Bees talk through dance (? .)

Write **SC** for series comma, **DA** for direct address, **SD** for set-off dialogue, or **MA** for multiple adjectives.

6. _____ The customer asked, "How much will the repairs cost?"

7. _____ I had a sweet, juicy apple for lunch.

8. _____ Finish your homework before playing video games, Craig.

9. _____ Shawn had a long, difficult homework assignment.

10. _____ Chloe, your song in the concert was beautiful.

---

11. Write three sentences with commas. One should be a compound sentence, one should be a complex sentence, and one should include a quotation.

_____

_____

_____

_____

_____

_____

Language Arts

The sentences in Column A contain words with apostrophes. Match these sentences to the types of apostrophes used in Column B. Draw a line to make your match.

Column A	Column B
12. The parents' cars lined the street.	contraction
13. Patty's blanket is nearly done.	singular possessive
14. The children's toys are in the toy box.	plural possessive ending in **s**
15. Teddy's missed the presentation.	plural possessive not ending in **s**

Rewrite the following sentences to include colons, semicolons, or parentheses.

16. Although the score was tied, our team looked strong we knew we would win.

_____

17. There are many reasons to adopt from a shelter it saves animals' lives, they are seen by a vet, and they are spayed and neutered.

_____

_____

18. The manager told the customers "The Black Friday sale will begin at 5 o'clock in the morning."

_____

19. Mac must 1 wash the dishes, 2 do his homework, and 3 get ready for bed.

_____

Rewrite each word with a hyphen in the correct spot.

20. thirtythree _____		21. excoach _____	
22. greatuncle _____		23. selfaware _____	
24. exwife _____		25. seventyfive_____	

Rewrite the following sentences by adding periods, question marks, and exclamation marks where needed.

1. "Marsha," called A.J., "I heard you got your driver's license"

   _____

2. "Don't forget to put mustard ketchup and pickles on my sandwich" Mona exclaimed

   _____

3. EB White is the author of the book *Charlotte's Web*

   _____

4. The customer asked, "What comes on the garden salad"

   _____

5. Wow That was the best movie I've ever seen

   _____

6. **Add commas where needed in the business letter.**

> 1151 Davidson Street
> Chicago IL 40000
> April 8 2015
>
> Mrs. Jane Merrinan Director
> City Community Center
> 1200 Adams Street
> Chicago IL 30000
>
> Dear Mrs. Merrinan:
>
> My name is A.J. Byington. I am interested in applying as a summer counselor at the Civic Community Center and I would like to become a part-time volunteer during the school year. I am a freshman at Northwest High School. My experience has included tutoring coaching and counseling students in elementary school. Your varied well-rounded programs interest me. I have included my activities list and references. I look forward to talking with you in the near future. Thank you for your time.
>
> Sincerely
> A.J. Byington

Chapter Review

7. Proofread the following paragraphs by adding commas, quotation marks, apostrophes, colons, semicolons, hyphens, and parentheses where needed.

Sharon are you going to the community center after school? asked Susan.

Yes, Im going right after school to play some basketball our team is going to the tournament. My great-grandpa is going to cheer me on, answered Sharon.

Im so glad we have a center, said Sharon. We learned in school about the very first community center. It was started by two very brave women Jane Addams and Ellen Gates Starr.

Susan responded, I dont think I've heard of them.

They lived way back in the 1800s. Life in cities was not easy, Sharon continued. Thousands of people worked in factories even kids and received little money in return. Jane and Ellen both wanted to help people. They moved into one of the worst parts of town. They found a big house on Halstead Street. They rented it and turned it into the first community center Hull House. Hull House offered child care for working mothers eventually leading to kindergarten classes. After a while, many classes were offered to people of all ages art, music, drama, cooking, science math and languages. The people of the city were finally brought together in a place where they could socialize relax, and escape their working lives. Many of the people who came to Hull House went on to lead successful lives and help other people.

Well, Sharon, said Susan, today's game should be played in honor of Jane Addams and Ellen Gates Starr!

Write three sentences about your favorite sporting event, either as a participant or a spectator. Use each of the three types of parentheses in your sentences.

8. _____

_____

9. _____

_____

10. _____

_____

Use a dictionary to look up two words with the prefix **ex-**, two words with the prefix **great-**, and two words with the prefix **self-**. Write a sentence for each.

11. _____
_____

12. _____
_____

13. _____
_____

14. _____
_____

15. _____
_____

16. _____
_____

17. Write a review of a movie you have seen or a book you have read. Include at least two of the following uses of semicolons: between independent clauses, to separate clauses that contain clauses, and to separate groups of words that contain commas.

_____
_____
_____
_____
_____
_____
_____

Language Arts

Tricky Verb Usage

Some irregular verbs are confused with one another. It is important to use them correctly.

The irregular verbs bring and take are often confused with each other. When you bring something, it is coming in or toward you. When you take something, it is moving away.

The forms of bring are bring (present), brought (past), and brought (past participle).

The teacher asked her students, "Please bring in newspapers to class." (present)

Mom brought me lunch for my school trip. (past)

I wish I had brought my sunglasses with me. (past participle)

The forms of take are take (present), took (past), and taken (past participle).

Dad said, "Could you take my slippers upstairs?" (present)

Jessica took magazines to her sick friend. (past)

He had taken the tickets to the game. (past participle)

The irregular verbs lay and lie are also easily confused.

The verb lay means to place. The forms of the verb lay are lay (present), laid (past), and laid (past participle).

The teachers lay the papers on their desks.

Tommy laid his shirts on the bed.

Mother has laid her briefcase on the same table every night for years.

The verb lie means to recline. The forms of the verb lie are lie (present), lay (past), and lain (past participle).

The kittens lie by the window in the sun.

Yesterday, the kittens lay on the blankets in the laundry room.

She has lain on the same spot on the sofa all afternoon.

Practice

Circle the best verb in parentheses to complete each sentence. Then, rewrite the sentence using the correct tense.

1. Don't (bring, take) the library books out of the building.

    _____

2. Brian and Matt (bring, take) extra water to the baseball games.

    _____

3. Last year Lilly (bring, take) cupcakes on her birthday.

    _____

4. Grover (bring, take) six cookies out of the box.

    _____

5. Yesterday, we (bring, take) blankets and towels to the animal shelter.

    _____

6. Don't (lay, lie) in the sun without sunscreen!

    _____

7. It was unusual that the papers were missing; he had (lay, lie) them in the same spot every morning.

    _____

8. Meagan (lay, lie) in bed too long this morning and was late for work.

    _____

9. Jean (lay, lie) the covers over the plates before the rain hit.

    _____

10. Please (lay, lie) the cups and plates at the end of the table.

    _____

Adjective or Adverb?

Adjectives modify nouns. Adverbs modify verbs, adjectives, and other adverbs. Some adverbs are easily confused with adjectives.

Bad is an adjective, and badly is an adverb.	That was a bad concert; the music was too loud. (bad modifies the noun concert) Tyler drives badly; he almost ran that stop sign. (badly modifies the verb drives)
Good is an adjective, and well is an adverb.	We watched a good game. (good modifies the noun game) Both teams played well. (well modifies the verb played)
The word already is an adverb. It answers the question when. The phrase all ready means completely ready.	It was morning and already time to leave. The team was all ready to leave.

Practice

Fill in the blank with the correct word from the box. Not every word will be used.

already	all ready	badly
good	well	bad

1. I can't believe it's _____ Saturday.

2. If Jesse doesn't get a _____ grade on this test, he will have to retake it.

3. You sing that song _____ .

4. Don't feel _____ about missing the party.

5. The cast members are _____ for their first performance of the school play.

Language Arts

Practice

Circle the correct adjective or adverb in parentheses. Then, underline the word it modifies (except for numbers 5 and 6) and write what part of speech it is on the lines below.

1. We threw out the (bad, badly) bruised orange.

   _____

2. Celina played (good, well) and won her match.

   _____

3. I just finished a really (good, well) book; I couldn't put it down.

   _____

4. The instructions were (bad, badly), and we got lost.

   _____

5. By the time the bus picked us up, we were (all ready, already) late.

6. If everyone in the class is (all ready, already) to go, we'll line up at the door.

7. It was a (good, well) recipe; I'll make that again.

   _____

8. If our chorus sings (good, well), we'll advance to the semifinals.

   _____

9. Daryl (bad, badly) sang the last song.

   _____

10. Ally had a (bad, badly) excuse for not playing in the game.

   _____

Negatives and Double Negatives

It is important to understand the difference between a negative and a double negative. One is correct. The other is not.

A negative sentence states the opposite. Negative words include not, no, never, nobody, nowhere, nothing, barely, hardly, and scarcely.

I do not like horror movies.

I never like to ride my bike after dark.

I can hardly wait until baseball season.

Negative sentences can also include contractions containing the word *not*.

We won't go anywhere without you.

Double negatives happen when two negative words are used in the same sentence. Don't use double negatives; doing so will make your sentence positive again, and it is poor grammar.

Incorrect: I'm not going nowhere until it stops raining.

Correct: I'm not going anywhere until it stops raining.

Practice

Rewrite the following sentences to correct the double negatives.

1. I love breakfast; I can't imagine not skipping it.

   _____

2. I can't scarcely believe I made it all the way down the slope without falling.

   _____

3. Samantha doesn't never like to wear her coat outside.

   _____

Synonyms and antonyms are two types of word relationships.

Synonyms describe things that are similar.

Synonyms are words that have the same, or almost the same, meaning.	Here are some examples of synonyms: clever/smart reply/answer wreck/destroy applaud/clap
Using synonyms can help you avoid repeating words and can make your writing more interesting.	"I think this is such a pretty prom dress," Jessica said. Her friend Marisa agreed, "It looks beautiful."

Antonyms describe things that are different.

Antonyms are words that have opposite, or almost opposite, meanings.	Here are some examples of antonyms: wide/narrow accept/decline break/repair borrow/lend
Using antonyms can help you show how people, places, situations, and things are different.	Jefferson Street is very crowded and has lots of stores. On the other side of town, Washington Street is almost empty.

Language Arts

Synonyms and Antonyms

Practice

Read each set of words below. Circle the two words in each set that are synonyms.

1. pardon forget forgive ordinary

2. damage mend repair mock

3. likely unlikely probable rarely

4. depart leave arrival mingle

5. heal insist injure wound

6. accept decline formula refuse

7. remorse regret replace joy

8. thin obese slender flexible

Rewrite each sentence below. Use a synonym for **boldface** words and an antonym for <u>underlined</u> words.

1. The police officer had to **pursue** the **criminal**, who **hopped** in his car and sped away.

   _____

2. Harriet <u>enjoys</u> cooking with foods that have <u>bold</u> flavors.

   _____

3. When Enzo **finished** his book, he felt quite <u>satisfied</u> with the <u>ending</u>.

   _____

4. Dr. Williams asked the **nervous** little girl to <u>exhale</u> <u>slowly</u>.

   _____

An **analogy** is a comparison between two pairs of words. To complete an analogy, figure out how the pairs of words are related.

In this **analogy**, a **coop** is a home for a **chicken**, just as a **hive** is a home for a **bee**.

Coop is to **chicken** as **hive** is to **bee**.

In this **analogy**, a **petal** is part of a **flower**, just as a **wing** is part of a **bird**.

Petal is to **flower** as **wing** is to **bird**.

In this **analogy**, **excited** is the opposite of **bored**, just as **silence** is the opposite of **noise**.

Excited is to **bored** as **silence** is to **noise**.

Practice

Complete each analogy below with a word from the box.

apple	forest	necklace
page	peddle	broken

1. **Pedal** is to _____ as **write** is to **right**.

2. **Neck** is to _____ as **finger** is to **ring**.

3. _____ is to **book** as **blade** is to **fan**.

4. **Sand** is to **beach** as **tree** is to _____.

5. **Spaghetti** is to **noodle** as _____ is to **fruit**.

6. **Fixed** is to _____ as **full** is to **empty**.

Analogies

Practice

Underline the word from each pair that completes the analogy.

1. **Teacher** is to (school, books) as **lifeguard** is to **pool**.

2. (Bark, Tail) is to **dog** as **neigh** is to **horse**.

3. **Shy** is to (bold, timid) as **guest** is to **visitor**.

4. **Orlando** is to **Florida** as (Wisconsin, Detroit) is to **Michigan**.

5. **King** is to (queen, kingdom) as **prince** is to **princess**.

6. **Stove** is to (kitchen, cook) as **tub** is to **bathroom**.

7. **Liz** is to **Elizabeth** as **Danny** is to (Tommy, Daniel).

8. (Spring, Fall) is to **winter** as **lunch** is to **dinner**.

9. **Copper** is to **penny** as **wool** is to (sheep, sweater).

10. **Four** is to **quarter** as (one, five) is to fifth.

Follow the directions to write your own analogies.

1. Write an analogy in which the words are synonyms.

   _____

2. Write an analogy that shows a part-to-whole relationship.

   _____

3. Write an analogy that shows a numerical relationship.

   _____

Language Arts

Homophones are words that sound the same but have different spellings and different meanings. If you are unsure about which homophone to use, look up the definitions in a dictionary.

There are hundreds of homophones in the English language. Here are some examples.

cereal: food made from grain serial: of a series	My favorite breakfast is a big bowl of cereal. My favorite TV shows are serial dramas with plots that continue from episode to episode.
council: a group elected to pass laws counsel: to give guidance	The council meets every Wednesday evening to discuss city plans. My teacher will counsel me on what subjects to take next year.
coarse: rough course: the path over which something moves	This material has a smooth texture, but that one is coarse. I like to ride my bike on the scenic course along the river.

Practice

Complete the following sentences with one of the homophones from the box.

cent	scent	sent

1. I bid one _____ more and won the item.

2. The flowers have a beautiful _____.

3. The letter was _____ to the wrong address.

Multiple-Meaning Words

Multiple-meaning words, or homographs, are words that are spelled the same but have different meanings. They may also sometimes have different pronunciations. In many cases, a homograph can be used as different parts of speech. If you are unsure about which multiple-meaning word to use, look up the definitions in a dictionary.

The word **bow** can be a noun that means "a looped piece of ribbon or cloth."	Lexi put a **bow** on top of her gift for Chandler.
Or, **bow** can be a verb that means "to bend at the waist."	Be sure you **bow** to the audience at the end of the performance.

Practice

Read each sentence. Then, circle the definition that describes the meaning of the underlined homograph as it is used in the sentence.

1. Before leaving the house, my mother always makes sure her <u>compact</u> is in her purse.

   a. dense and tightly packed

   b. a small case with a mirror

2. Juan added vanilla <u>extract</u> to the cookie dough.

   a. take out

   b. concentrated form

3. The <u>proceeds</u> from the auction will be used to provide art scholarships.

   a. money from a sale

   b. moves forward

4. Officer Wilkins talked calmly with the man who was <u>upset</u> about the accident.

   a. spilled or overturned

   b. distressed or anxious

Denotations and Connotations

Denotations and connotations relate to the meaning of words.

A word's denotation is its actual, literal meaning. It is the meaning you would find if you looked up the word in a dictionary.

The words **house**, **home**, **shack**, and **residence** all mean approximately the same thing.

Their denotation is "a place where people live."

A word's connotation is the meaning associated with the word. It may be more emotional, or tied to an idea or feeling about the word.

Connotations can be positive, negative, or neutral.

The **connotations** of the words **house**, **home**, **shack**, and **residence** are different.

House and **residence** both have a neutral connotation. These words do not cause a strong feeling in either direction.

Home has a positive connotation—it sounds cozy and reassuring.

Shack, on the other hand, has a negative connotation—it sounds run-down and shabby.

Practice

Write a sentence for each word below. The words in each pair have similar denotations but different connotations.

1. puny _____

   small _____

2. smile _____

   smirk _____

Denotations and Connotations

Practice

For each set of words below, write the denotation (or literal definition) on the top line. On the line beside each word, write **P** for positive connotation, **N** for neutral connotation, and **NG** for negative connotation.

1. ask   demand   request

   denotation: _____

   connotation: ask _____   demand _____   request _____

2. confident   cocky

   denotation: _____

   connotation: confident _____   cocky _____

3. slender   skinny

   denotation: _____

   connotation: slender _____   skinny _____

4. odd   special   unique

   denotation: _____

   connotation: odd _____   special _____   unique _____

5. curious   nosy   interested

   denotation: _____

   connotation: curious _____   nosy _____   interested _____

6. borrow   steal

   denotation: _____

   connotation: borrow _____   steal _____

7. cheap   thrifty   stingy

   denotation: _____

   connotation: cheap _____   thrifty _____   stingy _____

Similes, Metaphors, and Personification

Similes, metaphors, **and** personification **are three types of figures of speech. They make writing more interesting and vivid for the reader.**

A **simile** is a figure of speech that compares two things using the words **like** or **as**.

The summer sky was as blue as the inside of a swimming pool.

The sound of the papers rustling was like crisp leaves in autumn.

From above, the animal tracks looked like scribbles drawn across the snow.

A **metaphor** is a figure of speech that compares two unlike things that are similar in some way. Metaphors do not use **like** or **as**.

When Mr. Yang turned off the ignition, the car immediately became an icebox.

The city lights were a constellation against the inky sky.

The blazing sun cooked the landscape.

Personification is a figure of speech that gives human characteristics to something that is not human, such as an animal or an object.

The church bells sang through the valley.

Nell watched the flowers dance in the soft breeze.

The dog gave a knowing wink, then chased after the Frisbee.

Language Arts

Similes, Metaphors, and Personification

Practice

Read each sentence below. On the line, write **S** if it contains a simile, **M** if it contains a metaphor, and **P** if it contains personification.

1. _____ Clouds raced each other across the horizon.

2. _____ The tall trees on the edge of the forest were like the columns of a Greek temple.

3. _____ Carson was as still as a statue, waiting for the bee to fly away.

4. _____ The thunderstorm was a freight train rumbling through the night.

5. _____ On the trampoline, Malia was a rocket launching into the sky.

6. _____ Her irritating laugh sounded like a barking dog.

Complete each sentence below with a simile.

1. The jet soared through the air like _____.

2. The kitten's fur felt soft as _____.

3. Mr. Robinson's laugh rang out like _____.

4. The rooster stood on the fence and crowed like _____.

5. After the spring storm, the forest smelled as fresh as _____.

6. Maya tripped as she stepped onto the stage, and her face turned as red as

_____.

7. With each step, Rowan's boots crunched the snow, sounding like _____

_____.

8. Hannah's new scissors cut through fabric like _____.

Similes, Metaphors, and Personification

Practice

Each sentence below contains personification. Underline the part of the sentence that shows that the writer is personifying something that is an animal or an object.

1. The candle's flame leaped and danced as a breeze blew in the open window.

2. The moon smiled down at the small village in the mountains.

3. The drooping plant begged for water as the sun rose higher in the sky.

4. Winter's long icy fingers clawed at Baxter's face.

5. The metal detector beeped loudly, anxiously demanding to be noticed.

6. The old car sputtered to a stop, closed its eyes, and gave up.

7. At the crack of dawn, several birds cheerily demanded that I get up and start the day.

8. The portly hedgehog rubbed his belly and sighed happily. "That was a lovely meal, my dear, just splendid," he said.

9. The jagged streaks of lightning raced across the sky, each intent on being faster than the others.

_____

Write five sentences that include metaphors.

1. _____

2. _____

3. _____

4. _____

5. _____

Root Words

Knowing root words can help you understand the definitions of unfamiliar words. When you know what part of a word means, you may be able to figure out the meaning of the rest of the word. Here are examples of root words and their meanings.

The root word act means "to do." It is the root of the word actor, which means "a person who performs."	Jim wants to become an actor and make movies and TV shows.
The root word aqua means "water." It is the root of the word aquarium, which means "a container filled with water to hold saltwater or freshwater plants or animals."	Do you want to visit to the aquarium downtown to see dolphins?
The root word auto means "self." It is the root of the word automobile, which means "a vehicle to move oneself."	Sarah wants to get an automobile so she can drive herself places and not rely on public transportation.
The root word centi means "a hundred." It is the root of the word centennial, which means "a 100th anniversary."	Next year, we will celebrate the centennial of our school, which opened almost 100 years ago.
The root word duct means "to lead." It is the root of the word conduct, which means "to lead from a position of command."	I'm studying music to learn how to conduct an orchestra.

Practice

Look at each word equation below. The meaning of one part is shown in parentheses. Consult the chart of root words on the previous page to find the meaning of the other part.

Write the meaning in the first blank. Then, combine the two meanings in the second blank. Write the dictionary definition in the space provided. The first one has been done for you.

1. react   re (again) + act _____to do_____ = _____again to do_____

    Dictionary definition: _____to act or do again_____

2. automatic   auto _____ + matic (having a mind) = _____

    Dictionary definition: _____

3. transact   trans (across) + act _____ = _____

    Dictionary definition: _____

4. centimeter   centi _____ + meter (meter) = _____

    Dictionary definition: _____

5. aquanaut   aqua _____ + naut (sailor) = _____

    Dictionary definition: _____

6. induct   in (into) + duct _____ = _____

    Dictionary definition: _____

Language Arts

Greek Roots

Many words in the English language have Greek roots. Learning the meanings of these roots can help you determine the meanings of some unfamiliar words. Here are some examples of words with Greek roots.

chron means "time"	After Jed's alarm clock broke, he was chronically late to class.
bio means "life"	My favorite class is biology because I enjoy studying animal and plant life.
phon means "sound"	I think this telephone is broken because I can hardly hear you.
cycl means "circle"	A cyclone is a storm that creates a huge funnel of wind that spins in a circle.
therm means "heat"	According to the thermometer, you have a fever of 100 degrees.

Practice

Read the clues below. Then, choose the word with the Greek root from the box that best fits each clue and write it on the line.

biography	chronological	homophones
thermos	tricycle	

1. _____ arranged by order of time

2. _____ the story of a person's life

3. _____ a bottle that keeps liquids hot

4. _____ a vehicle that has three circular wheels

5. _____ words that sound the same but are spelled differently

Many words in the English language have Latin roots. Learning the meanings of these roots can help you determine the meanings of some unfamiliar words. Here are some examples of words with Latin roots.

aud means "hear"	The **audience** at the rock concert was excited to hear a great show.
vid and **vis** mean "see"	I recorded a **video** of the party, so we can watch it later.
ped means "foot"	This street is just for **pedestrians** and is only open to foot traffic.
ann and **enn** mean "year"	Each year, my parents go camping to celebrate their **anniversary**.
liber means "free"	The Statue of **Liberty** is one of the symbols of freedom in the United States.

Practice

Circle the word with the Latin root that matches each definition below.

1. a large room where people go to hear or see a performance

   auditorium   videography

2. freedom

   liberty   impede

3. an insect that has many pairs of legs

   pedestrian   millipede

4. the part of a bicycle that is operated by the foot

   liberate   pedal

Using a Dictionary

You can use the dictionary to look up unfamiliar words and better understand them. Here is an example of how a word appears in the dictionary.

laboratory (\\'la-b(ə-)rə-,tor-ē\\) *noun* a room in which scientific research and experiments are done

An entry in a dictionary includes several parts.

The first part is the word itself. When you look up a word in the dictionary, you are looking up an entry word.	laboratory
Entry words, which are usually printed in **bold**, are often base words. For example, you would look for pretty, not prettier, and silly, not silliness.	
The next part of an entry in a dictionary is the pronunciation of the word in parentheses. It shows how to pronounce the word phonetically and the number of syllables in the word.	(\\'la-b(ə-)rə-,tor-ē\\)
The part of speech explains if the word is a noun, verb, adverb, adjective, preposition, or interjection.	noun
The final part of a dictionary entry is the definition. It explains the meaning of the word. Some words have more than one meaning. In that case, several definitions will appear for the entry word.	a room in which scientific research and experiments are done
The top of each page in a dictionary includes **guide words** that show the first and last entry words on that page.	laboratory • lacrosse

Practice

Write the entry word that you would look up in a dictionary beside each bold word below.

1. crickets _____

2. contains _____

3. rubbing _____

4. dragonflies _____

5. divided _____

6. mosquitoes _____

7. found _____

8. soaring _____

Use the dictionary entries below to answer the questions that follow.

sincere (\sin-'sir\) *adj.* honest; genuine, *noun* sincerity

squash (\skwäsh\) 1. *noun* a fruit that is related to pumpkins and gourds 2. *verb* to crush or press flat

refrigerator (\ri-'fri-jə-,rā-tər\) *noun* a machine or appliance that keeps food cold

1. On the line below, write a sentence using the word *squash* as a verb.

   _____

   _____

2. Which is an entry word—*sincere* or *sincerity*?

   _____

3. Which guide words would you find on the same page as *refrigerator*?

   reef • refresh   reflection • regal   refugee • rehearse

   _____

4. How many syllables are there in *refrigerator*?

   _____

Language Arts

Chapter Review

Circle the best verb in parentheses to complete each sentence. Then, rewrite it using the correct tense.

1. The children were (bring, take) home when it started to thunder.

   _____

2. Marv was (bring, take) to the hospital when he sprained his ankle.

   _____

3. Grandma said, "Aubrey, (bring, take) me a glass of water, please."

   _____

4. (lay, lie) on the blanket on the sand.

   _____

5. Barbara (lay, lie) her blanket near the bed.

   _____

6. Maggie (lay, lie) down for a quick nap yesterday.

   _____

Write a sentence using each of the following words: *bad*, *badly*, *good*, *well*, *all ready*, *already*.

7. _____

8. _____

9. _____

10. _____

11. _____

12. _____

Rewrite the following sentences to correct the double negatives.

13. The triplets' parents won't go nowhere without the babysitter.

   _____

14. Sheila doesn't never wake up before 8 o'clock in the morning.

   _____

15. Nora didn't not like the pizza, but it wasn't her favorite.

   _____

Complete the following sentences by circling the best answer in parentheses.

16. Sydney likes raisins and granola in his (cereal, serial).

17. Stacy liked the (scent, sent) of the flowers in the window box.

18. Please (ring, wring) out the towels before placing them in the dryer.

19. Zola loved to eat fresh (mussels, muscles) with lemon and butter.

20. Look at the weather (vane, vein) to see which way the wind is blowing.

21. I need to select one more (coarse, course) to take next semester.

Read each pair of sentences. Circle N for noun or V for verb to identify the part of speech for the word in boldface. Each pair of sentences will have two different answers.

22. Horace dusted the **display** of books in the store's front window.   N   V

   The schools in our district **display** student artwork throughout their halls.   N   V

23. Please **number** your answer 1 through 10.   N   V

   Dr. Patel analyzed the **number** of tadpoles living in the pond.   N   V

24. Louisa made the goal, **evening** the score and making the crowd go wild.   N   V

   Later this **evening**, we will go to my grandparents' house for a party.   N   V

Language Arts

Read each question below. Write your answer on the line.

25. Which two words in this sentence are synonyms?

    Aliyah finished one book in three days and completed the other just two days later.

    _____

26. In this analogy, how are the two pairs of words related?

    Wheat is to flour as chicken is to egg.

    _____

27. Which two words in this sentence have a similar denotation but different connotations?

    Uncle Drew's family just bought a new house, but I'll really miss the pool and tennis courts at their old mansion.

    _____

28. What is the meaning of the boldface word in each sentence?

    Don't forget to turn off the **light** before bed. This package is not **light** enough to be sent by first-class mail.

    _____

29. Which two words in this sentence are antonyms?

    Although Kiara always felt clumsy as a child, she grew up to be a graceful young woman.

    _____

30. How are the boldface words in these two sentences related?

    In the movie, the spy tried to **defect** to the U.S. Unfortunately, there was a **defect** in his passport, and he was arrested.

    _____

On the lines, tell which two things in each simile or metaphor are being compared.

31. Desmond's face was as still as wood as he listened to the bad news.

    _____   _____

Complete each sentence below by writing the correct pronoun or pronouns on the line.

1. As an Olympic hopeful, she must train nearly every day if ________ wants to compete.
2. They did not go to the meeting, so ________ didn't get ________ assignments.
3. As a chef, she must be willing to experiment if ________ wants to develop new dishes.
4. Since he is only 10 years old, ________ needs to be accompanied by ________ older brother to go on the roller coaster.

---

5. **Write a nonfiction paragraph about a reptile or an insect that interests you. Underline the subjects of each sentence and circle the verbs.**

____

____

____

____

---

6. **Identify common nouns (CN), proper nouns (PN), adjectives (ADJ), adverbs (ADV), conjunctions (C), prepositions (P), and articles (A) in the following biography. Write the abbreviation on the line next to the word.**

Leonardo da Vinci

One of the _____ greatest _____ artists of _____ all time was more than just an ____ artist. He was a sculptor _____, scientist, inventor, engineer _____, astronomer, architect, musician, philosopher, and _____ mathematician _____. Leonardo da Vinci _____ (1452–1519) was born in Vinci, Italy _____. Da Vinci was a _____ genius. During his lifetime, he sketched objects that were ahead of his time: the _____ airplane, the tank, and the submarine _____. Da Vinci brilliantly _____ and beautifully _____ painted the human _____ body and other natural _____ objects. Leonardo da Vinci painted the famous _____ Mona Lisa and The Last Supper _____, both of which now hang in _____ The Louvre _____ in Paris, France.

Language Arts Review

Write different types of sentences.

7. Declarative Sentence:

   _____

8. Interrogative Sentence:

   _____

9. Exclamatory Sentence:

   _____

10. Imperative Sentence:

    _____

11. Simple Sentence:

    _____

12. Compound Sentence:

    _____

13. Complex Sentence:

    _____

14. Write a paragraph about your favorite meal or snack. Include a variety of sentences in your writing.

    _____

    _____

    _____

    _____

    _____

    _____

    _____

Complete the following sentences by circling the correct answer in parentheses. Hint: Not all choices are proper nouns and need to be capitalized.

15. The (Civil War, civil war) was fought from 1861 to 1865.

16. The (mayor, Mayor) of our town was just re-elected to a second term.

17. The (Arabic, arabic) language uses a different alphabet.

18. My great-grandparents lived through the (great depression, Great Depression).

19. Maybe that (Police Officer, police officer) over there can give us directions.

Complete the following sentences by circling the best end punctuation in parentheses.

20. Look how fast that race car driver took the curve (. ? !)

21. Can you please turn down your music (. ? !)

22. The trapeze performer is so far from the ground (. ? !)

23. It's cold outside, and it looks like it might snow (. ? !)

24. The astronauts are working to repair a telescope in space (. ? !)

Read each sentence below. Then, write a new sentence using a different meaning for the underlined word. Use a dictionary if you need help.

25. The book's <u>content</u> is too difficult for children under five years old to understand.

_____

26. The water contains <u>minute</u> amounts of chlorine and fluoride.

_____

27. King Alfred ordered his <u>subjects</u> to work through the night to finish the bridge.

_____

Page 7

Multi-Digit Multiplication

Multiplication is the way to find the sum of equal groups of numbers. Follow these steps to multiply numbers with more than one digit.

Solve: 3263 × 43

First, write the problem vertically. Place the factor with the most digits on top.

$$\begin{array}{r} 3263 \\ \times\ 43 \end{array}$$

Next, use place value to break the smaller factor up. 43 can be broken up into 40 and 3.

$$\begin{array}{r} 3263 \\ \times\ 40 \end{array} \qquad \begin{array}{r} 3263 \\ \times\ 3 \end{array}$$

Then, multiply 3263 by 40 and then by 3. Work from right to left.

$$\begin{array}{r} 3263 \\ \times\ 40 \\ \hline 130520 \end{array} \qquad \begin{array}{r} 3263 \\ \times\ 3 \\ \hline 9789 \end{array}$$

Finally, add the results to find the final product.

$$\begin{array}{r} 130520 \\ +\ 9789 \\ \hline 140309 \end{array} \qquad \begin{array}{r} 3263 \\ \times\ 43 \\ \hline 140,309 \end{array}$$

Practice

Solve the following problems.

1. $\begin{array}{r} 324 \\ \times\ 27 \\ \hline 8748 \end{array}$
2. $\begin{array}{r} 5150 \\ \times\ 22 \\ \hline 113,300 \end{array}$
3. $\begin{array}{r} 886 \\ \times\ 374 \\ \hline 331,364 \end{array}$

4. $\begin{array}{r} 763 \\ \times\ 618 \\ \hline 471,534 \end{array}$
5. $\begin{array}{r} 2186 \\ \times\ 342 \\ \hline 747,612 \end{array}$
6. $\begin{array}{r} 1898 \\ \times\ 475 \\ \hline 901,550 \end{array}$

Simple Steps · Sixth Grade   Multiplication and Division   7

Page 8

Multi-Digit Division

Division is the way to subtract equal groups of numbers from one larger number. Follow these steps to divide numbers with more than one digit.

Solve: 983 ÷ 28

First, divide the first digit of the dividend by the divisor. If the divisor will not go into the first digit, use both the first and second digit.

Next, subtract the result from the first two digits in the dividend. Bring down the final digit in the dividend and write it beside the difference. Divide this number by the divisor and repeat the same steps as for the first digit.

Finally, write the final difference, or remainder, as part of the quotient at the top of the answer line following the letter r. Make sure that this remainder is not divisible by the the divisor.

Practice

Solve the following problems.

1. 18)94 → 5 r4
2. 43)88 → 2 r2
3. 12)125 → 10 r5

4. 27)815 → 30 r5
5. 54)725 → 13 r23
6. 45)880 → 19 r25

8   Multiplication and Division   Simple Steps · Sixth Grade

Page 9

Reciprocal Operations

Reciprocal operations are opposite operations. Multiplication and division are reciprocal operations, just like addition and subtraction are reciprocal operations. You can use reciprocal operations to check your answers when you solve math problems.

Solve: 392 × 22

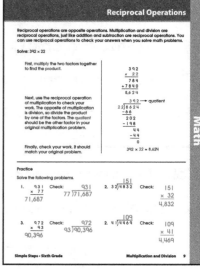

Practice

Solve the following problems.

1. $\begin{array}{r} 931 \\ \times\ 77 \\ \hline 71,687 \end{array}$ Check: 77)71,687 → 931

2. 32)4832 → 151   Check: $\begin{array}{r} 151 \\ \times\ 32 \\ \hline 4,832 \end{array}$

3. $\begin{array}{r} 972 \\ \times\ 93 \\ \hline 90,396 \end{array}$ Check: 93)90,396 → 972

4. 41)4469 → 109   Check: $\begin{array}{r} 109 \\ \times\ 41 \\ \hline 4,469 \end{array}$

Simple Steps · Sixth Grade   Multiplication and Division   9

Page 10

Multiplying Decimals

When multiplying decimals, the number of digits to the right of the decimal point in the product is the sum of the number of digits to the right of the decimal point in both factors.

Solve: 0.4 × 0.2

Practice

Solve the following problems.

1. $\begin{array}{r} 0.08 \\ \times\ 0.5 \\ \hline 0.040 \end{array}$
2. $\begin{array}{r} 0.7 \\ \times\ 8 \\ \hline 5.6 \end{array}$
3. $\begin{array}{r} 0.5 \\ \times\ 0.6 \\ \hline 0.30 \end{array}$

4. $\begin{array}{r} 0.03 \\ \times\ 0.4 \\ \hline 0.012 \end{array}$
5. $\begin{array}{r} 0.6 \\ \times\ 0.06 \\ \hline 0.036 \end{array}$
6. $\begin{array}{r} 0.09 \\ \times\ 0.7 \\ \hline 0.063 \end{array}$

10   Multiplication and Division   Simple Steps · Sixth Grade

Page 11

Multiplying Decimals

You can multiply a larger decimal and a whole number by a decimal by following these steps.

Solve: 2.8 × 0.6

Practice

Solve the following problems.

1. $\begin{array}{r} 1.68 \\ \times\ 8 \\ \hline 13.44 \end{array}$
2. $\begin{array}{r} 25 \\ \times\ 0.7 \\ \hline 17.5 \end{array}$
3. $\begin{array}{r} 9.806 \\ \times\ 31 \\ \hline 303.986 \end{array}$

4. $\begin{array}{r} 895 \\ \times\ 0.63 \\ \hline 563.85 \end{array}$
5. $\begin{array}{r} 27.1 \\ \times\ 3.54 \\ \hline 95.934 \end{array}$
6. $\begin{array}{r} 76.4 \\ \times\ 3.6 \\ \hline 275.04 \end{array}$

Simple Steps · Sixth Grade   Multiplication and Division   11

Page 12

Dividing Decimals

You can divide a decimal by a whole number by following these steps.

Solve: 25.84 ÷ 4

Practice

Solve the following problems.

1. 3)37.08 → 12.36
2. 8)9.976 → 1.247
3. 2)0.0214 → 0.0107

4. 11)20.614 → 1.874
5. 16)376.32 → 23.52
6. 12)230.16 → 19.18

12   Multiplication and Division   Simple Steps · Sixth Grade

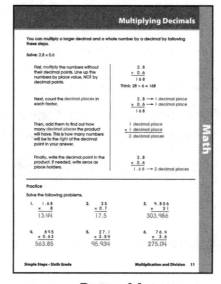
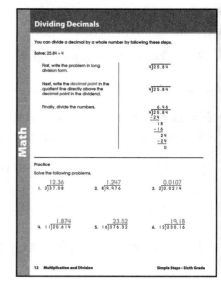

Page 13

Dividing Decimals

You can divide a decimal by another decimal. Multiply the divisor and dividend by a power of ten (10, 100, or 1,000) so that the divisor is a whole number.

Solve: 14 ÷ 3.5

First, change the divisor to a whole number by multiplying by a power of ten. Multiply the dividend by that same power of ten.

$3.5 \times 10 = 35$
$14 \times 10 = 140$

Next, write the division problem with the "new" numbers.

$35\overline{)140}$

Finally, solve the problem.

$$35\overline{)140}$$
$$-140$$
$$0$$

Practice

Solve the following problems.

1. $2.3\overline{)5.06}$ = 2.2
2. $7.2\overline{)10.8}$ = 1.5
3. $0.22\overline{)1.166}$ = 5.3
4. $0.015\overline{)0.45}$ = 30
5. $0.85\overline{)5.1}$ = 6
6. $0.035\overline{)7.7}$ = 220

Page 14

Problem Solving

You can use the multiplication and division strategies you have learned so far to solve more difficult problems.

First, underline the <u>important information</u> that you will need to solve the problem.

A package weighs <u>2.6</u> pounds. How much do <u>8</u> of the <u>same-sized</u> packages weigh?

Next, determine which operation is best for solving the problem.

We will use multiplication because finding 8 of the same-sized groups means to multiply.

Then, write a math sentence using the information.

2.6 pounds × 8 = total weight of packages

Finally, solve the problem.

$$2.6 \times 8 = 20.8 \text{ pounds}$$

Practice

Solve the problems. Show your work in the space provided.

1. A collection of nickels is worth $18.60. How many nickels are in the collection? — 372
2. A box of grass seed weighs 0.62 pounds. How much does a box containing 0.75 times as much grass seed weigh? — 0.465 pounds
3. Each prize for a carnival booth costs $0.32. How many prizes can you buy with $96? — 300

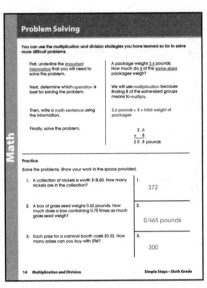

Page 15

Review

Use all of the multiplication and division skills you have learned so far to solve the problems.

Solve the problems.

1. 213 × 362 = 77,106
2. 248 × 231 = 57,288
3. 2851 × 261 = 744,111
4. 3732 × 531 = 1,981,692
5. $76\overline{)6308}$ = 83
6. $45\overline{)8329}$ = 185 r4
7. $26\overline{)45702}$ = 1,757 r20
8. $86\overline{)99588}$ = 1,158

Solve the following problems and use the reciprocal operation to check your work.

9. 465 × 26 = 12,090   Check: $26\overline{)12,090}$ = 465
10. $23\overline{)9798}$ = 426   Check: 426 × 23 = 9,798

Solve the problems.

11. 365.3 × 5.2 = 1,899.56
12. 0.76 × 0.53 = 0.4028
13. $67.45 × 23 = $1,551.35
14. 4.26 × 7.62 = 32.4612
15. $0.6\overline{)78}$ = 130
16. $0.09\overline{)738}$ = 8,200
17. $0.07\overline{)50.4}$ = 720
18. $18\overline{)$13.50}$ = $0.75

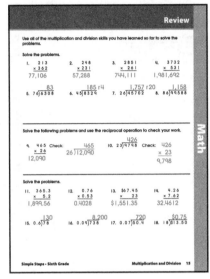

Page 16

Greatest Common Factor

A factor is a divisor of a number. A common factor is a factor that two or more numbers have in common. The greatest common factor is the largest factor that the numbers have in common. Use the following steps to find the greatest common factor of two numbers.

Solve: Find the greatest common factor of 32 and 40.

First, list all of the factors of each number in order.
Think: 1 × 32, 2 × 16, and 4 × 8.
Factors of 32: 1, 2, 4, 8, 16, 32
Think: 1 × 40, 2 × 20, 4 × 10, and 5 × 8.
Factors of 40: 1, 2, 4, 5, 8, 10, 20, 40

Next, underline the common factors of the numbers.
Factors of 32: 1, 2, 4, 8, 16, 32
Factors of 40: 1, 2, 4, 5, 8, 10, 20, 40

Finally, circle the greatest common factor of the numbers.
Factors of 32: 1, 2, 4, 8, 16, 32
Factors of 40: 1, 2, 4, 5, 8, 10, 20, 40

The greatest common factor of 32 and 40 is 8.

Practice

Find the greatest common factor of the following numbers.

1. 8, 12 — 4
2. 6, 18 — 6
3. 24, 15 — 3
4. 4, 6 — 2
5. 5, 12 — 1
6. 16, 12 — 4

Page 17

Least Common Multiple

A multiple is a product of a number multiplied by another number. A common multiple is a multiple that two or more numbers have in common. The least common multiple is the smallest multiple that the numbers have in common. Use the following steps to find the least common multiple of two numbers.

Solve: Find the least common multiple of 3 and 6.

First, list some multiples of each number in order.
Multiples of 3: 3, 6, 9, 12, 15, 18, 21, 24...
Multiples of 6: 6, 12, 18, 24, 30, 36, 42...

Next, underline the common multiples of the numbers.
Multiples of 3: 3, 6, 9, 12, 15, 18, 21, 24...
Multiples of 6: 6, 12, 18, 24, 30, 36, 42...

Finally, circle the least common multiple of the numbers.
Multiples of 3: 3, 6, 9, 12, 15, 18, 21, 24...
Multiples of 6: 6, 12, 18, 24, 30, 36, 42...

The least common multiple of 3 and 6 is 6.

Practice

Find the least common multiple of the following numbers.

1. 8, 12 — 24, 24
2. 12, 16 — 48, 48
3. 4, 7 — 28, 28
4. 2, 10 — 10, 10
5. 5, 7 — 35, 35
6. 4, 9 — 36, 36

Page 18

Multiplying Fractions

Multiply a fraction by another fraction by following these steps.

Solve: $\frac{3}{8} \times \frac{2}{3}$

First, multiply the numerators.
$$\frac{3}{8} \times \frac{2}{3} = \frac{3 \times 2}{\Box} = \frac{6}{\Box}$$

Next, multiply the denominators.
$$\frac{3}{8} \times \frac{2}{3} = \frac{3 \times 2}{8 \times 3} = \frac{6}{24}$$

Finally, simplify. To simplify, divide the numerator and the denominator by the greatest common factor.
$$\frac{6}{24} = \frac{1}{4}$$
The greatest common factor of 6 and 24 is 6.
$6 \div 6 = 1$
$24 \div 6 = 4$

Practice

Solve the following problems. Write the answers in simplest form.

1. $\frac{2}{5} \times \frac{2}{3} = \frac{4}{15}$
2. $\frac{3}{4} \times \frac{5}{6} = \frac{15}{24} = \frac{5}{8}$
3. $\frac{7}{8} \times \frac{5}{7} = \frac{35}{56} = \frac{5}{8}$
4. $\frac{2}{3} \times \frac{8}{9} = \frac{16}{27}$
5. $\frac{3}{4} \times \frac{3}{7} = \frac{9}{28}$
6. $\frac{11}{12} \times \frac{2}{3} = \frac{22}{36} = \frac{11}{18}$

Page 19

Multiplying Fractions

When you multiply with fractions, you are finding a piece of a piece. Follow these steps to multiply a fraction by a whole number.

Solve: $\frac{2}{3} \times 5$

First, rewrite the whole number as a fraction.
$$5 = \frac{5}{1}$$

Next, multiply the numerators.
$$\frac{2}{3} \times \frac{5}{1} = \frac{2 \times 5}{\square} = \frac{10}{\square}$$

Then, multiply the denominators.
$$\frac{2}{3} \times \frac{5}{1} = \frac{2 \times 5}{3 \times 1} = \frac{10}{3}$$

Finally, simplify.
$$\frac{10}{3} = 3\frac{1}{3}$$

Practice

Solve the following problems. Write the answers in simplest form.

1. $\frac{3}{4} \times 4$ — 3
2. $\frac{7}{8} \times 6$ — $5\frac{1}{4}$
3. $3 \times \frac{2}{5}$ — $1\frac{1}{5}$
4. $\frac{5}{12} \times 3$ — $1\frac{1}{4}$
5. $9 \times \frac{5}{8}$ — $5\frac{5}{8}$
6. $\frac{10}{11} \times 12$ — $10\frac{10}{11}$

Simple Steps • Sixth Grade Multiplication and Division 19

Page 20

Multiplying Mixed Numbers

A mixed number is a whole number with a fractional part. You can multiply a mixed number by another mixed number by rewriting them both as improper fractions. Follow these steps to multiply mixed numbers.

Solve: $2\frac{3}{4} \times 3\frac{1}{3}$

First, rewrite each mixed number as an improper fraction. An improper fraction is a fraction greater than one. Its numerator is greater than its denominator.
$$2\frac{3}{4} = \frac{11}{4} \qquad 3\frac{1}{3} = \frac{10}{3}$$

Next, multiply the numerators and then multiply the denominators.
$$\frac{11}{4} \times \frac{10}{3} = \frac{110}{12}$$

Finally, simplify.
$$\frac{110}{12} = \frac{55}{6} = 9\frac{1}{6}$$

Practice

Solve the following problems. Write the answers in simplest form.

1. $1\frac{1}{3} \times 2\frac{1}{8}$ — $2\frac{5}{6}$
2. $2\frac{1}{2} \times 1\frac{3}{4}$ — $4\frac{3}{8}$
3. $2\frac{5}{8} \times 2\frac{2}{5}$ — $6\frac{33}{40}$
4. $1\frac{1}{2} \times 2\frac{2}{3}$ — 4
5. $3\frac{1}{5} \times 5\frac{2}{3}$ — $18\frac{2}{15}$
6. $4\frac{1}{2} \times 4\frac{1}{2}$ — $20\frac{1}{4}$
7. $2\frac{1}{5} \times 3\frac{1}{4}$ — $7\frac{7}{12}$
8. $2\frac{4}{5} \times 3\frac{1}{8}$ — $8\frac{3}{4}$

20 Multiplication and Division Simple Steps • Sixth Grade

Page 21

Dividing Fractions

Fraction bars can help you divide fractions. Follow these steps to divide fractions.

Solve: $\frac{1}{3} \div \frac{1}{6}$

First, determine how many groups of the divisor are in the dividend.
$\frac{1}{3}$ is the dividend and $\frac{1}{6}$ is the divisor. How many sixths are in $\frac{1}{3}$?

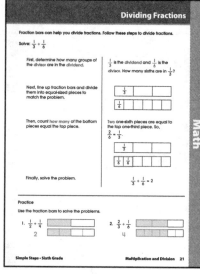

Next, line up fraction bars and divide them into equal-sized pieces to match the problem.

Then, count how many of the bottom pieces equal the top piece.
Two one-sixth pieces are equal to the top one-third piece. So, $\frac{2}{6} = \frac{1}{3}$.

Finally, solve the problem.
$$\frac{1}{3} \div \frac{1}{6} = 2$$

Practice

Use the fraction bars to solve the problems.

1. $\frac{1}{2} \div \frac{1}{4}$ — 2
2. $\frac{2}{3} \div \frac{1}{6}$ — 4

Simple Steps • Sixth Grade Multiplication and Division 21

Page 22

Dividing Fractions

Dividing fractions means to find how many groups of the divisor are in the dividend. To divide a fraction by another fraction, follow these steps.

Solve: $\frac{4}{5} \div \frac{8}{9}$

First, change the divisor into its reciprocal. The divisor is the second fraction in the problem. A reciprocal is when you switch the numerator and denominator.
The reciprocal of $\frac{8}{9}$ is $\frac{9}{8}$.

Then, multiply the dividend by the reciprocal.
$$\frac{4}{5} \div \frac{8}{9} = \frac{4}{5} \times \frac{9}{8} = \frac{36}{40}$$

Finally, simplify. The greatest common factor of 36 and 40 is 4, so divide both the numerator and the denominator by 4.
$$\frac{36}{40} = \frac{9}{10}$$

Practice

Divide the fractions. Write the answers in simplest form.

1. $\frac{1}{2} \div \frac{3}{5}$ — $\frac{5}{6}$
2. $\frac{1}{2} \div \frac{7}{8}$ — $\frac{4}{7}$
3. $\frac{7}{8} \div \frac{1}{3}$ — $2\frac{5}{8}$
4. $\frac{3}{5} \div \frac{2}{3}$ — $\frac{9}{10}$
5. $\frac{3}{4} \div \frac{1}{6}$ — $4\frac{1}{2}$
6. $\frac{1}{7} \div \frac{1}{2}$ — $\frac{2}{7}$

22 Multiplication and Division Simple Steps • Sixth Grade

Page 23

Dividing Fractions

You can divide a fraction by a whole number and a whole number by a fraction by following these steps.

Solve: $12 \div \frac{1}{5}$

First, rewrite the whole number as a fraction.
$$12 = \frac{12}{1}$$

Next, multiply the whole number in its fraction form by the reciprocal of the second fraction.
The reciprocal of $\frac{1}{5}$ is $\frac{5}{1}$.
$$\frac{12}{1} \times \frac{5}{1} = \frac{60}{1}$$

Finally, simplify.
$$\frac{60}{1} = 60$$
$$12 \div \frac{1}{5} = 60$$

Practice

Divide. Write the answers in simplest form.

1. $2 \div \frac{2}{3}$ — 3
2. $5 \div \frac{1}{4}$ — 20
3. $\frac{1}{4} \div 3$ — $\frac{1}{12}$
4. $\frac{1}{6} \div 4$ — $\frac{1}{24}$
5. $7 \div \frac{1}{3}$ — 21
6. $\frac{3}{7} \div 6$ — $\frac{1}{14}$

Simple Steps • Sixth Grade Multiplication and Division 23

Page 24

Dividing Mixed Numbers

You can divide a mixed number by another mixed number by following these steps.

Solve: $4\frac{1}{3} \div 2\frac{3}{4}$

First, rewrite each mixed number as an improper fraction.
$$4\frac{1}{3} \div 2\frac{3}{4} = \frac{13}{3} \div \frac{11}{4}$$

Next, multiply the dividend by the reciprocal of the divisor.
$$\frac{13}{3} \times \frac{4}{11} = \frac{52}{33}$$

Finally, simplify.
$$\frac{52}{33} = 1\frac{19}{33}$$

Practice

Divide. Write the answers in simplest form.

1. $2\frac{1}{2} \div 3\frac{1}{3}$ — $\frac{3}{4}$
2. $4\frac{1}{2} \div 1\frac{1}{6}$ — $3\frac{6}{7}$
3. $6 \div 2\frac{1}{2}$ — $2\frac{2}{5}$
4. $3\frac{3}{5} \div 4$ — $\frac{9}{10}$
5. $4\frac{5}{6} \div 2\frac{2}{5}$ — $2\frac{1}{72}$
6. $4\frac{1}{3} \div 6$ — $\frac{13}{18}$
7. $1\frac{1}{2} \div 3\frac{1}{8}$ — $\frac{12}{25}$
8. $3\frac{1}{3} \div 2\frac{3}{8}$ — $1\frac{23}{57}$

24 Multiplication and Division Simple Steps • Sixth Grade

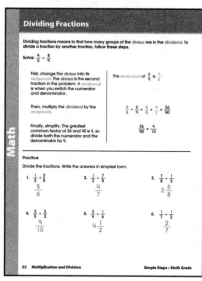

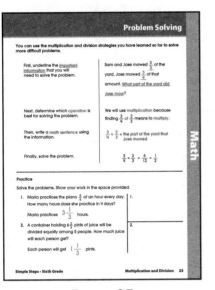

Page 25

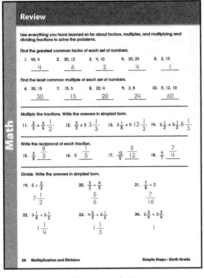

Page 26

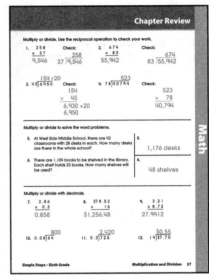

Page 27

Page 28

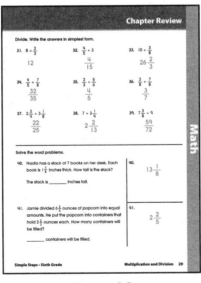

Page 29

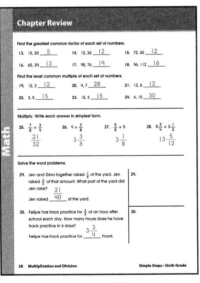

Page 30

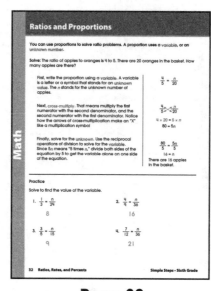
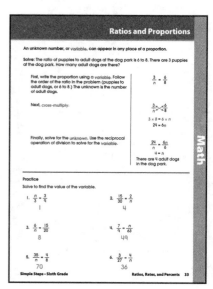
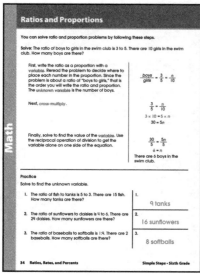
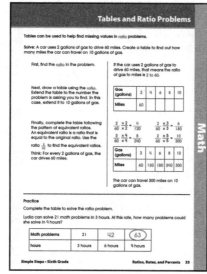
Answer Key

Page 37

Unit Rates

A rate is a special ratio that compares quantities of two different units, such as 340 miles per 10 gallons. In a unit rate, one of those quantities is 1, such as 34 miles per gallon.

Solve: If there are 160 students and 4 buses, how many students should go on each bus?

First, write the ratio in the problem as a fraction.	$\frac{160}{4}$
Next, write the equivalent unit rate as a variable over one. Use a variable as the numerator, and 1 as the denominator. Here, we will use s for students.	$\frac{160}{4} = \frac{s}{1}$
Finally, cross-multiply and solve to find the unit rate.	$4s = 160$ $s = 40$ The unit rate is $\frac{40}{1}$, or 40 students per bus

Practice.

Solve each problem by finding the unit rate.

1. John can create 20 paintings in 4 weeks. How many paintings can he create each week?
   1. 5 paintings

2. Sasha can walk 6 miles in 3 hours. If she has to walk 1 mile, how long will it take her?
   2. $\frac{1}{2}$ hour

3. Victoria can make 8 necklaces in 4 days. How long does it take her to make one necklace?
   3. $\frac{1}{2}$ a day

Simple Steps • Sixth Grade   Ratios, Rates, and Percents 37

Page 38

Unit Rates

You can use unit rates to solve real-world problems. Extend the unit rate to solve the problem.

Solve: Chelsea walked a total of 6 miles making 3 trips to school. How many more trips to school will Chelsea have to make to walk a total of 10 miles?

| First, find the unit rate. | $\frac{6 \text{ miles}}{3 \text{ trips}} = 2 \text{ miles per trip}$ |
| Next, use the unit rate to solve the problems. | 10 total miles ÷ 2 miles per trip = 5 trips |

Practice

Solve each problem by finding the unit rate.

1. Charlie downloads 3 songs for $3.90. If each song costs the same amount, how much would he pay to download 5 songs?
   1. $6.50

2. Kendra read 40 pages in 2 hours. At this rate, in how many hours will she have read 100 pages?
   2. 5 hours

3. Jaxon buys 5 cheeseburgers for $15.00. How many cheeseburgers can he buy with $24.00?
   3. 8 cheeseburgers

4. Carli knits 3 scarves in 6 weeks. How many weeks will it take her to knit 7 scarves?
   4. 14 weeks

5. Mateo baked a dozen muffins with 3 cups of flour. How many cups of flour will he need to bake 36 muffins?
   5. 9 cups

38 Ratios, Rates, and Percents   Simple Steps • Sixth Grade

Page 39

Graphing Ratios

You can graph a ratio on a coordinate grid.

Solve: Tom deposits $10 into his savings account each week. Complete the table to show the ratio of dollars to weeks, then graph the ratio.

| First, determine the ratio. | In one week, Tom saves $10. The ratio of weeks to dollars is 1:10. |

Next, complete the table following the ratio.

Weeks (x-values)	Dollars (y-values)
1	10
2	20
3	30
4	40
5	50

Then, graph the points on the coordinate grid. The points are in (x,y) order, or (weeks, dollars).

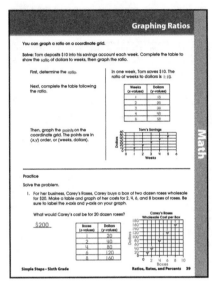

Practice

Solve the problem.

1. For her business, Carey's Roses, Carey buys a box of two dozen roses wholesale for $20. Make a table and graph of her costs for 2, 4, 6, and 8 boxes of roses. Be sure to label the x-axis and y-axis on your graph.

What would Carey's cost be for 20 dozen roses?

$200

Boxes (x-values)	Dollars (y-values)
1	20
2	40
4	80
6	120
8	160

Simple Steps • Sixth Grade   Ratios, Rates, and Percents 39

Page 40

Converting Measurements

You can use what you know about ratios to convert measurements. Use the conversion chart to write the equivalent measurements.

Solve: How many feet are equal to 24 inches?

1 foot (ft.) = 12 inches (in.)	1 in. = $\frac{1}{12}$ ft.
1 yard (yd.) = 3 ft.	1 ft. = $\frac{1}{3}$ yd.
1 yd. = 36 in.	1 in. = $\frac{1}{36}$ yd.
1 mile (mi.) = 5,280 ft.	1 mi. = 1,760 yd.

First, set up a proportion with the two measurements.	1 inch = $\frac{1}{12}$ ft.
Next, use a variable to set up the proportion.	24 in. = n ft.
Finally, decide if you need to multiply or divide to solve. Since 1 inch is equal to $\frac{1}{12}$ of a foot, 24 inches is 24 × $\frac{1}{12}$ feet.	24 in. = (24 × $\frac{1}{12}$) ft. 24 in. = 2 ft.

Practice

Complete the following measurement conversions.

1. 7 ft. = **84** in.
2. 72 in. = **6** ft.
3. 15 yd. = **45** ft.
4. 108 in. = **3** yd.
5. 4 mi. = **21,120** ft.
6. 4 mi. = **7,040** yd.
7. 3 yd. = **9** ft.
8. 120 in. = **10** ft.
9. 42 ft. = **14** yd.
10. 4 ft. 7 in. = **55** in.
11. 2 yd. 9 in. = **81** in.
12. 30 in. = **2½** ft.
13. 15,840 ft. = **3** mi.
14. 6 yd. = **18** ft.
15. 6 yd. = **216** in.
16. 2,640 ft. = **½** mi.

40 Ratios, Rates, and Percents   Simple Steps • Sixth Grade

Page 41

Problem Solving

You can use the strategies about ratios and proportion you have learned so far to solve more difficult problems.

First, underline the important information that you will need to solve the problem.	Peaches are 8 for $2. Jill bought 12 peaches. How much did she spend?
Next, determine which operation is best for solving the problem.	The ratio is $2 for 8 peaches, or 2 to 8, or $\frac{$2}{8 \text{ peaches}}$. Divide to find the unit rate, or the cost of one peach.
Then, write a math sentence using the information.	$\frac{$2}{8 \text{ peaches}}$ = $0.25 per peach 12 peaches × cost per peach = total spent
Finally, solve the problem.	12 × 0.25 = 3 Jill spent $3 on 12 peaches.

Practice

Solve the problems. Show your work in the space provided.

1. A frozen-yogurt factory makes 100 quarts of frozen yogurt in 5 hours. How many quarts could be made in 36 hours? What was the rate per day?
   1. 720 quarts; 480 quarts per day

2. A jet travels 590 miles in 5 hours. At this rate, how far could the jet fly in 10 hours? What is the rate of speed of the jet?
   2. 1,180 miles; 118 miles per hour

3. You can buy 5 cans of green beans at Village Market for $2.30, or you can buy 10 of them at Best Food for $5.10. Which place has the better deal?
   3. Village Market

Simple Steps • Sixth Grade   Ratios, Rates, and Percents 41

Page 42

Review

Use everything you have learned so far about ratios, proportions, unit rates, ratio graphing, and measurement conversion to solve the problems.

Complete the proportion equations.

1. $\frac{15}{12} = \frac{5}{4}$
2. $\frac{15}{21} = \frac{5}{7}$
3. $\frac{5}{6} = \frac{20}{24}$
4. $\frac{14}{10} = \frac{21}{15}$

Solve each problem.

5. A ferris wheel can accommodate 55 people in 15 minutes. How many people could ride the ferris wheel in 2 hours? What is the rate per hour?
   5. 440 people; 220 people per hour

6. Laura earns $7 per hour babysitting for her neighbor. How much will Laura make if she babysits for 4 hours?
   6. $28

7. Sweaters are 3 for $50. Leslie and her mother spent $100 on sweaters. How many did they buy?
   7. 6 sweaters

8. Jamal can ride his bike 5 miles in 2 hours. At this rate, how long will it take him to ride 20 miles? Complete the table to solve.

Miles	5	10	15	20
Hours	2	4	6	8

   8. 8 hours

9. Genny can make 7 bracelets in 3 hours. At this rate, how many bracelets can she make in 9 hours? Complete the table to solve.

Bracelets	7	14	21
Hours	3	6	9

   9. 21 bracelets

42 Ratios, Rates, and Percents   Simple Steps • Sixth Grade

Page 37   Page 38   Page 39
Page 40   Page 41   Page 42

Answer Key

Page 43

Percents

A percent is a part of 100. The symbol % (percent) means $\frac{1}{100}$ or 0.01 (one hundredth). Use the following steps to find the percent as a fraction and as a decimal.

Solve: Write 7% as a fraction and as a decimal.

First, write the percent as a fraction over 100. Write it in simplest form.

$$7\% = 7 \times \frac{1}{100}$$
$$= \frac{7}{1} \times \frac{1}{100}$$
$$= \frac{7}{100}$$

Next, write the percent as a decimal in the hundredths place.

$$7\% = 7 \times 0.01$$
$$= 0.07$$

Practice

Write each percent as a fraction and as a decimal.

	Percent	Fraction	Decimal
1.	2%	$\frac{2}{100}$ or $\frac{1}{50}$	0.02
2.	8%	$\frac{8}{100}$ or $\frac{2}{25}$	0.08
3.	27%	$\frac{27}{100}$	0.27
4.	13%	$\frac{13}{100}$	0.13
5.	68%	$\frac{68}{100}$ or $\frac{17}{25}$	0.68
6.	72%	$\frac{72}{100}$ or $\frac{18}{25}$	0.72
7.	56%	$\frac{56}{100}$ or $\frac{14}{25}$	0.56
8.	11%	$\frac{11}{100}$	0.11

Simple Steps • Sixth Grade — Ratios, Rates, and Percents 43

Page 44

Percents and Fractions

You can find a percent of a number by multiplying fractions.

Solve: Find 35% of 60.

First, write the percent as a fraction over 100.

$$35\% = \frac{35}{100}$$

Next, multiply the fraction by the whole number. The word "of" tells us to multiply because we are finding a part "of" a whole.

$$\frac{35}{100} \times 60 = \frac{35}{100} \times \frac{60}{1}$$

Finally, solve and write the answer in simplest form. You can simplify the fraction before you multiply for an easier problem.

$$\frac{35}{100} \times \frac{7}{20}$$
$$\frac{7}{20} \times \frac{60}{1} = \frac{420}{20} = \frac{42}{2} = 21$$
$$35\% \text{ of } 60 = 21$$

Practice

Solve the following problems. Write the answers as fractions in simplest form.

1. 40% of 20 = 8
2. 80% of 80 = 64
3. 40% of 32 = $12\frac{4}{5}$
4. 8% of 65 = $5\frac{1}{5}$
5. 30% of 32 = $9\frac{3}{5}$
6. 90% of 60 = 54
7. 28% of 7 = $1\frac{24}{25}$
8. 12% of 40 = $4\frac{4}{5}$
9. 45% of 50 = $22\frac{1}{2}$
10. 18% of 45 = $8\frac{1}{10}$
11. 36% of 80 = $28\frac{4}{5}$
12. 27% of 60 = $16\frac{1}{5}$
13. 14% of 70 = $9\frac{4}{5}$
14. 38% of 50 = 19

44 Ratios, Rates, and Percents — Simple Steps • Sixth Grade

Page 45

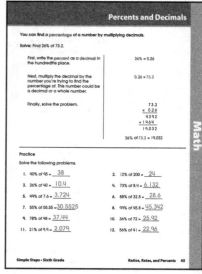

Percents and Decimals

You can find a percentage of a number by multiplying decimals.

Solve: Find 26% of 73.2.

First, write the percent as a decimal in the hundredths place.

$$26\% = 0.26$$

Next, multiply the decimal by the number you're trying to find the percentage of. This number could be a decimal or a whole number.

$$0.26 \times 73.2$$

Finally, solve the problem.

$$
\begin{array}{r}
73.2 \\
\times\ 0.26 \\
\hline
4392 \\
+1464 \\
\hline
19.032
\end{array}
$$

$$26\% \text{ of } 73.2 = 19.032$$

Practice

Solve the following problems.

1. 40% of 95 = 38
2. 12% of 200 = 24
3. 26% of 40 = 10.4
4. 73% of 8.4 = 6.132
5. 49% of 7.6 = 3.724
6. 88% of 32.5 = 28.6
7. 55% of 55.55 = 30.5525
8. 99% of 45.8 = 45.342
9. 78% of 48 = 37.44
10. 36% of 72 = 25.92
11. 21% of 9.9 = 2.079
12. 56% of 41 = 22.96

Simple Steps • Sixth Grade — Ratios, Rates, and Percents 45

Page 46

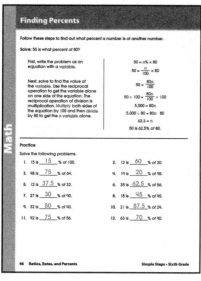

Finding Percents

Follow these steps to find out what percent a number is of another number.

Solve: 50 is what percent of 80?

First, write the problem as an equation with a variable.

$$50 = n\% \times 80$$
$$50 = \frac{n}{100} \times 80$$

Next, solve to find the value of the variable. Use the reciprocal operation to get the variable alone on one side of the equation. The reciprocal operation of division is multiplication. Multiply both sides of the equation by 100 and then divide by 80 to get n variable alone.

$$50 = \frac{80n}{100}$$
$$50 \times 100 = \frac{80n}{100} \times 100$$
$$5,000 = 80n$$
$$5,000 \div 80 = 80n \div 80$$
$$62.5 = n$$
$$50 \text{ is } 62.5\% \text{ of } 80.$$

Practice

Solve the following problems.

1. 15 is 15 % of 100.
2. 12 is 60 % of 20.
3. 48 is 75 % of 64.
4. 19 is 20 % of 95.
5. 12 is 37.5 % of 32.
6. 35 is 62.5 % of 56.
7. 27 is 30 % of 90.
8. 18 is 45 % of 45.
9. 32 is 80 % of 40.
10. 21 is 87.5 % of 24.
11. 42 is 75 % of 56.
12. 63 is 70 % of 90.

46 Ratios, Rates, and Percents — Simple Steps • Sixth Grade

Page 47

Finding Percents

Follow these steps to find out what percent a number is of a fraction or a decimal.

Solve: $\frac{1}{4}$ is what percent of $\frac{5}{8}$?

First, write the problem as an equation with a variable.

$$\frac{1}{4} = n\% \times \frac{5}{8}$$
$$\frac{1}{4} = \frac{n}{100} \times \frac{5}{8}$$

Next, solve to find the value of the variable. Use the reciprocal operation to get the variable alone on one side of the equation. The reciprocal operation of division is multiplication. Multiply both sides of the equation by 800 and then divide by 5 to get the n variable alone.

$$\frac{1}{4} = \frac{5n}{800}$$
$$\frac{1}{4} \times 800 = \frac{5n}{800} \times 800$$
$$\frac{800}{4} = 5n$$
$$200 = 5n$$
$$200 \div 5 = 5n \div 5$$
$$40 = n$$
$$\frac{1}{4} \text{ is } 40\% \text{ of } \frac{5}{8}.$$

Practice

Solve the following problems.

1. $\frac{1}{3}$ is 40 % of $\frac{5}{6}$.
2. 1.8 is 30 % of 6.
3. 0.9 is 20 % of 4.5.
4. $\frac{1}{5}$ is 25 % of $\frac{8}{10}$.
5. 2.4 is 15 % of 16.
6. 0.72 is 60 % of 1.2.

Simple Steps • Sixth Grade — Ratios, Rates, and Percents 47

Page 48

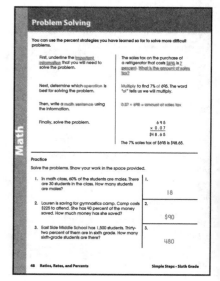

Problem Solving

You can use the percent strategies you have learned so far to solve more difficult problems.

First, underline the important information that you will need to solve the problem.

The sales tax on the purchase of a refrigerator that costs $695 is 7 percent. What is the amount of sales tax?

Next, determine which operation is best for solving the problem.

Multiply to find 7% of 695. The word "of" tells us we will multiply.

Then, write a math sentence using the information.

$0.07 \times 695 = $ amount of sales tax

Finally, solve the problem.

$$
\begin{array}{r}
695 \\
\times\ 0.07 \\
\hline
\$48.65
\end{array}
$$

The 7% sales tax of $695 is $48.65.

Practice

Solve the problems. Show your work in the space provided.

1. In math class, 60% of the students are males. There are 30 students in the class. How many students are males?
   1. 18

2. Lauren is saving for gymnastics camp. Camp costs $225 to attend. She has 40 percent of the money saved. How much money has she saved?
   2. $90

3. East Side Middle School has 1,500 students. Thirty-two percent of them are in sixth grade. How many sixth-grade students are there?
   3. 480

48 Ratios, Rates, and Percents — Simple Steps • Sixth Grade

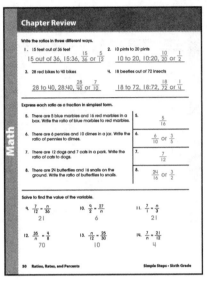

Page 49

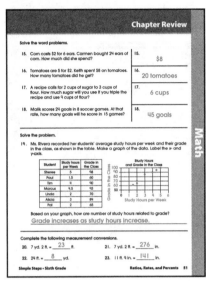

Page 50

Page 51

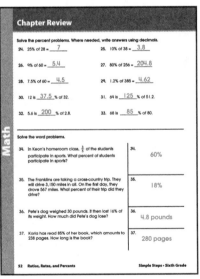

Page 52

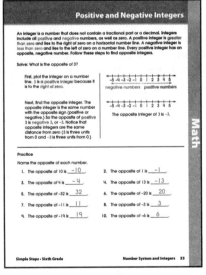

Page 53

Page 54

Page 55

Integer Values in Real Life

Integers can be used to describe real-life situations. Think about what the situation is describing and how it relates to positive and negative integers.

Solve: A driver is going 15 miles per hour below the speed limit. How can this be represented by an integer?

First, underline the word in the problem that tells you if this is a positive or negative integer. Here, the word "below" tells us that it is less than, or under, the speed limit.

A driver is going 15 miles per hour below the speed limit.

Next, write the number as a positive or negative integer. This situation can be described with a negative integer, so we will write a negative sign in front of the number.

15 miles per hour below the speed limit can be shown with the integer –15.

Practice

Use integers to represent each real-life situation.

1. 45 feet below sea level
   −45

2. a gain of 8 yards on a play
   8

3. $528 deposit into a checking account
   528

4. 62° above zero
   62

5. 10 units to the left on a number line
   −10

6. withdrawal of $95 from an ATM
   −95

7. stock market decrease of 97 points
   −97

8. 34° below zero
   −34

9. 6,000 feet above sea level
   6,000

Simple Steps • Sixth Grade   Number System and Integers 55

Page 56

Absolute Value

The absolute value of a number is its distance from zero. Therefore, the absolute value of a number is always positive. Absolute value is represented by vertical lines on either side of an integer. Find the absolute value of an integer by following these steps.

Solve: What is |−8|? Or, what is the absolute value of −8?

First, think of the distance from zero of the given integer on a number line.

The distance from zero of −8 on a number line is 8 units.

Next, write the number as an absolute value.

The absolute value of −8 is 8.
|−8| = 8
|−8| means "the absolute value of −8."

Practice

Find the absolute value of each integer.

1. |4| = 4
2. |−13| = 13
3. |11| = 11
4. |−2| = 2
5. |−21| = 21
6. |1| = 1
7. −|8| = −8   Think: This is the opposite of the absolute value of 8.
8. −|−15| = −15
9. −|−41| = −41

56   Number System and Integers   Simple Steps • Sixth Grade

Page 57

Comparing and Ordering Integers

You can compare and order integers on a number line. A negative integer is always less than a positive integer. The farther away a negative integer is from zero, the less its value is. When comparing two negative integers, the integer that is closer to zero is greater. To compare integers, follow these steps.

Solve: Compare the following integers: 4, −4, −4, and −2. List them from greatest to least.

First, plot the integers on a number line.

Next, compare the size of the integers based on their distance from zero.

4 is the greatest because it is a positive integer. −2 is only 2 units away from 0, while −4 is 4 units away, and −4 is 4 units away.

Finally, list the integers in the order the problem states.

The integers listed from greatest to least are 4, −2, −4, and −4.

Practice

Use the number line to list the integers in order from least to greatest.

1. −3, −5, 0   −5, −3, 0
2. 8, −8, 2   −8, 2, 8
3. 0, 5, −2, −3, 2   −3, −2, 0, 2, 5
4. −6, 5, −2, −3, 2   −6, −3, −2, 2, 5

Simple Steps • Sixth Grade   Number System and Integers 57

Page 58

Comparing and Ordering Integers

You can compare integers using a <, >, or = sign.

Solve: Compare −4 and −6 using <, >, or =.

First, compare the size of the integers based on their distance from zero.

−4 is 4 units away from 0, while −6 is 6 units away from 0. Since 4 is closer to 0 than 6 units away, −4 is greater than −6.

Next, write a <, >, or = sign between the integers to show the comparison.

−4 is greater than −6
−4 > −6

Practice

Compare the integers using <, >, or =.

1. 66 > 3
2. −24 < 82
3. 88 > −99
4. 99 > −84
5. −37 = −37
6. −33 > −90
7. −27 > −52
8. −49 > −69
9. −8 > −45
10. −1 < 0
11. 8 > −18
12. −4 < −1
13. −7 > −9
14. −83 < 81
15. −11 = −11

58   Number System and Integers   Simple Steps • Sixth Grade

Page 59

Ordered Pairs and the Coordinate Plane

Positive and negative integers can be graphed as ordered pairs on a coordinate plane. An ordered pair is two numbers written in (x,y) order. The first number in an ordered pair represents its point on the x-axis, or the horizontal axis. The second number represents the point on the y-axis, or the vertical axis.

Solve: Name the ordered pairs on the coordinate plane shown here.

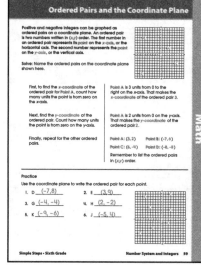

First, to find the x-coordinate of the ordered pair for Point A, count how many units the point is from zero on the x-axis.

Point A is 3 units from 0 to the right on the x-axis. That makes the x-coordinate of the ordered pair 3.

Next, find the y-coordinate of the ordered pair. Count how many units the point is from zero on the y-axis.

Point A is 2 units from 0 on the y-axis. That makes the y-coordinate of the ordered pair 2.

Finally, repeat for the other ordered pairs.

Point A: (3, 2)   Point B: (−7, 6)
Point C: (6, −4)   Point D: (−8, −8)

Remember to list the ordered pairs in (x,y) order.

Practice

Use the coordinate plane to write the ordered pair for each point.

1. D (−7,8)
2. E (3,9)
3. G (−4, −4)
4. H (2, −2)
5. K (−9, −6)
6. J (−5, 4)

Simple Steps • Sixth Grade   Number System and Integers 59

Page 60

Ordered Pairs and the Coordinate Plane

You can use coordinate planes to answer questions about the distance between two points.

Solve: What is the distance between Point F and Point C? Use the coordinate plane to solve.

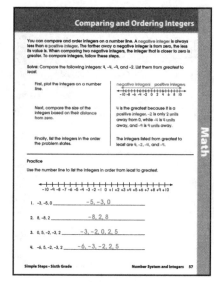

First, count along the x-axis between the two points. Begin at the first point in the problem (Point F.) Stop when you are in line with the other point (Point C.)

Starting at Point F, move 15 units left along the x-axis to be on the same y-coordinate line as Point C.

Next, count along the y-axis between the two points.

From Point F, move 4 units up along the y-axis to get to Point C.

Finally, add the distances together to find out the total distance between two points.

15 + 4 = 19
Point F and Point C are 19 units apart.

Practice

Use the coordinate plane above and the key shown here to answer the questions.

A = stream
D = school
B = home
E = park
C = bookstore
F = fire station

1. How far is it from school to the park? 11 units
2. How far is it from the fire station to the stream? 15 units
3. How far is it from the bookstore to home? 15 units
4. How far is it from the stream to the park? 23 units
5. How far is it from home to the fire station? 4 units

60   Number System and Integers   Simple Steps • Sixth Grade

Page 61

Problem Solving

You can use the integer strategies you have learned so far to solve more difficult problems.

First, underline the _important information_ that you will need to solve the problem.

Next, determine which operation is best for solving the problem.

Then, write a math sentence using the information.

Finally, solve the problem.

An elevator _started at the first floor_ and went _up 18_ floors. It then came _down 11_ floors and went _back up 16_. At what floor was it stopped?

This problem involves adding and subtracting, or the positive and negative integers 18, –11, and 16.

1 + 18 – 11 + 16 = the final floor

1 + 18 = 19
19 – 11 = 8
8 + 16 = 24
The elevator stopped on the 24th floor.

Practice

Solve the problems. Show your work in the space provided.

1. At midnight, the temperature was 30°F. By 6:00 a.m., it had dropped 5° and by noon, it had increased by 11°. What was the temperature at noon?

1. 36°

2. During one week, the stock market did the following: Monday rose 18 points, Tuesday rose 31 points, Wednesday dropped 5 points, Thursday rose 27 points, and Friday dropped 38 points. If it started out at 1,196 on Monday, what did it end up at on Friday?

2. 1,229 points

3. A submarine was located 350 feet below sea level. If it descends 125 feet, and then ascends 75 feet, what is its new location?

3. 400 feet below sea level

Simple Steps • Sixth Grade — Number System and Integers 61

Page 61

Page 62

Chapter Review

Name the opposite of each number.

1. The opposite of 8 is -8.
2. The opposite of –1 is 1.
3. The opposite of 5 is -5.
4. The opposite of 35 is -35.
5. The opposite of –21 is 21.
6. The opposite of –16 is 16.

Find the absolute value of each integer.

7. $|-3| = 3$
8. $|10| = 10$
9. $|5| = 5$
10. $|-9| = 9$
11. $|23| = 23$
12. $|-7| = 7$
13. $|-13| = 13$
14. $|-5| = 5$
15. $|-1| = 1$

Compare the integers using <, >, or =.

16. $82 < 91$
17. $31 > -27$
18. $-44 > -84$
19. $23 < 74$
20. $-10 < 70$
21. $51 > 24$
22. $74 > -42$
23. $99 > 66$
24. $-23 < -21$

Write the numbers in order from least to greatest.

25. –84, 42, –26, 8 $-89, -26, 8, 42$
26. –84, 91, –57, –90 $-90, -84, -57, 91$
27. 20, –81, –5, 87 $-81, -5, 20, 87$
28. 73, 53, 89, 55 $53, 55, 73, 89$
29. –91, –46, 52, 12 $-91, -46, 12, 52$
30. 22, 41, –23, –38 $-38, -23, 22, 41$

62 Number System and Integers — Simple Steps • Sixth Grade

Page 62

Page 63

Chapter Review

Use the coordinate plane to answer the questions.

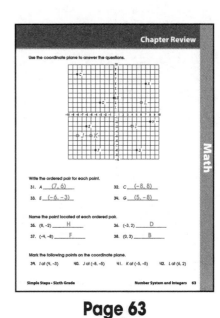

Write the ordered pair for each point.

31. A $(7, 6)$
32. C $(-8, 8)$
33. E $(-6, -3)$
34. G $(5, -8)$

Name the point located at each ordered pair.

35. (8, –2) H
36. (–3, 2) D
37. (–4, –8) F
38. (0, 3) B

Mark the following points on the coordinate plane.

39. I at (4, –3)
40. J at (–8, –5)
41. K at (–5, –5)
42. L at (6, 2)

Simple Steps • Sixth Grade — Number System and Integers 63

Page 63

Page 64

Properties: Commutative and Associative

The Commutative Properties of addition and multiplication state that the order in which numbers are added or multiplied does not change the result, or $a + b = b + a$. The Associative Properties of addition and multiplication state that the way in which addends or factors are grouped (by parentheses) does not change the result, or $(a \times b) \times c = a \times (b \times c)$.

Solve: Identify the property of the following statement: $(2 \times 4) \times 5 = 2 \times (4 \times 5)$

First, determine whether the statement shows an addition or a multiplication property.

$(2 \times 4) \times 5 = 2 \times (4 \times 5)$
This is a multiplication problem, so it shows a multiplication property.

Next, determine whether the statement shows the Commutative or Associative Property.

$(2 \times 4) \times 5 = 2 \times (4 \times 5)$
Since this statement shows the numbers in the same order but grouped in two different ways, (first with parentheses around the 2 and 4, and then with parentheses around 4 and 5) this is an Associative Property of Multiplication problem.

Practice

Name the property shown by each statement.

1. $2 \times 8 = 8 \times 2$ — Commutative Property of Multiplication
2. $2 + (3 + 4) = (2 + 3) + 4$ — Associative Property of Addition
3. $32 + 25 = 25 + 32$ — Commutative Property of Addition
4. $119 \times 120 = 120 \times 119$ — Commutative Property of Multiplication
5. $\times (2 \times 3) = (\ \times 2) \times 3$ — Associative Property of Multiplication
6. $5 \times (5 \times 5) = (5 \times 5) \times 5$ — Associative Property of Multiplication

64 Expressions and Equations — Simple Steps • Sixth Grade

Page 64

Page 65

Properties: Identity and Zero

The Identity Property of Addition states that the sum of an addend and 0 is the addend, or $a + 0 = a$. The Identity Property of Multiplication states that the product of a factor and 1 is that factor, or $a \times 1 = a$. The Properties of Zero state that the product of a factor and 0 is 0, or $a \times 0 = 0$. The Properties of Zero also state that the quotient of zero and any non-zero divisor is 0, or $0 \div 5 = 0$. Numbers cannot be divided by zero.

Solve: Identify the property of the following statement: $5 + 0 = 5$

First, determine whether the statement shows an addition or a multiplication property.

$5 + 0 = 5$
This is an addition problem, so it shows an addition property.

Next, determine whether the statement shows the Identity or Zero Property.

$5 + 0 = 5$
Since this statement shows an addend (5) plus 0 this shows the Identity Property of Addition.

Practice

Name the property shown by each statement.

1. $35 \times 1 = 35$ — Identity Property of Multiplication
2. $0 \times 9 = 0$ — Property of Zero
3. $45 + 0 = 45$ — Identity Property of Addition
4. $18 \times 0 = 0$ — Property of Zero
5. $0 + 12 = 0$ — Property of Zero
6. $1 \times 1 = 1$ — Identity Property of Multiplication

Simple Steps • Sixth Grade — Expressions and Equations 65

Page 65

Page 66

Distributive Property

The Distributive Property combines addition and multiplication operations. It states that multiplying a number by a group of numbers added together is the same as doing each multiplication step separately, or $a \times (b + c) = (a \times b) + (a \times c)$. Follow these steps to rewrite an expression using the Distributive Property.

Solve: Rewrite the following expression using the Distributive Property: $3 \times (2 + 5)$

First, distribute the first number to the other numbers in the expression. (An expression is a mathematical phrase that does not include an equal sign or answer.) So, the 3 can be distributed to the 2 and the 5 in the expression.

$3 \times (2 + 5)$
$3 \times (2 + 5) = (3 \times 2) + (3 \times 5)$

Next, solve both sides of the equation to check your work. They should be equal.

$3 \times (2 + 5) = (3 \times 2) + (3 \times 5)$
$3 \times 7 = 6 + 15$
$21 = 21$

Practice

Rewrite each expression using the Distributive Property.

1. $4 \times (6 + 2) = (4 \times 6) + (4 \times 2)$
2. $(2 \times 5) + (2 \times 4) = 2 \times (5 + 4)$
3. $(5 \times 1) + (5 \times 6) = 5 \times (1 + 6)$
4. $4 \times (2 + 6) = (4 \times 2) + (4 \times 6)$
5. $8 \times (4 + 3) = (8 \times 4) + (8 \times 3)$
6. $(5 \times \ ) + (5 \times 1) = 5 \times (0 + 1)$

66 Expressions and Equations — Simple Steps • Sixth Grade

Page 66

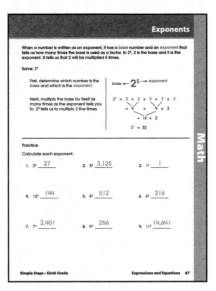

Page 67

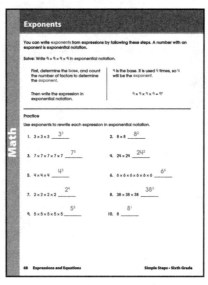

Page 68

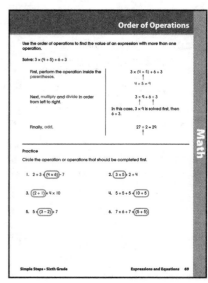

Page 69

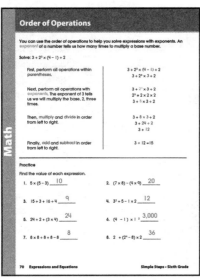

Page 70

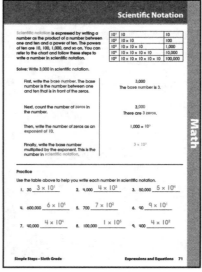

Page 71

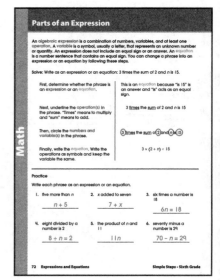

Page 72

Answer Key

Page 73

Parts of an Expression

There are two parts of an expression— a term and a coefficient. A term is a number, variable, product, or quotient in an expression. There can be more than one term in an expression. A coefficient is a number used to multiply a variable. Use the following steps to identify the parts of an expression.

Solve: Identify the parts of the expression $3a + 5$.

First, identify the terms. This expression has two terms. Terms are separated by a plus or minus sign.

$3a + 5$
$3a$ and 5 are both terms.

Next, identify the coefficient. A coefficient is the number that is used to multiply a variable.

$3a + 5$
The coefficient is 3 because it is used to multiply the variable a.

Practice

Identify the terms and the coefficient of each expression.

1. $2 + 6x$

terms: __2__ and __6x__

coefficient: __6__

2. $42 - 4b$

terms: __42__ and __4b__

coefficient: __4__

3. $12n - (4 \times 3)$

terms: __12n__ and __(4 × 3)__

coefficient: __12__

4. $5a + (2 - 1)$

terms: __5a__ and __(2 - 1)__

coefficient: __5__

5. $10y + 10$

terms: __10y__ and __10__

coefficient: __10__

6. $(2 + 3) + 14n$

terms: __(2 + 3)__ and __14n__

coefficient: __14__

Simple Steps • Sixth Grade   Expressions and Equations   73

Page 74

Writing Expressions and Equations

You can write an equation or an algebraic expression in words using variables, terms, and coefficients.

Solve: Write an expression or equation for "four times a number, plus 2, is 6."

First, determine the variable. You can choose any letter you want for a variable to stand for an unknown. It's common to use the first letter of the word, so we can use n for "number."

Four times a number, plus 2, is 6.
The variable is n.

Next, determine the operation(s). Look for key words and vocabulary that tell you which operation to use.

Four times a number, plus 2, is 6.
This statement has two operations: multiplication (times) and addition (plus).

Finally, write the expression or equation. This statement is an equation because it includes an answer, 6.

$4 \times n + 2 = 6$ OR
$4n + 2 = 6$

Practice

Translate each phrase into an expression or an equation.

1. x increased by 5

__x + 5__

2. 11 decreased by a number is 7.

__11 - n = 7__

3. Seven times s

__7s__

4. c less than 7

__7 - c__

5. the product of 15 and m

__15m__

6. one-fourth of x is 5

__¼ x = 5__

7. 8 times a number, plus 4, is 84.

__8n + 4 = 84__

8. a number added to 12 is 23

__12 + n = 23__

9. A number divided by 5 is 6.

__n ÷ 5 = 6__

74   Expressions and Equations   Simple Steps • Sixth Grade

Page 75

Problem Solving

You can use the expressions and equations strategies you have learned so far to solve more difficult problems.

First, underline the important information that you will need to write the equation.

Martha bought 1 soft drink for $3.00 and 4 candy bars. She spent a total of $11.00. Write an equation that will help you find the cost for each candy bar.

Next, determine which operation and variable is best for solving the problem.

This is an equation because there is an answer (the total of $11.00.) The unknown is the cost of candy bars. Because Martha bought 4 of them, we will multiply 4 times a variable, c, for candy bar. We will add $3 for the soft drink to that and have it equal the total of $11.

Finally, write an equation using the information.

$4 \times$ candy bars $+ \$3$ soft drink $= \$11$
$4c + 3 = 11$

Practice

Write equations for each situation.

1. 248 students went on a trip to the zoo. All 6 buses were filled and 8 students had to travel in cars. Write an equation or expression that will help you find out how many students rode in each bus.

1. $(6 \times s) + 8 = 248$

2. Todd sold half of his comic books and then bought 6 more. He now has 16. Write an equation that will help you find out how many comic books Todd had at the beginning.

2. $\frac{c}{2} + 6 = 16$

3. A bike shop charges $12.00, plus $6.00 an hour, for renting a bike. Mike paid $48.00 to rent a bike. Write an equation that will help you find out how many hours Mike rented the bike.

3. $12 + 6h = 48$

Simple Steps • Sixth Grade   Expressions and Equations   75

Page 76

Review

Use everything you have learned so far about expressions and equations to solve the problems.

Name the property shown in each statement: Associative, Commutative, or Identity.

1. $3 \times (6 \times 2) = (3 \times 6) \times 2$ __Associative__

2. $15 \times 1 = 1$ __Identity__

3. $(3 + 5) + 2 = 3 + (5 + 2)$ __Associative__

4. $112 \times 12 = 12 \times 112$ __Commutative__

Rewrite each expression using the Distributive Property.

5. $3 \times (5 - 2)$ __(3 × 5) - (3 × 2)__

6. $(5 \times 2) + (8 \times 2)$ __(5 + 8) × 2__

Write each problem as a product of factors.

7. 2^4 __2 × 2 × 2 × 2__

8. 9^2 __9 × 9__

9. 5^3 __5 × 5 × 5__

10. 4^2 __4 × 4__

11. 8^5 __8 × 8 × 8 × 8 × 8__

12. 7^3 __7 × 7 × 7__

Solve each problem using the order of operations.

13. $2^3 \times 4 + (6 \div 2)$ __35__

14. $(12 \times 2) + 2 + 4^2$ __28__

15. $48 \div (12 - 8) \times (12 - 10)$ __24__

16. $(3^2 + 3) + (5 \times 2) - 3$ __0__

Write the expression for each statement.

17. The product of 4 and the difference between 8 and 3 __4 × (8 - 3)__

18. 4 increased by the product of 5 and 3 __4 + (5 × 3)__

19. The difference between 16 and the product of 4 and 2 __16 - (4 × 2)__

20. The quotient of 25 and 5 increased by 3 __(25 ÷ 5) + 3__

76   Expressions and Equations   Simple Steps • Sixth Grade

Page 77

Simplifying Expressions

You can use the Distributive Property or combine like terms to simplify expressions. Follow these steps. If there is more than one variable in an expression, use the Distributive Property to simplify. If there are at least two of the same variable in an expression, combine like terms to simplify.

Simplify: $3(x + 2y)$ using the Distributive Property.

First, use the Distributive Property to distribute the first factor to the other factors in the next term. Both x and 2y can be multiplied by 3.
Then, write the simplified expression.

$3x + 6y$

$3(x + 2y)$
$3x + (3 \times 2y)$

Simplify: Simplify $6m - 4m + 3p$ by combining like terms.

First, combine the like terms. Like terms are terms that have the same variable. Here, 6m and 4m are like terms.
Then, write the simplified expression.

$2m + 3p$

$6m - 4m + 3p$
$2m$

Practice

Use the Distributive Property to simplify.

1. $3(2a - 8b) =$ __6a - 24b__

2. $x(y - 4) =$ __xy - 4x__

3. $7(a + b) =$ __7a + 7b__

4. $7(5x + 8) =$ __35x + 56__

Combine like terms to simplify.

5. $y + y - 2 =$ __15y - 2__

6. $25x - x + 2y =$ __24x + 2y__

7. $4a + 8b + a - b =$ __15a + 8b__

8. $4a + 7 + 3a + 8 - 3a =$ __4a + 15__

Simple Steps • Sixth Grade   Expressions and Equations   77

Page 78

Simplifying Expressions

Equivalent expressions are created by simplifying values (using the Distributive Property) and combining like terms.

Simplify: $4(6x - 5)$

Use the Distributive Property to create an equivalent expression. Multiply each value by 4.

$4(6x - 5)$
$(4 \times 6x) - (4 \times 5)$
$24x - 20$

Simplify: $4(r + r + r)$

Combine like terms to create an equivalent expression.

$4(r + r + r)$
$4(4r)$
$16r$

Practice

Write an equivalent expression for each.

1. $7(4z + 8b)$ __28z + 56b__

2. $8(2x + 3^2)$ __16x + 72__

3. $9(3 + 8x)$ __27 + 72x__

4. $\frac{(t + t + t)}{4}$ __$\frac{3t}{4}$__

5. $7(c + c + c)$ __7 × 3c__

6. $10(y + 2)$ __10y + 20__

7. $5(3y + 8t + 2)$ __15y + 40t + 10__

8. $6(z + 6)$ __6z + 36__

9. $11(2r + 3)$ __22r + 33m__

10. $\frac{(2x + 2x)}{8}$ __$\frac{x}{2}$__

78   Expressions and Equations   Simple Steps • Sixth Grade

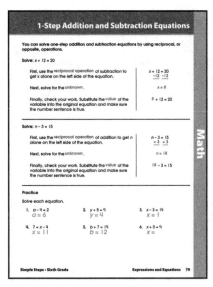

Page 79

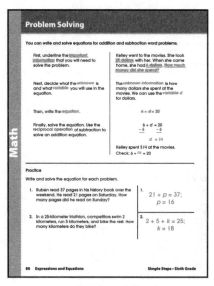

Page 80

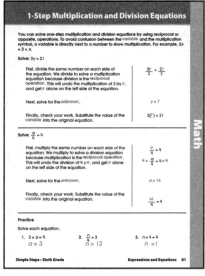

Page 81

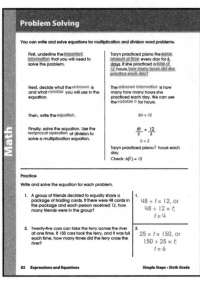

Page 82

Page 83

Page 84

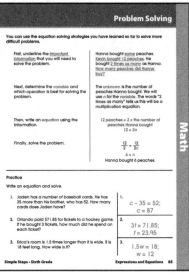

Page 85

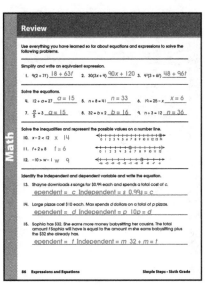

Page 86

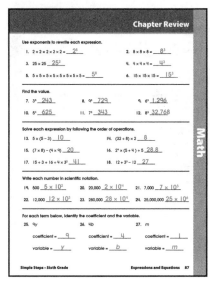

Page 87

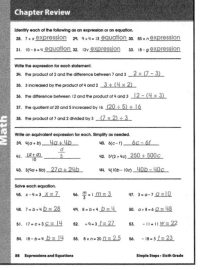

Page 88

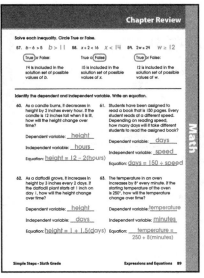

Page 89

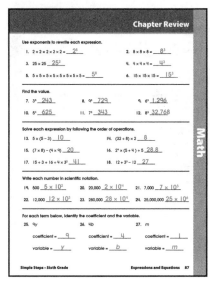

Page 90

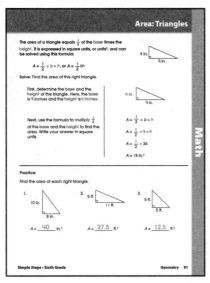

Page 91

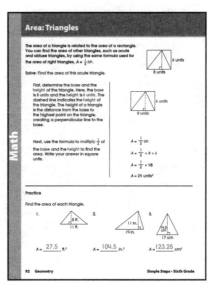

Page 92

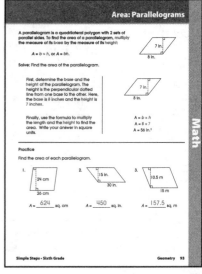

Page 93

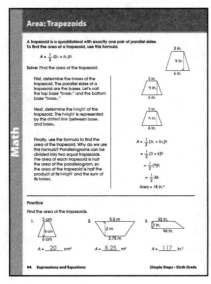

Page 94

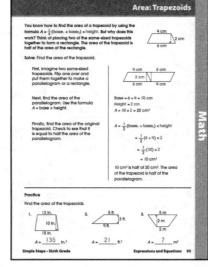

Page 95

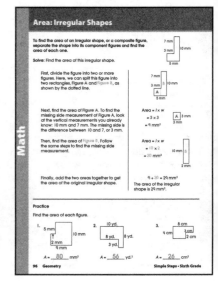

Page 96

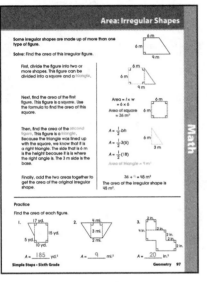

Page 97

Area: Irregular Shapes

Practice

Find the area of each figure.

1. $A = \underline{185}$ yd.²
2. $A = \underline{9}$ mi.²
3. $A = \underline{20}$ in.²

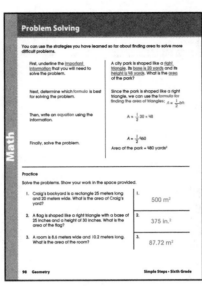

Page 98

Problem Solving

Practice

Solve the problems. Show your work in the space provided.

1. Craig's backyard is a rectangle 25 meters long and 20 meters wide. What is the area of Craig's yard?

    1. 500 m²

2. A flag is shaped like a right triangle with a base of 25 inches and a height of 30 inches. What is the area of the flag?

    2. 375 in.²

3. A room is 8.6 meters wide and 10.2 meters long. What is the area of the room?

    3. 87.72 m²

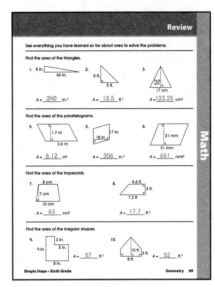

Page 99

Review

Use everything you have learned so far about area to solve the problems.

Find the area of the triangles.

1. $A = \underline{240}$ in.²
2. $A = \underline{12.5}$ ft.²
3. $A = \underline{123.25}$ cm²

Find the area of the parallelograms.

4. $A = \underline{6.12}$ m²
5. $A = \underline{306}$ in.²
6. $A = \underline{651}$ mm²

Find the area of the trapezoids.

7. $A = \underline{63}$ cm²
8. $A = \underline{17.7}$ ft.²

Find the area of the irregular shapes.

9. $A = \underline{57}$ ft.²
10. $A = \underline{52}$ ft.²

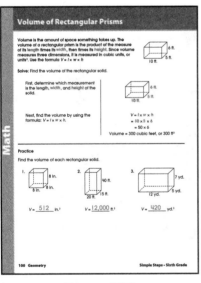

Page 100

Volume of Rectangular Prisms

Practice

Find the volume of each rectangular solid.

1. $V = \underline{512}$ in.³
2. $V = \underline{12,000}$ ft.³
3. $V = \underline{420}$ yd.³

Page 101

Volume of Rectangular Prisms

Practice

Find the volume of each rectangular solid.

1. $V = \frac{30}{343}$ cu. in.
2. $V = \frac{160}{729}$ cu. cm

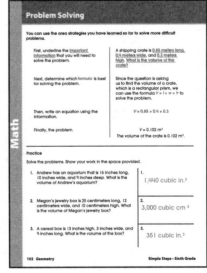

Page 102

Problem Solving

Practice

Solve the problems. Show your work in the space provided.

1. Andrew has an aquarium that is 16 inches long, 10 inches wide, and 9 inches deep. What is the volume of Andrew's aquarium?

    1. 1,440 cubic in.³

2. Megan's jewelry box is 25 centimeters long, 12 centimeters wide, and 10 centimeters high. What is the volume of Megan's jewelry box?

    2. 3,000 cubic cm³

3. A cereal box is 13 inches high, 3 inches wide, and 9 inches long. What is the volume of the box?

    3. 351 cubic in.³

Answer Key

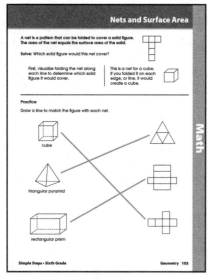

Page 103

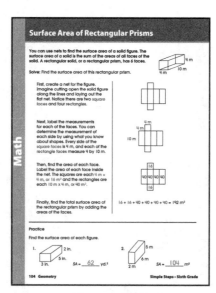

Page 104

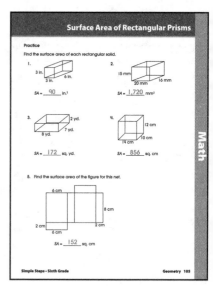

Page 105

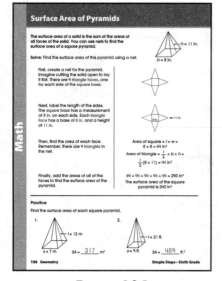

Page 106

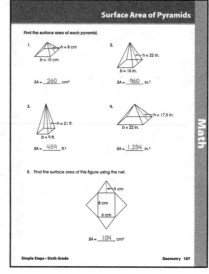

Page 107

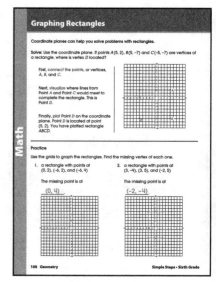

Page 108

Answer Key

Page 109

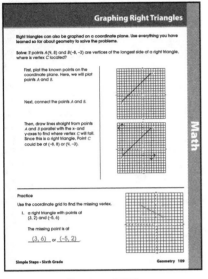

Graphing Right Triangles

Right triangles can also be graphed on a coordinate plane. Use everything you have learned so far about geometry to solve the problems.

Solve: If points A(4, 8) and B(-8, -3) are vertices of the longest side of a right triangle, where is vertex C located?

First, plot the known points on the coordinate plane. Here, we will plot points A and B.

Next, connect the points A and B.

Then, draw lines straight from points A and B parallel with the x- and y-axes to find where vertex C will fall. Since this is a right triangle, Point C could be at (-8, 8) or (4, -3).

Practice

Use the coordinate grid to find the missing vertex.

1. a right triangle with points at (3, 2) and (-5, 6)

   The missing point is at

   __(3, 6)__ or __(-5, 2)__

Page 110

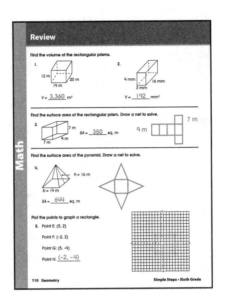

Review

Find the volume of the rectangular prisms.

1. 12 m, 14 m, 20 m
   V = __3,360__ m³

2. 4 mm, 3 mm, 16 mm
   V = __192__ mm³

Find the surface area of the rectangular prism. Draw a net to solve.

3. 7 m, 7 m, 7 m, 9 m
   SA = __350__ sq. m

Find the surface area of the pyramid. Draw a net to solve.

4. h = 16 m, b = 14 m
   SA = __644__ sq. m

Plot the points to graph a rectangle.

5. Point E: (5, 2)
   Point F: (-2, 2)
   Point G: (5, -4)
   Point H: __(-2, -4)__

Page 111

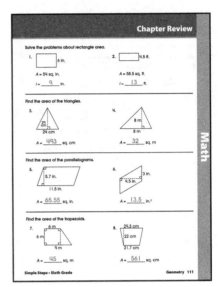

Chapter Review

Solve the problems about rectangle area.

1. 6 in.
   A = 54 sq. in.
   l = __9__ in.

2. 4.5 ft.
   A = 58.5 sq. ft.
   l = __13__ ft.

Find the area of the triangles.

3. 24 cm, 24 cm
   A = __493__ sq. cm

4. 8 m, 8 m
   A = __32__ sq. m

Find the area of the parallelograms.

5. 5.7 in., 11.5 in.
   A = __65.55__ sq. in.

6. 3 in., 4.5 in.
   A = __13.5__ in.²

Find the area of the trapezoids.

7. 6 m, 6 m
   A = __45__ sq. m

8. 24.3 cm, 22 cm, 21.7 cm
   A = __561__ sq. cm

Page 112

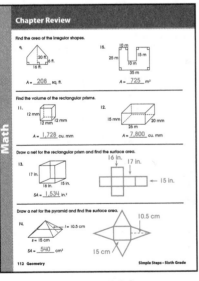

Chapter Review

Find the area of the irregular shapes.

9. 20 ft., 16 ft.
   A = __208__ sq. ft.

10. 10 m, 25 m, 15 m, 10 m, 35 m
    A = __725__ m²

Find the volume of the rectangular prisms.

11. 12 mm, 12 mm, 12 mm
    A = __1,728__ cu. mm

12. 15 mm, 26 mm, 20 mm
    A = __7,800__ cu. mm

Draw a net for the rectangular prism and find the surface area.

13. 17 in., 16 in., 15 in., 16 in., 17 in., 15 in.
    SA = __1,534__ in.²

Draw a net for the pyramid and find the surface area.

14. l = 10.5 cm, s = 15 cm, 10.5 cm, 15 cm
    SA = __540__ cm²

Page 113

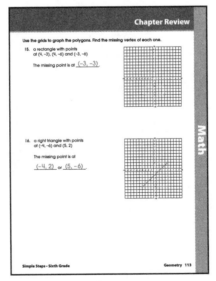

Chapter Review

Use the grids to graph the polygons. Find the missing vertex of each one.

15. a rectangle with points at (4, -3), (4, -6) and (-3, -6)

    The missing point is at __(-3, -3)__.

16. a right triangle with points at (-4, -6) and (5, 2)

    The missing point is at

    __(-4, 2)__ or __(5, -6)__

Page 114

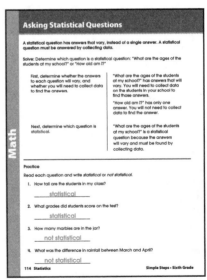

Asking Statistical Questions

A statistical question has answers that vary, instead of a single answer. A statistical question must be answered by collecting data.

Solve: Determine which question is a statistical question: "What are the ages of the students at my school?" or "How old am I?"

First, determine whether the answers to each question will vary, and whether you will need to collect data to find the answers.

"What are the ages of the students at my school?" has answers that will vary. You will need to collect data on the students in your school to find those answers.

"How old am I?" has only one answer. You will not need to collect data to find the answer.

Next, determine which question is statistical.

"What are the ages of the students at my school?" is a statistical question because the answers will vary and must be found by collecting data.

Practice

Read each question and write statistical or not statistical.

1. How tall are the students in my class?

   __statistical__

2. What grades did students score on the test?

   __statistical__

3. How many marbles are in the jar?

   __not statistical__

4. What was the difference in rainfall between March and April?

   __not statistical__

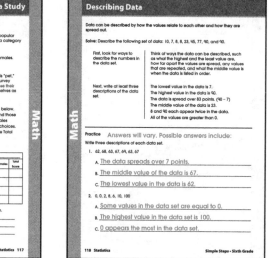

Page 117

Page 118

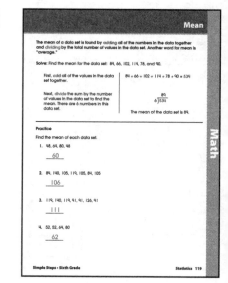

Page 119

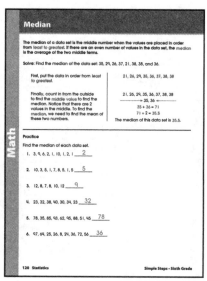

Page 120

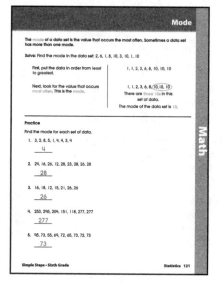

Page 121

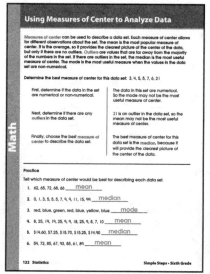

Page 122

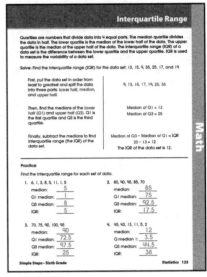

Page 123

Using Measures of Center to Analyze Data

Find the measures of center for each data set and decide which would be best to describe the data set. Remember to look for any outliers that can affect the mean!

1. Cesar's Test Scores: 84, 80, 78, 90, 76, 88, 86, 80, 94
   Which is the best measure of center?
   __mean__
   Mean: 84
   Median: 84
   Mode: 80

2. Basketball Team Scores: 78, 77, 81, 84, 67, 78, 75, 42
   Which is the best measure of center?
   __median__
   Mean: 72.75
   Median: 77.5
   Mode: 78

3. Daily Theater Attendance: 124, 127, 111, 119, 107, 99, 115
   Which is the best measure of center?
   __mean__
   Mean: 114.57
   Median: 115
   Mode: no mode

4. Marisa's Daily Tips: $15, $21, $18, $13, $52, $21, $25
   Which is the best measure of center?
   __median__
   Mean: $23.57
   Median: $21
   Mode: $21

Simple Steps • Sixth Grade   Statistics 123

Page 124

Range

Range is one way to describe a measure of variation, rather than a measure of center. A measure of variation describes how spread out a set of data is. The range of a data set is the difference between the largest and smallest values contained in the data set.

Solve: Find the range of the set of data: 11, 12, 15, 15, 13, and 12

First, put the values in the data set in order from least to greatest.   11, 12, 12, 13, 15, 15

Next, subtract to find the difference between the largest and the smallest value. This is the range.   15 – 11 = 4
The range of this set of data is 4.

Practice

Find the range of each data set.

1. 11, 10, 12, 9   3
2. 79, 79, 79, 84   5
3. 25, 30, 32, 23, 27, 22   10
4. 96, 94, 101, 96, 91, 92   10
5. 36, 33, 37, 37, 41, 33   8
6. 506, 508, 510, 509   4
7. 277, 280, 287, 276   11
8. 10, 8, 9, 12, 6, 8   6

124 Statistics   Simple Steps • Sixth Grade

Page 125

Interquartile Range

Quartiles are numbers that divide data into 4 equal parts. The median quartile divides the data in half. The lower quartile is the median of the lower half of the data. The upper quartile is the median of the upper half of the data. The interquartile range (IQR) of a data set is the difference between the lower quartile and the upper quartile. IQR is used to measure the variability of a data set.

Solve: Find the interquartile range (IQR) for the data set: 13, 15, 9, 35, 25, 17, and 19

First, put the data set in order from least to greatest and split the data into three parts: lower half, median, and upper half.   9, 13, 15, 17, 19, 25, 35

Then, find the medians of the lower half (Q1) and upper half (Q3). Q1 is the first quartile and Q3 is the third quartile.   Median of Q1 = 13
Median of Q3 = 25

Finally, subtract the medians to find interquartile range (the IQR) of the data set.   Median of Q3 – Median of Q1 = IQR
25 – 13 = 12
The IQR of the data set is 12.

Practice

Find the interquartile range for each set of data.

1. 6, 1, 3, 8, 5, 11, 1, 5
   median: 5
   Q1 median: 1
   Q3 median: 8
   IQR: 5

2. 80, 90, 95, 85, 70
   median: 85
   Q1 median: 75
   Q3 median: 92.5
   IQR: 17.5

3. 70, 75, 90, 100, 95
   median: 90
   Q1 median: 72.5
   Q3 median: 97.5
   IQR: 25

4. 45, 43, 13, 11, 5, 2
   median: 12
   Q median 1: 3.5
   Q3 median: 44.5
   IQR: 38

Simple Steps • Sixth Grade   Statistics 125

Page 126

Mean Absolute Deviation

The mean absolute deviation (MAD) of a data set is a value that shows if the data set is consistent. The closer the mean absolute deviation of a data set is to zero, the more consistent it is. MAD tells how far away each value in the set is from the middle.

Solve: Find the mean absolute deviation of the data set: 17, 19, 8, 32, 21, 24, 19.

First, put the data set in order from least to greatest.   8, 17, 19, 19, 21, 24, 32

Next, find the mean of the data set.   8 + 17 + 19 + 19 + 21 + 24 + 32 = 140
140 ÷ 7 = 20
Mean = 20

Then, find the absolute value of the difference between the mean and each value in the set.
20 – 8 = 12; |12| = 12
20 – 17 = 3; |3| = 3
20 – 19 = 1; |1| = 1
20 – 19 = 1; |1| = 1
20 – 21 = –1; |–1| = 1
20 – 24 = –4; |–4| = 4
20 – 32 = –12; |–12| = 12

Then, find the mean of those absolute values. This number is the mean absolute deviation.
12 + 3 + 1 + 1 + 1 + 4 + 12 = 34
34 ÷ 7 = 4.86
Mean absolute deviation = 4.86

Practice

Find the mean absolute deviation of each data set. Round each answer to two decimal places.

1. 10, 16, 18, 15, 15, 10, 23
   mean: 15.29
   value differences: 5.29; 5.29; 0.29; 0.29; 0.71; 2.71; 7.71
   MAD: 3.18

2. 41, 56, 38, 45, 55, 51, 52
   mean: 48.29
   value differences: 10.29; 7.29; 3.29; 2.71; 3.71; 6.71; 7.71
   MAD: 5.96

126 Statistics   Simple Steps • Sixth Grade

Page 127

Using Measures of Variability

A measure of center for a data set summarizes all of its values with a single number. A measure of variation describes how a data set's values vary with a single number. The range of a data set is a measure of variability.

Solve: Complete the table by listing the measures of variability for each data set. Round answers to two decimal places.

Data	Range	IQR	MAD
1. 43, 48, 80, 53, 59, 65, 58, 66, 70, 50, 76, 62	37	16.5	9
2. 12, 47, 26, 25, 38, 45, 35, 35, 41, 39, 32, 25, 18, 30	35	14	8
3. 99, 45, 23, 67, 45, 91, 82, 78, 62, 51	76	37	19.1
4. 10, 2, 5, 6, 7, 3, 4	8	4	2.04
5. 23, 56, 45, 65, 59, 55, 61, 54, 85, 25	62	16	13.08
6. 55, 63, 88, 97, 58, 90, 88, 71, 65, 77, 75, 88, 95, 86	42	23	12

Simple Steps • Sixth Grade   Statistics 127

Page 128

Using Measures of Variability

Use measures of center and variability to summarize this data set. Round answers to two decimal places.

A school keeps track of how many students are buying notebooks each month from the school store. They collected this information.

Month	Notebooks Sold
Jan.	25
Feb.	30
Mar.	15
Apr.	20
May	15
June	5
July	0
Aug.	35
Sept.	20
Oct.	15
Nov.	20
Dec.	30

mode: 15, 20
median: 20
mean: 19.17
range: 35
IQR: 12.5
MAD: 7.64

Write 2 to 3 sentences that describe the data set.
Answers will vary but could include information about the outliers in June and July, the jump in data from July to August, the highest data value in August, etc.

Which would be a better measure of center for this data: mean or median? Why?
Median, because the data has some outliers.

128 Statistics   Simple Steps • Sixth Grade

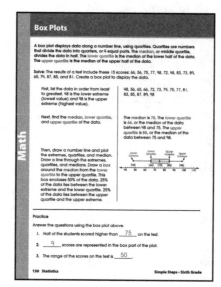

Page 129

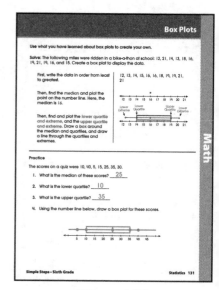

Page 130

Page 131

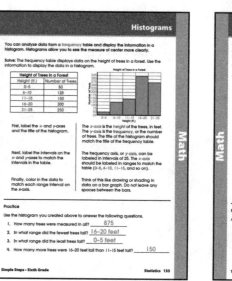

Page 132

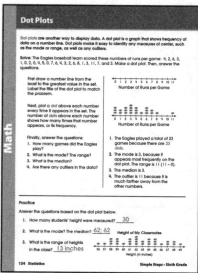

Page 133

Page 134

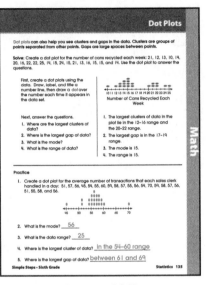

Page 135

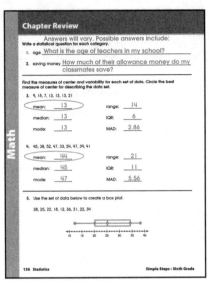

Page 136

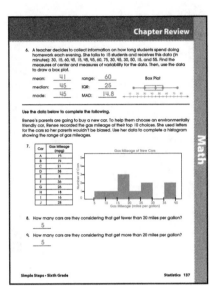

Page 137

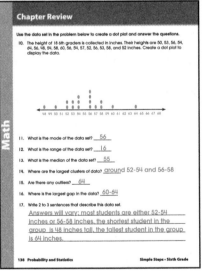

Page 138

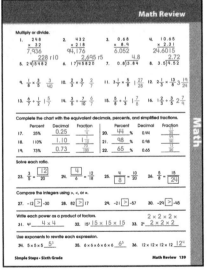

Page 139

Page 140

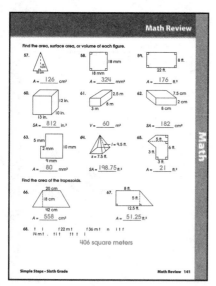

Page 141

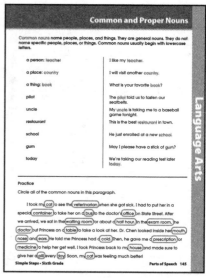

Page 142

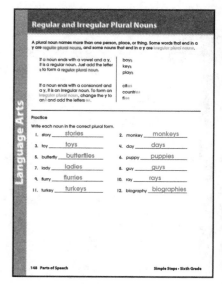

Page 145

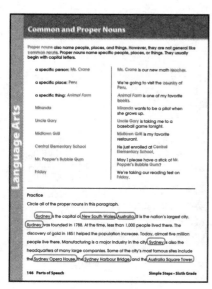

Page 146

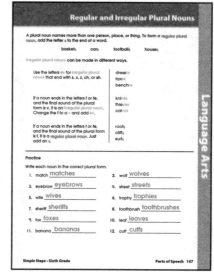

Page 147

Page 148

Page 149

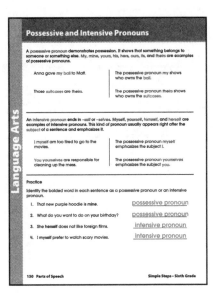

Page 150

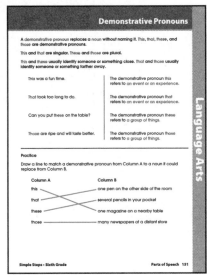

Page 151

Page 149 — Subject and Object Pronouns

A pronoun is a word used in place of a noun. A subject pronoun replaces a noun that is the subject of a sentence. I, you, he, she, and it are subject pronouns.

James found the ball. (James is the subject of the sentence.)	He found the ball. (He is the subject pronoun.)
Baseball is my favorite sport. (Baseball is the subject of the sentence.)	It is my favorite sport. (It is the subject pronoun.)

An object pronoun replaces a noun that is the object of a sentence. Me, you, him, her, and it are object pronouns.

Give the book to Keisha. (Keisha is the object of the sentence.)	Give the book to her. (her is the object pronoun.)
James put the book away. (book is the object of the sentence.)	James put it away. (It is the object pronoun.)

Practice

Identify the bolded word in each sentence as a subject pronoun or an object pronoun.

1. Jessica, please put it over there. — object pronoun
2. I have practice after school today. — subject pronoun
3. He doesn't like string beans. — subject pronoun
4. Tommy gave his old jacket to me. — object pronoun

Page 150 — Possessive and Intensive Pronouns

A possessive pronoun demonstrates possession. It shows that something belongs to someone or something else. My, mine, yours, his, hers, ours, its, and theirs are examples of possessive pronouns.

Anna gave my ball to Matt.	The possessive pronoun my shows who owns the ball.
Those suitcases are theirs.	The possessive pronoun theirs shows who owns the suitcases.

An intensive pronoun ends in –self or –selves. Myself, yourself, himself, and herself are examples of intensive pronouns. This kind of pronoun usually appears right after the subject of a sentence and emphasizes it.

I myself am too tired to go to the movies.	The possessive pronoun myself emphasizes the subject I.
You yourselves are responsible for cleaning up the mess.	The possessive pronoun yourselves emphasizes the subject you.

Practice

Identify the bolded word in each sentence as a possessive pronoun or an intensive pronoun.

1. That new purple hoodie is mine. — possessive pronoun
2. What do you want to do on your birthday? — possessive pronoun
3. She herself does not like foreign films. — intensive pronoun
4. I myself prefer to watch scary movies. — intensive pronoun

Page 151 — Demonstrative Pronouns

A demonstrative pronoun replaces a noun without naming it. This, that, these, and those are demonstrative pronouns.

This and that are singular. These and those are plural.

This and these usually identify someone or something close. That and those usually identify someone or something farther away.

This was a fun time.	The demonstrative pronoun this refers to an event or an experience.
That took too long to do.	The demonstrative pronoun that refers to an event or an experience.
Can you put these on the table?	The demonstrative pronoun these refers to a group of things.
Those are ripe and will taste better.	The demonstrative pronoun those refers to a group of things.

Practice

Draw a line to match a demonstrative pronoun from Column A to a noun it could replace from Column B.

Column A	Column B
this	one pen on the other side of the room
that	several pencils in your pocket
these	one magazine on a nearby table
those	many newspapers at a distant store

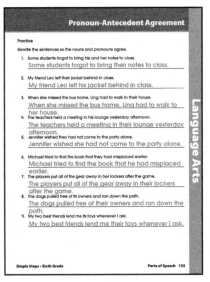

Page 152

Page 153

Page 155

Page 152 — Relative Pronouns

Relative pronouns are related to nouns that have already been stated. Who, whose, that, and which are relative pronouns. They are used to combine two sentences that share a common noun.

Carmen is a doctor. Carmen lives next door to me.	Carmen is the doctor who lives next door to me. (who refers to Carmen)
Miguel is a barber. Miguel's shop is on Elm Street.	Miguel is the barber whose shop is on Elm Street. (whose refers to Miguel)
You just read a report. The report is incorrect.	The report that you just read is correct. (that refers to the report)
The magazine articles are too long. The magazine articles must be cut.	The magazine articles, which are too long, must be cut. (which refers to the magazine articles)

Practice

Complete the sentences by circling the correct relative pronoun in parentheses.

1. Someone (who, which) likes bananas might like kiwi too.
2. She likes movies (which, that) have a lot of action.
3. Racers (whose, which) cars are ready can drive to the starting line.
4. The bananas, (who, which) are the ripest fruits we have in the house, should be used in the recipe.

Page 153 — Indefinite Pronouns

An indefinite pronoun does not specifically name the noun that it replaces. Here are some examples of indefinite pronouns.

all	everybody	one
another	everyone	several
any	everything	some
anybody	few	somebody
anyone	many	something
anything	nobody	
each	none	

Many were invited to the party, but only a few came.	The indefinite pronoun many does not identify who or what came to the party.
We donated everything from the attic to the charity event.	The indefinite pronoun everything does not identify what was donated.
They let us buy anything we wanted.	The indefinite pronoun anything does not identify what was bought.

Practice

Underline all of the indefinite pronouns in this paragraph.

Each of the cooks in town made ice cream cones for the fair. The cooks were put in pairs. One made the ice cream while another made the cones. You wouldn't think there would be any problems. However, there were some. Different customers wanted different things. One wanted cherry, while another wanted chocolate. Several wanted two scoops with different flavors. But the cooks were ready for anything. They also made snow cones. They even made milkshakes that were a big hit. By the end of the day, everything had been eaten.

Page 155 — Pronoun-Antecedent Agreement

Practice

Rewrite the sentences so the nouns and pronouns agree.

1. Some students forgot to bring his and her notes to class.
   Some students forgot to bring their notes to class.
2. My friend Leo left their jacket behind in class.
   My friend Leo left his jacket behind in class.
3. When she missed the bus home, Ling had to walk to their house.
   When she missed the bus home, Ling had to walk to her house.
4. The teachers held a meeting in his lounge yesterday afternoon.
   The teachers held a meeting in their lounge yesterday afternoon.
5. Jennifer wished they had not come to the party alone.
   Jennifer wished she had not come to the party alone.
6. Michael tried to find the book that they had misplaced earlier.
   Michael tried to find the book that he had misplaced earlier.
7. The players put all of the gear away in her lockers after the game.
   The players put all of the gear away in their lockers after the game.
8. The dogs pulled free of its owners and ran down the path.
   The dogs pulled free of their owners and ran down the path.
9. My two best friends lend me its toys whenever I ask.
   My two best friends lend me their toys whenever I ask.

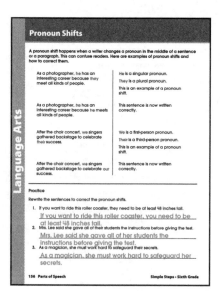

Page 156

Pronoun Shifts

A pronoun shift happens when a writer changes a pronoun in the middle of a sentence or a paragraph. This can confuse readers. Here are examples of pronoun shifts and how to correct them.

As a photographer, he has an interesting career because they meet all kinds of people.	He is a singular pronoun. They is a plural pronoun. This is an example of a pronoun shift.
As a photographer, he has an interesting career because he meets all kinds of people.	This sentence is now written correctly.
After the choir concert, we singers gathered backstage to celebrate their success.	We is a first-person pronoun. Their is a third-person pronoun. This is an example of a pronoun shift.
After the choir concert, we singers gathered backstage to celebrate our success.	This sentence is now written correctly.

Practice

Rewrite the sentences to correct the pronoun shifts.

1. If you want to ride this roller coaster, they need to be at least 48 inches tall.
   If you want to ride this roller coaster, you need to be at least 48 inches tall.
2. Mrs. Lee said she gave all of their students the instructions before giving the test.
   Mrs. Lee said she gave all of her students the instructions before giving the test.
3. As a magician, she must work hard to safeguard their secrets.
   As a magician, she must work hard to safeguard her secrets.

156 Parts of Speech • Simple Steps · Sixth Grade

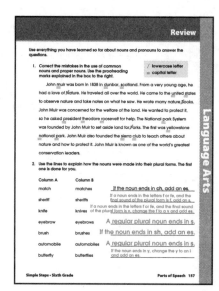

Page 157

Review

Use everything you have learned so far about nouns and pronouns to answer the questions.

1. Correct the mistakes in the use of common nouns and proper nouns. Use the proofreading marks explained in the box to the right.

   ✓ lowercase letter
   ≡ capital letter

   John muir was born in 1838 in dunbar, scotland. From a very young age, he had a love of Nature. He traveled all over the world. He came to the united states to observe nature and take notes on what he saw. He wrote many nature books. John Muir was concerned for the welfare of the land. He wanted to protect it, so he asked president theodore roosevelt for help. The National park System was founded by John Muir to set aside land for parks. The first was yellowstone national park. John Muir also founded the sierra club to teach others about nature and how to protect it. John Muir is known as one of the world's greatest conservation leaders.

2. Use the lines to explain how the nouns were made into their plural forms. The first one is done for you.

Column A	Column B	
match	matches	If the noun ends in ch, add an es.
sheriff	sheriffs	If a noun ends in the letters f or fe, and the final sound of the plural form is f, add an s.
knife	knives	If a noun ends in the letters f or fe, and the final sound of the plural form is v, change the f to a v and add es.
eyebrow	eyebrows	A regular plural noun ends in s.
brush	brushes	If the noun ends in sh, add an es.
automobile	automobiles	A regular plural noun ends in s.
butterfly	butterflies	If the noun ends in y, change the y to an i and add an es.

Simple Steps · Sixth Grade • Parts of Speech 157

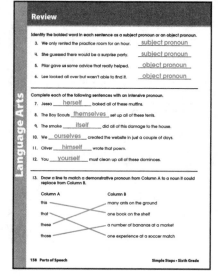

Page 158

Review

Identify the bolded word in each sentence as a subject pronoun or an object pronoun.

3. We only rented the practice room for an hour. ___subject pronoun___
4. She guessed there would be a surprise party. ___subject pronoun___
5. Pilar gave us some advice that really helped. ___object pronoun___
6. Lee looked all over but wasn't able to find it. ___object pronoun___

Complete each of the following sentences with an intensive pronoun.

7. Jessa ___herself___ baked all of these muffins.
8. The Boy Scouts ___themselves___ set up all of these tents.
9. The smoke ___itself___ did all of this damage to the house.
10. We ___ourselves___ created the website in just a couple of days.
11. Oliver ___himself___ wrote that poem.
12. You ___yourself___ must clean up all of these dominoes.

13. Draw a line to match a demonstrative pronoun from Column A to a noun it could replace from Column B.

Column A	Column B
this	many ants on the ground
that	one book on the shelf
these	a number of bananas at a market
those	one experience at a soccer match

158 Parts of Speech • Simple Steps · Sixth Grade

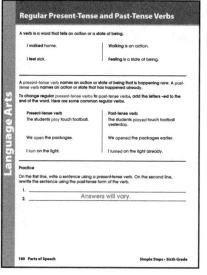

Page 159

Review

Complete each sentence by choosing the correct relative pronoun in parentheses. Circle the correct answer.

14. Bicyclers (which, **whose**) bikes are ready can follow the path.
15. He likes novels (**who**, that) are set in other countries.
16. The man (**who**, whose) lives across the street is an actor.
17. The car (who, **that**) you drove is blocking the driveway.

18. Rewrite the following school news report. Replace the underlined words with indefinite pronouns. More than one answer is acceptable in many sentences.

   The whole community attended the fundraiser for the school. The bake sale was a big success. Not a single item was left at the end of the evening. Chris and his friends looked for more brownies. Most of the students enjoyed the food, music, and art. Six or seven of the attendees promised to help with next year's fundraiser.

   Sample Answer: Everyone attended the fundraiser for the school. The bake sale was a big success. Nothing was left at the end of the evening. Some looked for more brownies. Many enjoyed the food, music, and art. Almost everybody promised to help with next year's fundraiser.

Complete each sentence below by writing the correct pronoun on the line. In some cases, there may be more than one acceptable answer.

19. They did not go to the Girl Scouts meeting, so ___they___ didn't hear the news.
20. Since he is leaving for college this fall, ___he___ is getting a car.
21. I met with the soccer coach, and ___she___ said I could to join the team.
22. When they got home, ___they___ wanted to have a snack.
23. I need to get my permission slip signed if ___I___ want to go to the art museum.
24. Is Jorge going to join you and me at the pool, or will he call ___you___ first?

Simple Steps · Sixth Grade • Parts of Speech 159

Page 160

Regular Present-Tense and Past-Tense Verbs

A verb is a word that tells an action or a state of being.

I walked home.	Walking is an action.
I feel sick.	Feeling is a state of being.

A present-tense verb names an action or state of being that is happening now. A past-tense verb names an action or state that has happened already.

To change regular present-tense verbs to past-tense verbs, add the letters –ed to the end of the word. Here are some common regular verbs.

Present-tense verb	Past-tense verb
The students play touch football.	The students played touch football yesterday.
We open the packages.	We opened the packages earlier.
I turn on the light.	I turned on the light already.

Practice

On the first line, write a sentence using a present-tense verb. On the second line, rewrite the sentence using the past-tense form of the verb.

1.
2. Answers will vary.

160 Parts of Speech • Simple Steps · Sixth Grade

Page 161

Regular Present-Tense and Past-Tense Verbs

Practice

Write each verb in present tense in the first sentence. Then, write it in past tense in the second sentence.

1. mend — Today, I **mend.** — Yesterday, I **mended.**
2. cook — Today, I **cook.** — Yesterday, I **cooked.**
3. bake — Today, I **bake.** — Yesterday, I **baked.**
4. answer — Today, I **answer.** — Yesterday, I **answered.**
5. wave — Today, I **wave.** — Yesterday, I **waved.**
6. scream — Today, I **scream.** — Yesterday, I **screamed.**
7. bike — Today, I **bike.** — Yesterday, I **biked.**
8. jump — Today, I **jump.** — Yesterday, I **jumped.**
9. whisper — Today, I **whisper.** — Yesterday, I **whispered.**
10. divide — Today, I **divide.** — Yesterday, I **divided.**
11. act — Today, I **act.** — Yesterday, I **acted.**
12. cycle — Today, I **cycle.** — Yesterday, I **cycled.**
13. mow — Today, I **mow.** — Yesterday, I **mowed.**
14. yell — Today, I **yell.** — Yesterday, I **yelled.**
15. rake — Today, I **rake.** — Yesterday, I **raked.**

Simple Steps · Sixth Grade • Parts of Speech 161

Answer Key

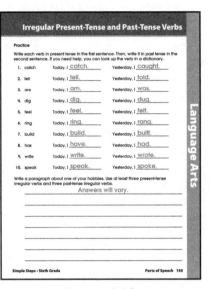

Page 163

Irregular Present-Tense and Past-Tense Verbs

Practice
Write each verb in present tense in the first sentence. Then, write it in past tense in the second sentence. If you need help, you can look up the verb in a dictionary.

1. catch — Today, I _catch._ — Yesterday, I _caught._
2. tell — Today, I _tell._ — Yesterday, I _told._
3. are — Today, I _am._ — Yesterday, I _was._
4. dig — Today, I _dig._ — Yesterday, I _dug._
5. feel — Today, I _feel._ — Yesterday, I _felt._
6. ring — Today, I _ring._ — Yesterday, I _rang._
7. build — Today, I _build._ — Yesterday, I _built._
8. has — Today, I _have._ — Yesterday, I _had._
9. write — Today, I _write._ — Yesterday, I _wrote._
10. speak — Today, I _speak._ — Yesterday, I _spoke._

Write a paragraph about one of your hobbies. Use at least three present-tense irregular verbs and three past-tense irregular verbs.
Answers will vary.

Simple Steps • Sixth Grade — Parts of Speech 163

Page 165

Subject-Verb Agreement

Here are some rules to remember for subject-verb agreement.

If the subject is a compound subject and includes the word and, a plural verb is needed.	Tyler and Inez bake a pie together.
If the subject is a compound subject and includes the words nor or or, then the verb must agree with the subject closest to it.	Neither Tyler nor Inez likes blueberry pie.
If the subject and the verb are separated by a number of words, the subject and the verb still must agree with each other.	Inez, along with her sisters, works at the bakery.

Practice
Circle the correct verb for each sentence.

1. Jill (jump, _jumps_) rope after school.
2. Jill and Katie (_jump_, jumps) rope after school.
3. Jill and her friends (_jump_, jumps) rope after school.
4. Jill, as well as her friends, (jump, _jumps_) rope after school.
5. Michael (practice, _practices_) the violin after school.
6. Michael and Mia (_practice_, practices) the violin after school.
7. Neither Michael nor Mia (practice, _practices_) the violin on weekends.

Simple Steps • Sixth Grade — Parts of Speech 165

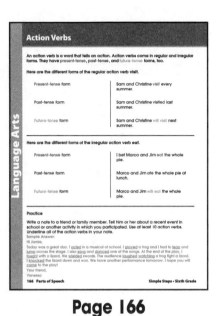

Page 166

Action Verbs

An action verb is a word that tells an action. Action verbs come in regular and irregular forms. They have present-tense, past-tense, and future-tense forms, too.

Here are the different forms of the regular action verb visit.

Present-tense form	Sam and Christine visit every summer.
Past-tense form	Sam and Christine visited last summer.
Future-tense form	Sam and Christine will visit next summer.

Here are the different forms of the irregular action verb eat.

Present-tense form	I bet Marco and Jim eat the whole pie.
Past-tense form	Marco and Jim ate the whole pie at lunch.
Future-tense form	Marco and Jim will eat the whole pie.

Practice
Write a note to a friend or family member. Tell him or her about a recent event in school or another activity in which you participated. Use at least 10 action verbs. Underline all of the action verbs in your note.
Sample Answer:
Hi Jamie,
Today was a great day. I acted in a musical at school. I played a frog and I had to leap and jump across the stage. I also sang and danced one of the songs. At the end of the play, I fought with a lizard. We wielded swords. The audience laughed watching a frog fight a lizard. I knocked the lizard down and won. We have another performance tomorrow. I hope you will come to the play!
Your friend,
Vanessa

166 Parts of Speech — Simple Steps • Sixth Grade

Page 167

Helping Verbs

A helping verb is not a main verb. It helps form some of the tenses of a main verb. The verb to be is one kind of helping verb. Here are the different forms.

is   are   was   were   am   been

Helping verbs often help express time or mood. Here are some examples.

shall	had	do
will	would	can
could	should	did
may	must	
have	has	

Main verbs that end in ing can be a clue that there is a helping verb in the sentence.
The athlete was training for hours.
The dancer had been practicing for days.

Practice
Underline the helping verb or verbs in each sentence.

1. I have been following her music career for years.
2. It has been days since we've seen each other.
3. We could ride this train to get home faster.
4. It will take a long time to finish all of these chores.
5. This assignment was given to us yesterday morning.

Simple Steps • Sixth Grade — Parts of Speech 167

Page 168

Linking Verbs

A linking verb does not name an action. It connects a subject to a noun or adjective. The most common linking verbs are the forms of the verb to be.

is   are   was   were   am   been

Here are other kinds of linking verbs.

Some linking verbs are those of the five senses.	The pencil feels sharp. You look pretty in that outfit. These roses smell the best. I sound weird when I have a cold. His soup tastes delicious.
Some linking verbs reflect a state of being.	I appear different than I once did. The man becomes angry when he has to wait. She grows tired of doing this assignment. I remain determined to finish. We seem upset, but we're not.

Practice
Circle the linking verb and underline the noun or adjective it links to in each sentence.

1. The crowd at the baseball game (appears) excited.
2. The audience thought the play (was) good.
3. The lettuce in this salad (tastes) bitter.
4. The line to get into the restaurant (seems) long.
5. Syd, Mitzi, and Deb (were) the top runners in the race.

168 Parts of Speech — Simple Steps • Sixth Grade

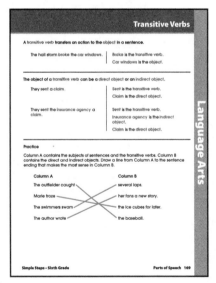

Page 169

Transitive Verbs

A transitive verb transfers an action to the object in a sentence.

The hail storm broke the car windows.	Broke is the transitive verb. Car windows is the object.

The object of a transitive verb can be a direct object or an indirect object.

They sent a claim.	Sent is the transitive verb. Claim is the direct object.
They sent the insurance agency a claim.	Sent is the transitive verb. Insurance agency is the indirect object. Claim is the direct object.

Practice
Column A contains the subjects of sentences and the transitive verbs. Column B contains the direct and indirect objects. Draw a line from Column A to the sentence ending that makes the most sense in Column B.

Column A
The outfielder caught
Marie froze
The swimmers swam
The author wrote

Column B
several laps.
her fans a new story.
the ice cubes for later.
the baseball.

Simple Steps • Sixth Grade — Parts of Speech 169

Simple Steps • Sixth Grade

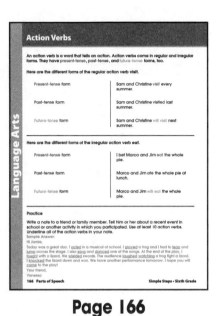
Answer Key

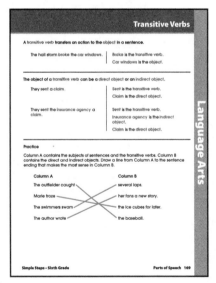

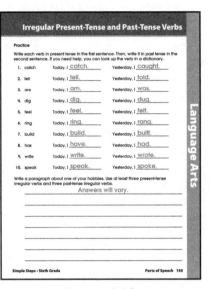

Answer Key 301

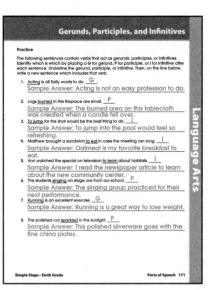

Page 171

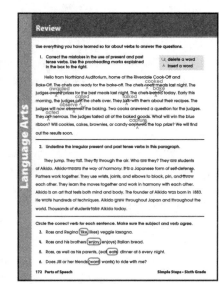

Page 172

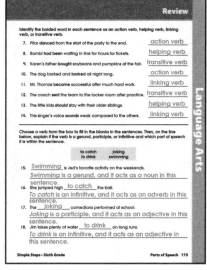

Page 173

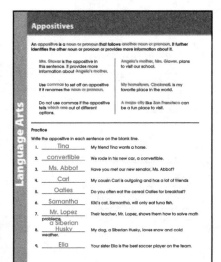

Page 174

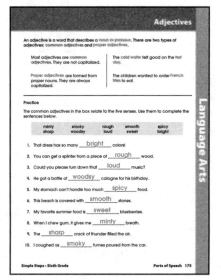

Page 175

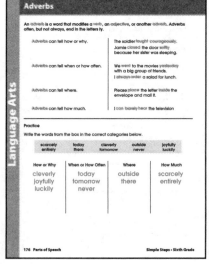

Page 176

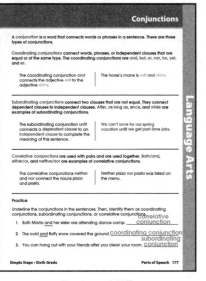

Page 177

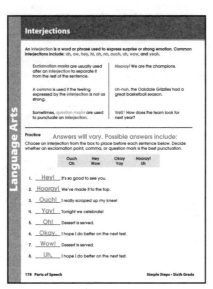

Page 178

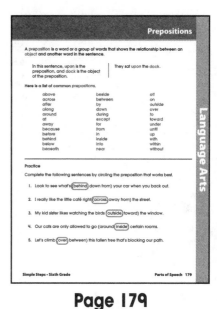

Page 179

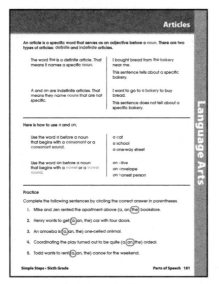

Page 180

Page 181

Page 182

Page 183

Review

7. Match the words in Column A with their relationship in Column B.

Column A
- both mushrooms and olives
- before it gets dark
- after the race
- neither pennies nor nickels
- music and dance
- purple or blue shirt

Column B
- equal (coordinate)
- pairs (correlative)
- dependent (subordinate)
- equal (coordinate)
- pairs (correlative)
- dependent (subordinate)

Write a sentence for each interjection in the box. Decide whether an exclamation point, comma, or question mark is the best punctuation.

| Aw | Eeek | Okay | Ouch | Wow |

8. _____
9. _____
10. _____ Answers will vary.
11. _____
12. _____

Circle the preposition and underline the entire prepositional phrase in each sentence.

13. A gray squirrel sat on the roof.
14. A jogger ran down the street.
15. The tree sat behind the white fence.
16. Lauren will be coming to my house later.
17. The clouds floated through the bright sky.

Simple Steps • Sixth Grade   Parts of Speech 183

Page 184

Chapter Review

Complete the following sentences by circling the best answer in parentheses.

1. I like to visit the (museum) Museum on Sundays.
2. The New York (museum) Museum of Art is one famous museum.
3. Paul Klee was a famous artist who loved and painted many (cats) cat).
4. (Women) Womans) were the subject of many of the paintings of Henri Matisse.
5. Claude Monet's parents did not want (he) him) to become an artist.
6. Marc Chagall liked to paint violins in memory of his uncle (which) who) played.
7. Pierre-Auguste Renoir believed (anyone) everyone) should work with his or her hands.
8. Karen (herself) yourself) has only visited this one art museum.
9. I (myself) ourselves) have visited more than a dozen.
10. An artist should always follow (their) his/her) heart.

Circle the regular past-tense verb and underline the irregular past-tense verb.

11. Last weekend we (played) ball and we built sand castles.

Circle the action verb and underline the helping verb phrase.

12. The golfer (hit) the ball to the left; he should have hit it straight ahead.

Circle the transitive verb and underline its object.

13. The artist (drew) many paintings.

Circle the infinitive.

14. The author is going (to write) at the beach.

184 Parts of Speech   Simple Steps • Sixth Grade

Page 185

Chapter Review

Identify the part of speech underlined in each sentence as an adjective (ADJ), adverb (ADV), conjunction (CON), or interjection (INJ).

15. __ADJ__ Kay brought a huge orange to go with her lunch.
16. __INJ__ Really? Do you think the project will be ready in time?
17. __CON__ Lynn wants to buy the blue or red bracelet.
18. __ADV__ Annie can't babysit tomorrow because she's busy.
19. __ADJ__ The heavy rain made it difficult to see the road.
20. __INJ__ Awesome! We biked all the way to the top of the mountain.
21. __CON__ Bobcats hunt both during the night and during the day.
22. __ADJ__ The kids wanted to ride the newest roller coaster.
23. __ADV__ This assignment needs to be finished by this afternoon.
24. __INJ__ Oh no, I hope I do better on the next test.

25. Circle the prepositions and underline the objects of the prepositions in the paragraph.

The West Wing is located in the White House. The President of the United States has his office in the West Wing. It is called the Oval Office. The West Wing houses the executive staff's offices, in addition to the president's office. The chief of staff's office is across from the Oval Office. The vice president works beside the chief of staff. The press secretary and the communication director's offices are along the main corridor. The Roosevelt Room (a conference room), the Cabinet Room (the cabinet is a group of advisers who are heads of government departments), and the President's secretary's office are a little farther down the corridor. Outside of the press secretary's window is the Rose Garden. The West Colonnade runs alongside the Rose Garden. The Press Room is inside the West Colonnade. The Press Room sits on top of an old swimming pool. The swimming pool is a remnant of Franklin D. Roosevelt's administration. That completes the tour of the West Wing.

Simple Steps • Sixth Grade   Parts of Speech 185

Page 186

Chapter Review

26. Some of the sentences in the paragraph need helping verbs to make them complete. Insert helping verbs when needed. Use the proofreader mark from the box to the right. Answers may vary. Possible answers include:

A insert a word

Glacier National Park located in Montana. Glacier National Park aptly named. Glaciers left from the ice age remain in the park. Grizzly bears said to be the mascot of the park. Rangers said that they observed the bears' almost human-like behavior. The mountain goats of Glacier National Park live high in the mountains. The visitors go high up to find them. Glacier National Park known as one of the top night spots of the national parks. Because it is located far away from cities, the skies are dark and millions of stars seen at night. You visit Glacier National Park any time of year.

27. What is your favorite play, movie, or television show? Write a paragraph to describe it. Underline the articles you used.

_____
_____
_____ Answers will vary.
_____
_____
_____

186 Parts of Speech   Simple Steps • Sixth Grade

Page 187

Declarative Sentences

A declarative sentence makes a statement. Use a period at the end to punctuate a declarative sentence.

A declarative sentence can make a statement about a person.	Louise just won a scholarship to attend college.
A declarative sentence can make a statement about a place.	A new restaurant opened on Roosevelt Street this summer.
A declarative sentence can make a statement about a thing.	My necklace fell to the floor when the clasp broke.

Declarative sentences can be written in different tenses.

A declarative sentence can make a statement about the past.	Steve parked the car near the entrance to the park earlier.
A declarative sentence can make a statement about the present.	I am finishing up my homework right now.
A declarative sentence can make a statement about the future.	We will be visiting my grandmother in a month.

Practice

Write three declarative sentences about a subject of your choosing. Don't forget to use periods at the end of your sentences.

1. _____
2. _____ Answers will vary.
3. _____

Simple Steps • Sixth Grade   Sentences 187

Page 188

Declarative Sentences

Practice

Identify the declarative sentences by placing a ✓ on the line provided. Leave the other sentences blank.

1. ____ Have you ever heard of a red-eyed tree frog?
2. ✓ Red-eyed tree frogs are small, colorful, musical frogs with big red eyes.
3. ____ Where do red-eyed tree frogs live?
4. ✓ They primarily live in South America, Central America, and parts of Mexico.
5. ✓ They like lowland rain forests close to rivers and hills.
6. ____ How small are red-eyed tree frogs?
7. ✓ Female red-eyed tree frogs grow to be 3 inches long.
8. ✓ Males grow to be only 2 inches long.
9. ____ Do they have any color other than red eyes?
10. ✓ Their bodies are neon green with dashes of yellow and blue.
11. ✓ Their upper legs are bright blue and their feet are orange or red.
12. ____ How are these tree frogs musical?
13. ✓ Red-eyed tree frogs are nocturnal and can be heard in their trees at night.
14. ____ Why are these frogs called tree frogs?
15. ✓ They live mostly in trees.

188 Sentences   Simple Steps • Sixth Grade

Page 189

Interrogative Sentences

An interrogative sentence asks a question. Use a question mark at the end to punctuate an interrogative sentence.

An interrogative sentence can ask a question about a person.	Can Raj play on our team?
An interrogative sentence can ask a question about a place.	Is your hometown big or small?
An interrogative sentence can ask a question about a thing.	Do these pants come in blue?

Interrogative sentences can be written in different tenses.

An interrogative sentence can ask a question about the past.	Did you see that new superhero movie last night?
An interrogative sentence can ask a question about the present.	Can you help me carry these packages into the house?
An interrogative sentence can ask a question about the future.	Will dinner be at seven o'clock tonight?

Practice

Write three interrogative sentences about a subject of your choosing. Don't forget to use question marks at the end of your sentences.

1. ___
2. ___   Answers will vary.
3. ___

Simple Steps · Sixth Grade   Sentences 189

Page 190

Interrogative Sentences

Practice

Complete the following sentences by circling the correct punctuation at the end of each.

1. Who is your hero ⑦.
2. Do you have Mr. Bell for history this year ⑦.
3. What is your favorite food ⑦.
4. Can we leave first thing in the morning ⑦.
5. When does the bus leave ⑦.
6. Green is my favorite color ?Ⓞ
7. Where are we going on the field trip next week ⑦.
8. I'm going to have Mr. Stubbert for history next year ?Ⓞ
9. Why don't we go out for dinner ⑦.
10. Can Charlie come over for dinner ⑦.
11. How many stars are in the sky ⑦.
12. I'm going to take the bus downtown ?Ⓞ
13. What's your favorite color ⑦.
14. How many sisters and brothers do you have ⑦.
15. That building looks very unusual ?Ⓞ
16. Have you ever seen the Grand Canyon ⑦.
17. Are you going to take swimming lessons this summer ⑦.
18. I am so clumsy, I dropped my tray at lunch ?Ⓞ
19. How do you want to decorate the gym for the dance ⑦.
20. I like broccoli on my salad ?Ⓞ

190 Sentences   Simple Steps · Sixth Grade

Page 191

Exclamatory Sentences

An exclamatory sentence expresses urgency, surprise, or strong emotion. Use an exclamation mark at the end to punctuate an exclamatory sentence.

An exclamatory sentence can make a bold statement about a person.	I just won concert tickets on the radio!
An exclamatory sentence can make a bold statement about a place.	The mountain is hundreds of feet high!
An exclamatory sentence can make a bold statement about a thing.	Only one more test before summer break!
An exclamatory sentence can also be used in dialogue.	"I did it!" Kelly shouted when she learned she got an A on her exam.

Exclamatory sentence can be written in different tenses.

An exclamatory sentence can make a bold statement about the past.	I won first prize at the fair this afternoon!
An exclamatory sentence can make a bold statement about the present.	This is the best birthday party ever!
An exclamatory sentence can make a bold statement about the future.	I will be flying on an airplane for the first time next week!

Practice

Write two interrogative sentences about a subject of your choosing. Don't forget to use exclamation marks at the end of your sentences.

1. ___
2. ___   Answers will vary.

Simple Steps · Sixth Grade   Sentences 191

Page 192

Exclamatory Sentences

Practice

Proofread the following skit. Punctuate the sentences by adding periods, question marks, or exclamation marks on the spaces.

"Karen and Dave," shouted Sandra, "we're going to a planetarium!"

"What is a planetarium?" asked Karen.

"A planetarium," answered Sandra, "is a room with a large dome ceiling. Images of the sky are projected onto the ceiling with a star projector. Planetariums are amazing!"

Dave continued, "You can see the movements of the sun, moon, planets, and stars. I've always wanted to go to a planetarium."

Sandra said, "They shorten the time so you can see in just minutes what it takes the objects years to complete."

"Will we be able to see the constellations of the zodiac?" asked Karen.

"Yes, I believe so," answered Dave. "We will even be able to see how the objects in the sky will look thousands of years from now."

"We'll sit in seats like we're at the movie theater, but it will really look like we're outside," said Sandra.

Karen exclaimed, "I can't wait to go to the planetarium!"

Write two sentence pairs. Write two declarative sentences using periods as the end punctuation. Then, write two similar sentences that show stronger emotion or surprise. You can add interjections if you like. Be sure to change the end punctuation to an exclamation mark.

1. ___   Answers will vary.
2. ___

192 Sentences   Simple Steps · Sixth Grade

Page 193

Imperative Sentences

An imperative sentence makes a demand. It is often written in the present tense.

| The subject of an imperative sentence is often not expressed. It is usually the understood subject you. | Get on Bus #610. (You get on Bus #610.) Pick up that piece of paper. (You pick up that piece of paper.) Hand me your completed essays. (You hand me your completed essays.) |

Imperative sentences can use different kinds of punctuation.

| An imperative sentence can end with a period. | Help me move the sofa to the other side of the room. |
| An imperative sentence can end with an exclamation mark. | Answer the phone before it stops ringing! |

Practice

Write a paragraph that gives instructions on how to make or do something. Use at least three imperative sentences.

___
___   Answers will vary.
___

Simple Steps · Sixth Grade   Sentences 193

Page 194

Imperative Sentences

Practice

Identify the following sentences by writing D for declarative, IN for interrogative, E for exclamatory, or IM for imperative after each sentence.

1. Hop over that puddle! __IM__
2. How many more days until spring break? __IN__
3. I won the contest! __E__
4. I don't want anchovies on my pizza. __D__
5. Visit my lemonade stand this summer. __IM__
6. What is the distance of a century bicycle ride? __IN__
7. Announce the winners as they come across the finish line. __IM__
8. The firefighter saved everyone in the house! __E__
9. Think about what you want to serve at the party. __IM__
10. My favorite appetizer is vegetable stuffed mushrooms. __D__
11. Whom do you admire most? __IN__
12. The fundraiser was a huge success! __E__
13. Hand me the wrench. __IM__
14. Can you meet us at the zoo? __IN__
15. Wash the dishes after you clear off the table. __IM__
16. I can't wait to see this movie! __E__
17. Her parents said she could come over for dinner. __D__

194 Sentences   Simple Steps · Sixth Grade

Answer Key

Answer Key

Page 195

Review

Use everything you have learned so far about sentences to answer the questions.

The sentences in Column A are missing their punctuation. Add the correct punctuation. Then, draw a line to match them with their type of sentence in Column B.

Column A | Column B
1. I will be thirteen on my next birthday . — declarative
2. Hurry up and open your presents . or ! — interrogative
3. How old are you ? — imperative
4. Oh no, the wind just blew my hat away ! — exclamatory
5. Is it supposed to snow all weekend ? — interrogative
6. Autumn is my favorite season . — exclamatory
7. Where are my shoes ? — interrogative
8. We just won the state championship ! — interrogative
9. Watch where you're going . or ! — declarative
10. Basketball is my favorite sport . — imperative

Use periods, question marks, and exclamation marks to complete the following sentences.

11. What are the largest trees in the world ?
12. Redwood trees are the largest trees in the world .
13. Redwoods can grow to be 240 feet tall .
14. Find out how long redwoods live .
15. Redwoods can live more than 2000 years .
16. Redwood trees are located along the Pacific Coast in the United States .
17. Redwood fossils have been found all over the world .
18. Fossils from redwood trees have been found from as long ago as 160 million years .
19. Wow those are the tallest redwood trees I have ever seen !

Simple Steps • Sixth Grade   Sentences 195

Page 196

Simple Sentences

A simple sentence has one independent clause. It expresses one complete thought.

| An independent clause expresses a complete thought and can stand alone. | The city zoo recently closed. |
| A dependent clause expresses an incomplete thought and cannot stand alone. | because there haven't been many visitors |

Simple sentences can take different forms.

A simple sentence can have one or more simple subjects.	Goats live at the sanctuary. Goats and turkeys live at the sanctuary.
A simple sentence can have one or more simple predicates (verbs).	The goats played with the other animals. The turkeys played and talked with the other animals.
A simple sentence can have more than one simple subject and more than one simple predicate (verb).	The goats and the turkeys played and talked with the other animals.

Practice

Write S next to the sentences. Write DC next to the dependent clauses.

1. while I read a book DC
2. She's playing basketball with her friends. S
3. Baked fish tastes delicious. S
4. especially with roasted vegetables DC

196 Sentences   Simple Steps • Sixth Grade

Page 197

Simple Sentences

Practice

Match the simple sentences in Column A to the correct description of sentence parts in Column B.

Column A | Column B
1. Farm Sanctuary rescues and protects farm animals. — one subject
2. Farm Sanctuary members have helped to pass farm animal protection laws. — two subjects
3. The New York sanctuary and the California sanctuary are home to hundreds of rescued farm animals. — one predicate
4. Farm Sanctuary offers a humane education program to schools. — two predicates
5. At Farm Sanctuary, people and animals work and play together. — two subjects/two predicates

Write simple sentences as described below.

1. one subject
   Answers will vary.
2. more than one subject
   Answers will vary.
3. one predicate
   Answers will vary.
4. more than one predicate
   Answers will vary.
5. more than one subject and more than one predicate
   Answers will vary.

Simple Steps • Sixth Grade   Sentences 197

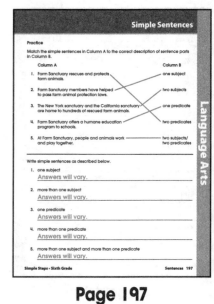

Page 198

Compound Sentences

A compound sentence has two or more independent clauses joined together. It expresses more than one complete thought.

| This compound sentence contains two independent clauses. | He didn't think he was a fan of Shakespeare, yet he enjoyed the play. |
| Each independent clause could be written as a separate sentence. | He didn't think he was a fan of Shakespeare. He enjoyed the play. |

There are two ways to form a compound sentence.

| A compound sentence can be two independent clauses joined by a semicolon. | Joan wanted to watch the basketball game; her roommate wanted to watch a baking show. |
| A compound sentence can be two independent clauses joined by a comma and a coordinate conjunction. | Joan wanted to watch the basketball game, but her roommate wanted to watch a baking show. |

Practice

Identify whether each sentence is a compound sentence or a simple sentence. Write CS for compound sentence and SS for simple sentence.

1. I'd like to visit Yellowstone National Park. SS
2. Jamie tries to clean her room, but her brother keeps interrupting her. CS
3. I helped my dad mow the grass today; I also pulled weeds in the garden. CS
4. It's too hot to play outside SS

198 Sentences   Simple Steps • Sixth Grade

Page 199

Compound Sentences

Practice

Match the independent clauses in Column A with the independent clauses in Column B to create compound sentences. Write the compound sentences on the lines below. Remember to punctuate the sentence correctly and to include coordinate conjunctions if needed.

Column A | Column B
1. The football game was exciting. — They have a good record this year.
2. My favorite team is playing. — I'm going to get pizza after the game.
3. My school's colors are blue and white. — The score was close.
4. I'm going to get a pretzel at halftime. — The season isn't over yet.
5. My team won the game. — The opposing team's colors are green and gold.

Sample Answers:

1. The football game was exciting; the score was close.
2. My favorite team is playing, and they have a good record this year.
3. My school's colors are blue and white, and the opposing team's colors are green and gold.
4. I'm going to get a pretzel at halftime, or I'm going to get pizza after the game.
5. My team won the game, but the season isn't over yet.

Simple Steps • Sixth Grade   Sentences 199

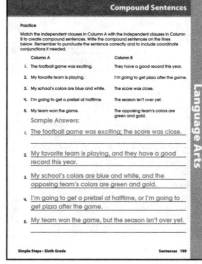

Page 201

Complex Sentences

Practice

Put a check mark ✓ on the line in front of any complex sentences below.

1. ✓ I like biking because it is good exercise.
2. ✓ Tony is going to order pasta with mushrooms, which is his favorite dish.
3. ___ History is my favorite subject.
4. ✓ Mr. Baum, who is also the baseball coach, is my favorite teacher.
5. ✓ While Kim is a good speller, Jerry is better.
6. ___ I would like a salad for lunch, yet soup sounds good too.
7. ✓ Erin made the basketball team after two weeks of tryouts.
8. ✓ Although it's going to snow, I think we should still hike the trails.
9. ✓ Unless it rains, we'll walk, not ride.
10. ✓ We can continue hiking until it gets icy.

Write four complex sentences on the lines below. Remember to include either a relative pronoun or a subordinate conjunction.

11. _____
12. _____   Answers will vary.
13. _____
14. _____

Simple Steps • Sixth Grade   Sentences 201

Answer Key

Page 202

Sentence Fragments

A sentence fragment is not a complete sentence. It is a group of words that is missing a subject, a predicate, or both. A sentence fragment is also a group of words that does not express a complete thought, as in a dependent clause.

This sentence fragment has no subject.	Doesn't have good insulation.
This is a complete sentence with a subject.	The **window** doesn't have good insulation.
This sentence fragment has no predicate.	The flowers in the spring.
This is a complete sentence with a predicate.	The flowers will **bloom** in the spring.
This sentence fragment has no subject or predicate. It is a dependent clause because it does not express a complete thought.	Since the lemonade was too sour.
This is a complete sentence with a subject and a predicate.	**We drank** water since the lemonade was too sour.

Practice

Write CS next to the complete sentences. Write SF next to the sentence fragments.

1. into the woods SF
2. The meadow was swarming with birds and insects. CS
3. don't know how to swim SF
4. Tell me how to solve this puzzle. CS

202 Sentences · Simple Steps · Sixth Grade

Page 203

Sentence Fragments

Practice

Complete the following sentence fragments by choosing a phrase from the box.

> It was presented
> The statue's height
> Construction began
> is "Liberty Enlightening the World."
> stands on Liberty Island in the New York Harbor.

1. The Statue of Liberty stands on Liberty Island in the New York Harbor. (look for a verb phrase)
2. Construction began in France in 1875. (look for a subject and a verb)
3. It was presented to the United States on July 4, 1884. (look for a subject and verb)
4. The official name of the Statue of Liberty is "Liberty Enlightening the World." (look for a verb phrase)
5. The statue's height from base to torch is 152 feet, 2 inches. (look for a subject)

Create your own sentences from these sentence fragments.

1. In the summer, I like
   Answers will vary.
2. Is one of my favorite winter activities
   Answers will vary.
3. During the fall
   Answers will vary.
4. When the weather turns warm in the spring
   Answers will vary.

Simple Steps · Sixth Grade · Sentences 203

Page 205

Combining Sentences and Sentence Variety

Practice

Rewrite the following paragraphs by combining sentences. Turn simple sentences into compound or complex sentences to create sentence variety.

Charles Schulz was one of America's most famous cartoonists. He created the most popular comic strip ever. He wrote the most popular comic strip ever: *Peanuts*. The *Peanuts* characters are some of the most popular characters ever seen in comic strips. The characters are also popular in books. The characters are popular on television too. The *Peanuts* comic strip made its debut in seven newspapers in 1950.

Charles Schulz based much of *Peanuts* on his own life. He actually had a black and white dog named Spike. Spike was the inspiration for Snoopy. Snoopy is the world's most famous beagle. The *Peanuts* characters teach us all lessons about ourselves. They teach us about the world around us. That is one reason why the characters have remained popular for so many years.

Answers will vary. Possible answer:

Charles Schulz was one of America's most famous cartoonists because he created the most popular comic strip ever: *Peanuts*. The *Peanuts* characters are some of the most popular characters ever seen in comic strips, and they are also popular in books and on television too. The *Peanuts* comic strip made its debut in seven newspapers in 1950.

Charles Schulz based much of *Peanuts* on his own life. He actually had a black and white dog named Spike that was the inspiration for Snoopy, the world's most famous beagle. The *Peanuts* characters teach us all lessons about ourselves and about the world around us. That is one reason why the characters have remained popular for so many years.

Simple Steps · Sixth Grade · Sentences 205

Page 206

Review

Use everything you have learned so far about sentences to answer the questions.

Write one simple sentence, two compound sentences, and two complex sentences on the lines below.

1. Simple Sentence:
   Answers will vary.
2. Compound Sentence:
   Answers will vary.
3. Compound Sentence:
   Answers will vary.
4. Complex Sentence:
   Answers will vary.
5. Complex Sentence:
   Answers will vary.

Identify the following sentences as either sentence fragments or complete sentences. Write F for fragment and CS for complete sentence. Then, for the sentences that are fragments, tell why they are fragments (for example, missing a subject). Write your answer on the line below each sentence.

6. CS The satellite is orbiting Mars.
7. F As though the sun were shining.
   This sentence fragment is missing a subject and a predicate.
8. F Since the whole class is going on the field trip.
   This sentence fragment is missing a subject and a predicate.

206 Sentences · Simple Steps · Sixth Grade

Page 207

Chapter Review

1. Rewrite the exclamatory sentence as an imperative sentence.
   You should drink the hot tea slowly!
   Sample Answer: Please drink the hot tea slowly.
2. Rewrite the interrogative sentence as a declarative sentence.
   Are you going to the game on Saturday?
   Sample Answer: I heard you are going to the game on Saturday.
3. Rewrite the imperative sentence as an interrogative sentence.
   Hit the ball far!
   Sample Answer: Can you hit the ball far?
4. Rewrite the declarative sentence as an imperative sentence.
   We all should recycle the papers instead of putting them in the trash.
   Sample Answer: Recycle the papers instead of putting them in the trash.

Write whether the following sentences are simple, compound, complex, or a sentence fragment. If they are simple sentences or sentence fragments, rewrite them.

5. She jogged through the mist. She jogged slowly.
   They are simple sentences.
6. The chefs cooked and baked in the competition.
   This is a simple sentence.
7. After dinner, I'm going for a walk.
   This is a complex sentence.
8. Although I studied hard.
   This is a sentence fragment.
   Sample Sentence: Although I studied hard, I still barely passed the test.

Simple Steps · Sixth Grade · Sentences 207

Page 208

Chapter Review

Follow the directions below to write different kinds of sentences. Then, identify the type of sentence you wrote in parentheses.

9. Write a sentence with a simple subject.
   Answers will vary.
10. Write a sentence with compound subjects.
    Answers will vary.
11. Write a sentence with compound verbs.
    Answers will vary.
12. Write a sentence with combined adjectives.
    Answers will vary.
13. Write a sentence with combined adverbs.
    Answers will vary.
14. Write a sentence that uses a subordinate conjunction.
    Answers will vary.
15. Write a sentence that uses a coordinate conjunction.
    Answers will vary.
16. Write a sentence that uses a relative pronoun.
    Answers will vary.
17. Write a sentence that has a dependent clause and an independent clause.
    Answers will vary.
18. Write a sentence that has two independent clauses.
    Answers will vary.

208 Sentences · Simple Steps · Sixth Grade

Page 209

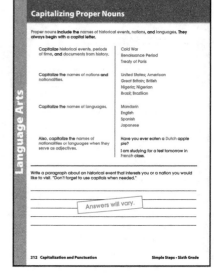

Chapter Review

19. Write a dialogue with four characters. They are attending an exciting activity at school, such as a game, a fair, or a dance. Have them interact and discuss what they see and do. In your skit, use declarative, interrogative, exclamatory, and imperative sentences. Remember to include the proper punctuation.

Answers will vary.

Simple Steps • Sixth Grade   Sentences 209

Page 211

Capitalizing Proper Nouns

Practice

Rewrite the following sentences after unscrambling the names of days of the week or months of the year.

1. The month of jeun is Adopt a Shelter Cat Month.
   The month of June is Adopt a Shelter Cat Month.

2. Earth Day, a day for environmental awareness, is celebrated in ipari.
   Earth Day, a day for environmental awareness, is celebrated in April.

3. Do you want to go to the movies on ywdeadsen?
   Do you want to go to the movies on Wednesday?

4. This year, Valentine's Day falls on the second naydom of barutrey.
   This year, Valentine's Day falls on the second Monday of February.

5. The state of Colorado has its own day, and it's celebrated in stuagu.
   The state of Colorado has its own day, and it's celebrated in August.

6. Shogatsu is the name for New Year in Japan; it is celebrated in najruay.
   Shogatsu is the name for New Year in Japan; it is celebrated in January.

Write a paragraph about your favorite day of the week or month of the year.

Answers will vary.

Simple Steps • Sixth Grade   Capitalization and Punctuation 211

Page 212

Capitalizing Proper Nouns

Proper nouns include the names of historical events, nations, and languages. They always begin with a capital letter.

Capitalize historical events, periods of time, and documents from history.	Cold War Renaissance Period Treaty of Paris
Capitalize the names of nations and nationalities.	United States; American Great Britain; British Nigeria; Nigerian Brazil; Brazilian
Capitalize the names of languages.	Mandarin English Spanish Japanese
Also, capitalize the names of nationalities or languages when they serve as adjectives.	Have you ever eaten a Dutch apple pie? I am studying for a test tomorrow in French class.

Write a paragraph about an historical event that interests you or a nation you would like to visit. *Don't forget to use capitals when needed.*

Answers will vary.

212 Capitalization and Punctuation   Simple Steps • Sixth Grade

Page 213

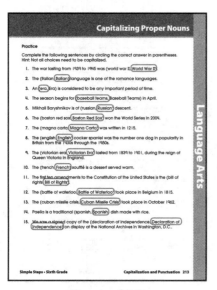

Capitalizing Proper Nouns

Practice

Complete the following sentences by circling the correct answer in parentheses. Hint: Not all choices need to be capitalized.

1. The war lasting from 1939 to 1945 was (world war II, **World War II**).
2. The (Italian, **Italian**) language is one of the romance languages.
3. An (**era**, Era) is considered to be any important period of time.
4. The season begins for (**baseball teams**, Baseball Teams) in April.
5. Mikhail Baryshnikov is of (russian, **Russian**) descent.
6. The (boston red sox, **Boston Red Sox**) won the World Series in 2004.
7. The (magna carta, **Magna Carta**) was written in 1215.
8. The (english, **English**) cocker spaniel was the number one dog in popularity in Britain from the 1930s through the 1950s.
9. The (victorian era, **Victorian Era**) lasted from 1839 to 1901, during the reign of Queen Victoria in England.
10. The (french, **French**) soufflé is a dessert served warm.
11. The first ten amendments to the Constitution of the United States is the (bill of rights, **Bill of Rights**).
12. The (battle of waterloo, **Battle of Waterloo**) took place in Belgium in 1815.
13. The (cuban missile crisis, **Cuban Missile Crisis**) took place in October 1962.
14. Paella is a traditional (spanish, **Spanish**) dish made with rice.
15. We saw a signed copy of the (declaration of Independence, **Declaration of Independence**) on display at the National Archives in Washington, D.C..

Simple Steps • Sixth Grade   Capitalization and Punctuation 213

Page 214

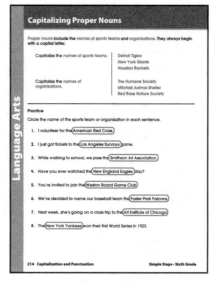

Capitalizing Proper Nouns

Proper nouns include the names of sports teams and organizations. They always begin with a capital letter.

Capitalize the names of sports teams.	Detroit Tigers New York Giants Houston Rockets
Capitalize the names of organizations.	The Humane Society Mitchell Animal Shelter Red Rose Nature Society

Practice

Circle the name of the sports team or organization in each sentence.

1. I volunteer for the **American Red Cross**.
2. I just got tickets to the **Los Angeles Sunrays** game.
3. While walking to school, we pass the **Smithson Art Association**.
4. Have you ever watched the **New England Eagles** play?
5. You're invited to join the **Weston Board Game Club**.
6. We've decided to name our baseball team the **Foster Park Falcons**.
7. Next week, she's going on a class trip to the **Art Institute of Chicago**.
8. The **New York Yankees** won their first World Series in 1923.

214 Capitalization and Punctuation   Simple Steps • Sixth Grade

Page 215

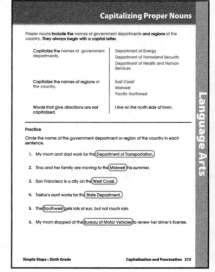

Capitalizing Proper Nouns

Proper nouns include the names of government departments and regions of the country. They always begin with a capital letter.

Capitalize the names of government departments.	Department of Energy Department of Homeland Security Department of Health and Human Services
Capitalize the names of regions of the country.	East Coast Midwest Pacific Northwest
Words that give directions are not capitalized.	I live on the north side of town.

Practice

Circle the name of the government department or region of the country in each sentence.

1. My mom and dad work for the **Department of Transportation**.
2. Tina and her family are moving to the **Midwest** this summer.
3. San Francisco is a city on the **West Coast**.
4. Tasha's aunt works for the **State Department**.
5. The **Southwest** gets lots of sun, but not much rain.
6. My mom stopped at the **Bureau of Motor Vehicles** to renew her driver's license.

Simple Steps • Sixth Grade   Capitalization and Punctuation 215

Page 216

Capitalizing Proper Nouns

Proper nouns include titles and geographic names. They always begin with a capital letter.

Capitalize the titles of books, songs, movies, plays, newspapers, and magazines. Most titles are also underlined or italicized in text.
Charlotte's Web
The Raven
Time
West Side Story

Place quotes around the titles of short works, such as songs, poems, short stories, and articles.
Song: "Stay with Me"
Story: "The Tortoise and the Hare"

Capitalize titles when directly followed by a name.
Mayor Franklin
Senator Santos
Professor Gupta

Capitalize geographic names, such as countries, states, cities, counties, bodies of water, public areas, roads, highways, and buildings.
Columbia
Hawaii
Athens
Queens County
Chesapeake Bay
Sierra Nevada Range
Main Street
Route 66
Globe Theatre

Practice

Complete the following sentences by circling the best answer in parentheses.

1. My favorite song is ("Firework," "firework") by Katy Perry.
2. The (President, president) of the organization is visiting on Tuesday.
3. At 2:00 pm, (Governor, governor) Spencer is making a speech.
4. Valerie and Gerald watched the sunset from the (Eiffel Tower, eiffel tower).

216 Capitalization and Punctuation   Simple Steps • Sixth Grade

Page 217

Capitalizing Sentences

Follow this capitalization rule for sentences.

Capitalize the first word of a sentence.
The wind blew through the trees.
Please clean your room today.
Watch out!
Can I borrow that pen?

Practice

Complete the following sentences by circling the best answer in parentheses.

1. (The, the) girls' team beat the boys' team by three seconds.
2. (The, the) airplane was going to be delayed.
3. (My, my) cousin is visiting us for the summer from England.
4. (Do, do) you know what time the (Movie, movie) is supposed to start?
5. Are you going to the (Mountains, mountains) or the beach for vacation?
6. (Be, be) careful because the sidewalk is very slippery!
7. (Monday, monday) is my least favorite day of the week.
8. (Help, help)! I can't lift this box by myself.
9. (Let's, let's) pack a picnic and take it to the park.

Simple Steps • Sixth Grade   Capitalization and Punctuation 217

Page 218

Capitalizing Direct Quotations

Follow these capitalization rules for direct quotations.

Capitalize the first word of a direct quotation.
My father said, "Finish your homework and then we'll go for a ride."
"I'm almost finished now," I happily answered.

If a continuous sentence in a direct quotation is split and the second half is not a new sentence, do not capitalize it.
"Keep your hands and arms inside the car," said the attendant, "and stay seated."

If a new sentence begins after the split in a direct quotation, then capitalize it as you would with any sentence.
"Roller coasters are my favorite rides," I said. "I can ride them all day."

Indirect quotations are not capitalized.
My father said he had been working on his car for weeks.

Practice

Complete the following sentences by circling the best answer in parentheses.

1. T.C. said, "(Baseball, baseball) is my favorite sport."
2. The technician said (The, the) car would be ready in a few hours.
3. "Don't rush through your homework," said the teacher, "(And, and) stay focused."
4. Mrs. Wilson told her husband that (He, he) should be careful shoveling the snow.

218 Capitalization and Punctuation   Simple Steps • Sixth Grade

Page 220

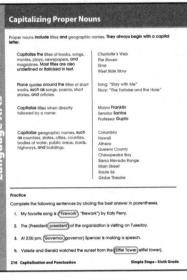

Capitalizing Personal Letters

Practice

Name the parts of the personal letter below by writing the names on the lines provided. Identify each section as the heading, salutation, body, closing, or signature. Then, circle the capital letters.

heading — 751 Hibernia Rd. / Seattle, WA 40000 / February 31, 2014

salutation — Dear Uncle Josh,

body — How are you? My ski trip has been great! I even learned how to snowboard. I think I'll be really sore tomorrow. All of the fundraising was worth it. Thanks for helping us out. I'm glad our class got to take this trip. I hope I'll get to come back someday.

closing — Thank you,
signature — Lucy

220 Capitalization and Punctuation   Simple Steps • Sixth Grade

Page 222

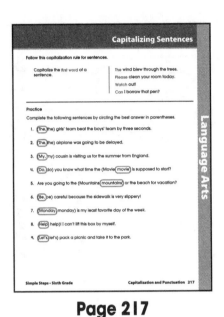

Capitalizing Business Letters

Practice

Write the heading, inside address, salutation, body, closing, and signature of a business letter. Make up the names and other information if needed, but be sure you capitalize correctly.

Answers will vary.

222 Capitalization and Punctuation   Simple Steps • Sixth Grade

Page 223

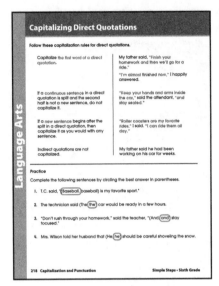

Review

Use everything you have learned so far about capitalization to answer the questions.

Complete the following sentences by circling the best answer in parentheses.

1. "Riley," called Gillian, "(Let's, let's) use carrots and raisins on our snowman."
2. Our teacher said the test will be on (Wednesday, wednesday).
3. (Winters, winters) in the north are cold and blustery.
4. The summer solstice occurs in the month of (June, june).
5. Drive (North, north) on Route 3 and then you'll be close to the community center.
6. The hostess said, "(Your, your) table will be ready in 10 minutes."
7. The U.S. (Constitution, constitution) was written in Philadelphia in 1787.
8. The (Peace Corps, peace corps) is a federal agency that reports to Congress and the executive branch.
9. "(My, my) shift starts at 3:00, so let's study when I'm finished," said Celia.
10. The high school offers (Italian, italian) as one of its languages.
11. The (Aveda Corporation, aveda corporation) is located in Minnesota.
12. North America is located in the (Northern, northern) hemisphere.
13. In the fairy tale, the princess said (She, she) was waiting for her prince.
14. The (Danish, danish) pastry is baked fresh every day.
15. My favorite baseball team is the (San Francisco Giants, San Francisco giants).
16. The pep rally will be held in the gym on (Friday, friday) afternoon.
17. The (Sierra Club, sierra club) is an environmental organization for people of all ages.
18. Doug said, "(My, my) Aunt Clara makes the best blueberry muffins."
19. The winter solstice occurs in the month of (December, december).

Simple Steps • Sixth Grade   Capitalization and Punctuation 223

Review

20. Write a personal letter or a business letter on the lines below. Be sure to include the required sections and follow the rules for capitalization.

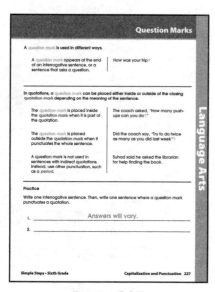

Answers will vary.

224 Capitalization and Punctuation   Simple Steps • Sixth Grade

Page 224

Periods: Sentences and Dialogue

A period is used at the end of different kinds of sentences.

A period appears at the end of a declarative sentence.

Louise just won a scholarship to attend college.

A period appears at the end of an imperative sentence when the statement is not urgent.

Please pick your clothes up off the floor.

A period can be used in dialogue. It appears inside the quotation mark.

Terrance said, "It seems like a great day for a picnic."

If the quote comes at the beginning of the sentence, use a comma at the end of the direct quotation and before the quotation mark. Place a period at the end of the sentence.

"If it gets cold, put on your jacket," said Robyn.

Practice

Rewrite the following sentences by adding periods where necessary.

1. Check out at the far counter
   Check out at the far counter.

2. Janet said, "Let's take a long walk"
   Janet said, "Let's take a long walk."

3. "Hiking is my favorite hobby," said Charlie
   "Hiking is my favorite hobby," said Charlie.

4. Reach a little farther, and you will have touched the top
   Reach a little farther, and you will have touched the top.

Simple Steps • Sixth Grade   Capitalization and Punctuation 225

Page 225

Periods: Abbreviations and Initials

A period is also used for abbreviations or initials.

Use a period after each part of an abbreviation. An abbreviation is a shortened form of a word or phrase.

M.A. (Master of Arts)

Use a period after each letter of an initial. An initial is the first letter of a name.

Samuel L. Jackson

Practice

Rewrite the following sentences by adding periods where necessary.

1. Kathryn received her MA from the University of Arizona.
   Kathryn received her M.A. from the University of Arizona.

2. My favorite actress is Vivica A Fox.
   My favorite actress is Vivica A. Fox.

3. JRR Tolkien is my favorite author.
   J.R.R. Tolkien is my favorite author.

4. My younger sister's favorite book is Junie B Jones Smells Something Fishy.
   My youngest sister's favorite book is Junie B. Jones Smells Something Fishy.

5. Franklin D Roosevelt was first elected president in 1932.
   Franklin D. Roosevelt was first elected president in 1932.

6. Mrs Obrador is the principal at my school.
   Mrs. Obrador is the principal at my school.

226 Capitalization and Punctuation   Simple Steps • Sixth Grade

Page 226

Question Marks

A question mark is used in different ways.

A question mark appears at the end of an interrogative sentence, or a sentence that asks a question.

How was your trip?

In quotations, a question mark can be placed either inside or outside of the closing quotation mark depending on the meaning of the sentence.

The question mark is placed inside the quotation mark when it is part of the quotation.

The coach asked, "How many push-ups can you do?"

The question mark is placed outside the quotation mark when it punctuates the whole sentence.

Did the coach say, "Try to do twice as many as you did last week"?

A question mark is not used in sentences with indirect quotations. Instead, use other punctuation, such as a period.

Suhad said he asked the librarian for help finding the book.

Practice

Write one interrogative sentence. Then, write one sentence where a question mark punctuates a quotation.

1. _____ Answers will vary. _____

2. _____

Simple Steps • Sixth Grade   Capitalization and Punctuation 227

Page 227

Question Marks

Practice

Draw a line to match the sentences in Column A with their descriptions in Column B.

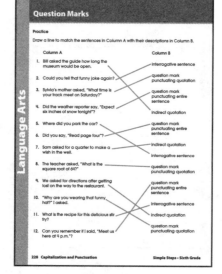

Column A

1. Bill asked the guide how long the museum would be open.
2. Could you tell that funny joke again?
3. Sylvia's mother asked, "What time is your track meet on Saturday?"
4. Did the weather reporter say, "Expect six inches of snow tonight"?
5. Where did you park the car?
6. Did you say, "Read page four"?
7. Sam asked for a quarter to make a wish in the well.
8. The teacher asked, "What is the square root of 64?"
9. We asked for directions after getting lost on the way to the restaurant.
10. "Why are you wearing that funny hat?" I asked.
11. What is the recipe for this delicious stir fry?
12. Can you remember if I said, "Meet us here at 4 p.m."?

Column B

interrogative sentence
question mark punctuating quotation
question mark punctuating entire sentence
indirect quotation
question mark punctuating entire sentence
indirect quotation
interrogative sentence
question mark punctuating quotation
question mark punctuating entire sentence
interrogative sentence
indirect quotation
question mark punctuating quotation

228 Capitalization and Punctuation   Simple Steps • Sixth Grade

Page 228

Exclamation Marks

An exclamation mark is used in different ways.

An exclamation mark is used at the end of an exclamatory sentence. This type of sentence expresses surprise.

We have to read all three chapters for homework tonight!

An exclamatory sentence can also express a strong emotion, such as anger or fear. It also requires an exclamation mark.

I think I just saw a ghost!

Interjections sometimes require exclamation marks.

Aha! I've come up with the answer!

It's important not to overuse exclamation marks. If a sentence does not express surprise, urgency, or strong emotion, use a period or other punctuation instead.

I don't feel like going to the park today.

Practice

Choose a word from the box to complete the following sentences to express strong emotion or surprise. Not all of the words will be used.

| warm | far | fast |
| loud | hot | soft |

1. Don't touch the stove; it is _____ hot _____!

2. Look how _____ fast _____ that race car driver took the curve!

3. Please turn down that _____ loud _____ music!

4. The trapeze performer is so _____ far _____ from the ground!

Simple Steps • Sixth Grade   Capitalization and Punctuation 229

Page 229

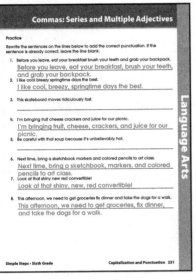

Page 231

Commas: Series and Multiple Adjectives

Practice

Rewrite the sentences on the lines below to add the correct punctuation. If the sentence is already correct, leave the line blank.

1. Before you leave, eat your breakfast brush your teeth and grab your backpack.
   Before you leave, eat your breakfast, brush your teeth, and grab your backpack.
2. I like cool breezy springtime days the best.
   I like cool, breezy, springtime days the best.
3. This skateboard moves ridiculously fast.
4. I'm bringing fruit cheese crackers and juice for our picnic.
   I'm bringing fruit, cheese, crackers, and juice for our picnic.
5. Be careful with that soup because it's unbelievably hot.
6. Next time, bring a sketchbook markers and colored pencils to art class.
   Next time, bring a sketchbook, markers, and colored pencils to art class.
7. Look at that shiny new red convertible!
   Look at that shiny, new, red convertible!
8. This afternoon, we need to get groceries fix dinner and take the dogs for a walk.
   This afternoon, we need to get groceries, fix dinner, and take the dogs for a walk.

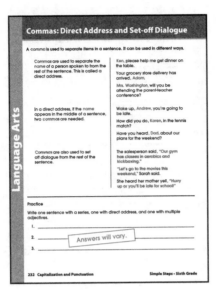

Page 232

Commas: Direct Address and Set-off Dialogue

A comma is used to separate items in a sentence. It can be used in different ways.

Commas are used to separate the name of a person spoken to from the rest of the sentence. This is called a direct address.

Ken, please help me get dinner on the table.
Your grocery store delivery has arrived, Adam.
Mrs. Washington, will you be attending the parent-teacher conference?

In a direct address, if the name appears in the middle of a sentence, two commas are needed.

Wake up, Andrew, you're going to be late.
How did you do, Karen, in the tennis match?
Have you heard, Dad, about our plans for the weekend?

Commas are also used to set off dialogue from the rest of the sentence.

The salesperson said, "Our gym has classes in aerobics and kickboxing."
"Let's go to the movies this weekend," Sarah said.
She heard her mother yell, "Hurry up or you'll be late for school!"

Practice

Write one sentence with a series, one with direct address, and one with multiple adjectives.

1.
2. Answers will vary.
3.

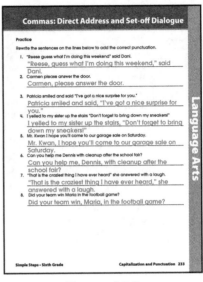

Page 233

Commas: Direct Address and Set-off Dialogue

Practice

Rewrite the sentences on the lines below to add the correct punctuation.

1. "Reese guess what I'm doing this weekend" said Dani.
   "Reese, guess what I'm doing this weekend," said Dani.
2. Carmen please answer the door.
   Carmen, please answer the door.
3. Patricia smiled and said "I've got a nice surprise for you."
   Patricia smiled and said, "I've got a nice surprise for you."
4. I yelled to my sister up the stairs "Don't forget to bring down my sneakers!"
   I yelled to my sister up the stairs, "Don't forget to bring down my sneakers!"
5. Mr. Kwan I hope you'll come to our garage sale on Saturday.
   Mr. Kwan, I hope you'll come to our garage sale on Saturday.
6. Can you help me Dennis with cleanup after the school fair?
   Can you help me, Dennis, with cleanup after the school fair?
7. "That is the craziest thing I have ever heard" she answered with a laugh.
   "That is the craziest thing I have ever heard," she answered with a laugh.
8. Did your team win Maria in the football game?
   Did your team win, Maria, in the football game?

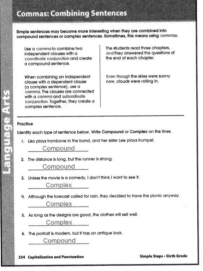

Page 234

Commas: Combining Sentences

Simple sentences may become more interesting when they are combined into compound sentences or complex sentences. Sometimes, this means using commas.

Use a comma to combine two independent clauses with a coordinate conjunction and create a compound sentence.

The students read three chapters, and they answered the questions at the end of each chapter.

When combining an independent clause with a dependent clause (a complex sentence), use a comma. The clauses are connected with a comma and subordinate conjunction. Together, they create a complex sentence.

Even though the skies were sunny now, clouds were rolling in.

Practice

Identify each type of sentence below. Write Compound or Complex on the lines.

1. Lisa plays trombone in the band, and her sister Lee plays trumpet.
   Compound
2. The distance is long, but the runner is strong.
   Compound
3. Unless the movie is a comedy, I don't think I want to see it.
   Complex
4. Although the forecast called for rain, they decided to have the picnic anyway.
   Complex
5. As long as the designs are good, the clothes will sell well.
   Complex
6. The portrait is modern, but it has an antique look.
   Compound

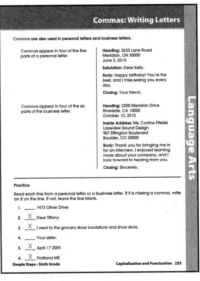

Page 235

Commas: Writing Letters

Commas are also used in personal letters and business letters.

Commas appear in four of the five parts of a personal letter.

Heading: 2633 Lane Road
Meridian, OH 30000
June 3, 2015
Salutation: Dear Kelly,
Body: Happy birthday! You're the best, and I miss seeing you every day.
Closing: Your friend,

Commas appear in four of the six parts of the business letter.

Heading: 2200 Meridian Drive
Riverside, CA 10000
October 10, 2015
Inside Address: Ms. Corrine Fifelski
Lakeview Sound Design
907 Effington Boulevard
Boulder, CO 20000
Body: Thank you for bringing me in for an interview. I enjoyed learning more about your company, and I look forward to hearing from you.
Closing: Sincerely,

Practice

Read each line from a personal letter or a business letter. If it is missing a comma, write an X on the line. If not, leave the line blank.

1. _____ 1473 Oliver Drive
2. _X_ Dear Tiffany
3. _X_ I went to the grocery store bookstore and shoe store.
4. _____ Your sister,
5. _X_ April 17 2004
6. _X_ Portland ME

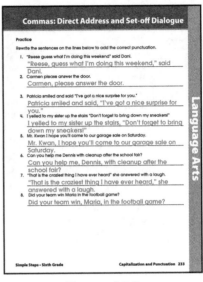

Page 236

Quotation Marks

Quotation marks are used in a sentence with dialogue or other kinds of quotations.

Quotation marks show the exact words of a speaker. They are placed before and after all of the words in the direct quotation.

"Let's go to the movies tonight," said Janice. "That new animated film was just released."

Quotation marks are also used when a direct quotation is made within a direct quotation. In this case, single quotation marks are used to set off the inside quotation.

John said, "Miss Robinson clearly said, 'The project is due tomorrow.'"

Quotation marks are used with some titles. Quotation marks are used with the titles of short works, including stories, poems, songs, and articles in magazines and newspapers.

"North Carolina Wins the Championship"
"Just Another Love Song"

Quotation marks are not used with the titles of long works, such as books or plays.

The Wizard of Oz
Romeo and Juliet

If a title is quoted within a direct quotation, then single quotation marks are used.

Melissa said, "Did you read the article 'Saving Our Oceans' in this magazine?"

Practice

Write one sentence of dialogue that includes a direct quotation by a character. Write one sentence that includes a title in quotation marks. Write one direct quotation of your own.

1.
2. Answers will vary.
3.

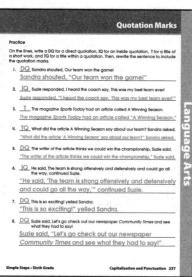

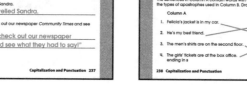

Answer Key

Quotation Marks

Practice

On the lines, write a DQ for a direct quotation, IQ for an inside quotation, T for a title of a short work, and TQ for a title within a quotation. Then, rewrite the sentence to include the quotation marks.

1. DQ Sandra shouted, Our team won the game!
Sandra shouted, "Our team won the game!"

2. IQ Suzie responded, I heard the coach say, This was my best team ever!
Suzie responded, "I heard the coach say, 'This was my best team ever!'"

3. T The magazine Sports Today had an article called A Winning Season.
The magazine Sports Today had an article called "A Winning Season."

4. TQ What did the article A Winning Season say about our team? Sandra asked.
"What did the article 'A Winning Season' say about our team?" Sandra asked.

5. DQ The writer of the article thinks we could win the championship, Suzie said.
"The writer of the article thinks we could win the championship," Suzie said.

6. IQ He said, the team is strong offensively and defensively and could go all the way, continued Suzie.
"He said, 'The team is strong offensively and defensively and could go all the way,'" continued Suzie.

7. DQ This is so exciting! yelled Sandra.
"This is so exciting!" yelled Sandra.

8. DQ Suzie said, Let's go check out our newspaper Community Times and see what they had to say!
Suzie said, "Let's go check out our newspaper Community Times and see what they had to say!"

Simple Steps • Sixth Grade — Capitalization and Punctuation 237

Page 237

Apostrophes

An apostrophe can be used in two ways.

Apostrophes are used in contractions, which are shortened forms of words. The words are shortened by leaving out letters. Apostrophes take the place of the omitted letters.	he is = he's can not = can't
Apostrophes are also used to form possessives, which show possession, or ownership. To form a singular possessive, or the possessive of a singular noun, add an apostrophe and an s.	I'll carry Harry's notebook.

There are two ways to form a plural possessive, or the possessive of a plural noun.

For plural nouns ending in s, simply add the apostrophe.	The puppies' guardians are very happy.
If the plural noun does not end in an s, add both the apostrophe and an s.	The women's team has won every game.

Practice

The sentences in Column A contain words with apostrophes. Match these sentences to the types of apostrophes used in Column B. Draw a line to make your match.

Column A
1. Felicia's jacket is in my car.
2. He's my best friend.
3. The men's shirts are on the second floor.
4. The girls' tickets are at the box office.

Column B
contraction
singular possessive
plural possessive ending in s
plural possessive not ending in s

238 Capitalization and Punctuation — Simple Steps • Sixth Grade

Page 238

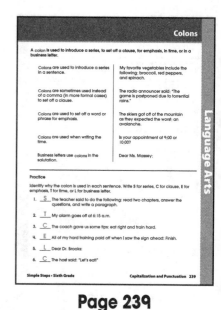

Colons

A colon is used to introduce a series, to set off a clause, for emphasis, in time, or in a business letter.

Colons are used to introduce a series in a sentence.	My favorite vegetables include the following: broccoli, red peppers, and spinach.
Colons are sometimes used instead of a comma (in more formal cases) to set off a clause.	The radio announcer said: "The game is postponed due to torrential rains."
Colons are used to set off a word or phrase for emphasis.	The skiers got off of the mountain as they expected the worst: an avalanche.
Colons are used when writing the time.	Is your appointment at 9:00 or 10:00?
Business letters use colons in the salutation.	Dear Ms. Massey:

Practice

Identify why the colon is used in each sentence. Write S for series, C for clause, E for emphasis, T for time, or L for business letter.

1. S The teacher said to do the following: read two chapters, answer the questions, and write a paragraph.
2. T My alarm goes off at 6:15 a.m.
3. C The coach gave us some tips: eat right and train hard.
4. E All of my hard training paid off when I saw the sign ahead: Finish.
5. L Dear Dr. Brooks:
6. C The host said: "Let's eat!"

Simple Steps • Sixth Grade — Capitalization and Punctuation 239

Page 239

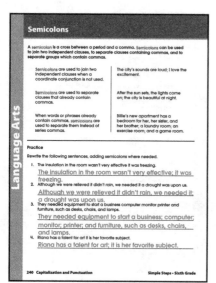

Semicolons

A semicolon is a cross between a period and a comma. Semicolons can be used to join two independent clauses, to separate clauses containing commas, and to separate groups which contain commas.

Semicolons are used to join two independent clauses when a coordinate conjunction is not used.	The city's sounds are loud; I love the excitement.
Semicolons are used to separate clauses that already contain commas.	After the sun sets, the lights come on; the city is beautiful at night.
When words or phrases already contain commas, semicolons are used to separate them instead of series commas.	Billie's new apartment has a bedroom for her, her sister, and her brother; a laundry room; an exercise room; and a game room.

Practice

Rewrite the following sentences, adding semicolons where needed.

1. The insulation in the room wasn't very effective it was freezing.
The insulation in the room wasn't very effective; it was freezing.

2. Although we were relieved it didn't rain, we needed it a drought was upon us.
Although we were relieved it didn't rain, we needed it; a drought was upon us.

3. They needed equipment to start a business computer monitor printer and furniture, such as desks, chairs, and lamps.
They needed equipment to start a business; computer monitor; printer; and furniture, such as desks, chairs, and lamps.

4. Riana has a talent for art it is her favorite subject.
Riana has a talent for art; it is her favorite subject.

240 Capitalization and Punctuation — Simple Steps • Sixth Grade

Page 240

Hyphens

Hyphens are used to divide words at the end of a line and to create new words. They are also used between numbers.

Use a hyphen to divide a word into syllables.	beau-ti-ful per-form
Do not divide one-syllable words with fewer than six letters.	through piece
Do not divide one letter from the rest of the word.	event-ful not: e-ventful
Divide syllables after the vowel if the vowel is a syllable on its own.	come-dy not: com-edy
Divide words with double consonants between the consonants.	swim-ming mir-ror
Hyphens can be used to create new words when combined with words and word parts such as self, ex, and great.	The pianist was self-taught. My great-grandmother is 105 years old. I just saw our ex-mayor at the store.
Hyphens are used between numbers.	twenty-one

Practice

Circle the word that includes the correct use of punctuation from the two choices for each item.

1. instru-ment / instrument
2. o-ceanographer / ocean-ographer
3. thirty two / thirty-two
4. char-ity / charit-y
5. ch-air / chair
6. run-ning / runn-ing
7. great aunt / great-aunt
8. sixty-four / sixty four

Simple Steps • Sixth Grade — Capitalization and Punctuation 241

Page 241

Parentheses

Parentheses are used to show supplementary material, to set off phrases in a stronger way than commas, and to enclose numbers.

Parentheses show supplementary material. Supplementary material is a word or phrase that gives additional information.	Theresa's mother (a dentist) will speak to our class next week.
Sometimes, words or phrases that might be set off with commas are set off with parentheses instead. It gives the information more emphasis.	Leo's apartment building, the one with the nice window boxes, was voted prettiest in the neighborhood. Leo's apartment building (the one with the nice window boxes) was voted prettiest in the neighborhood.
Parentheses are also used to enclose numbers.	Jacklyn wants to join the track team because (1) it is good exercise, (2) she can travel to other schools and cities, and (3) she can meet new friends.

Practice

Match the sentences in Column A with the reason why parentheses are used in Column B. Draw a line to make your match.

Column A
1. When cooking rice, don't forget to (1) rinse the rice, (2) steam the rice, and (3) eat the rice!
2. The preliminary findings (announced yesterday) are important to the study.
3. The dinosaur bones (a huge discovery) can be seen in the museum.

Column B
supplementary material
set off with emphasis
enclose numbers

242 Capitalization and Punctuation — Simple Steps • Sixth Grade

Page 242

Page 243

Review

Use everything you have learned so far about punctuation to answer the questions.

Complete the following sentences by circling the best end punctuation in parentheses.

1. Bees are fascinating creatures (. !) — (.)
2. Can bees talk (? .) — (?)
3. Scientists have discovered that bees talk to each other (? .) — (.)
4. How do they talk (? !) — (?)
5. Bees talk through dance (? .) — (.)

Write SC for series comma, DA for direct address, SD for set-off dialogue, or MA for multiple adjectives.

6. __SD__ The customer asked, "How much will the repairs cost?"
7. __MA__ I had a sweet, juicy apple for lunch.
8. __DA__ Finish your homework before playing video games, Craig.
9. __MA__ Shawn had a long, difficult homework assignment.
10. __DA__ Chloe, your song in the concert was beautiful.

11. Write three sentences with commas. One should be a compound sentence, one should be a complex sentence, and one should include a quotation.

Answers will vary.

Simple Steps • Sixth Grade
Capitalization and Punctuation 243

Page 244

Review

The sentences in Column A contain words with apostrophes. Match these sentences to the types of apostrophes used in Column B. Draw a line to make your match.

Column A | Column B
12. The parents' cars lined the street. — plural possessive ending in s
13. Patty's blanket is nearly done. — singular possessive
14. The children's toys are in the toy box. — plural possessive not ending in s
15. Teddy's missed the presentation. — contraction

Rewrite the following sentences to include colons, semicolons, or parentheses.

16. Although the score was tied, our team looked strong we knew we would win.
Although the score was tied, our team looked strong;
we knew we would win.

17. There are many reasons to adopt from a shelter it saves animals' lives, they are seen by a vet, and they are spayed and neutered.
There are many reasons to adopt from a shelter: it
saves animals' lives, they are seen by a vet, and they
are spayed or neutered.

18. The manager told the customers "The Black Friday sale will begin at 5 o'clock in the morning."
The manager told the customers: "The Black Friday
sale will begin at 5 o'clock in the morning."

19. Mac must 1 wash the dishes, 2 do his homework, and 3 get ready for bed.
Mac must (1) wash the dishes, (2) do his homework,
and (3) get ready for bed.

Rewrite each word with a hyphen in the correct spot.

20. thirtythree __thirty-three__   21. excoach __ex-coach__
22. greatuncle __great-uncle__   23. selfaware __self-aware__
24. exwife __ex-wife__   25. seventyfive __seventy-five__

244 Capitalization and Punctuation
Simple Steps • Sixth Grade

Page 245

Chapter Review

Rewrite the following sentences by adding periods, question marks, and exclamation marks where needed.

1. "Marsha," called A.J., "I heard you got your driver's license"
"Marsha," called A.J., "I heard you got your driver's
license."
2. "Don't forget to put mustard ketchup and pickles on my sandwich" Mona exclaimed
"Don't forget to put mustard, ketchup, and pickles on
my sandwich!" Mona exclaimed.
3. E.B White is the author of the book Charlotte's Web
E.B. White is the author of the book Charlotte's Web.
4. The customer asked, "What comes on the garden salad"
The customer asked, "What comes on the garden
salad?"
5. Wow That was the best movie I've ever seen
Wow! That was the best movie I've ever seen!

6. Add commas where needed in the business letter.

1151 Davidson Street
Chicago, IL 40000
April 8, 2015

Mrs. Jane Merrinan, Director
City Community Center
1200 Adams Street
Chicago, IL 30000

Dear Mrs. Merrinan:

My name is A.J. Byington. I am interested in applying as a summer counselor at the Civic Community Center, and I would like to become a part-time volunteer during the school year. I am a freshman at Northwest High School. My experience has included tutoring, coaching and counseling students in elementary school. Your varied, well-rounded programs interest me. I have included my activities list and references. I look forward to talking with you in the near future. Thank you for your time.

Sincerely,
A.J. Byington

Simple Steps • Sixth Grade
Capitalization and Punctuation 245

Page 246

Chapter Review

7. Proofread the following paragraphs by adding commas, quotation marks, apostrophes, colons, semicolons, hyphens, and parentheses where needed.

"Sharon, are you going to the community center after school?" asked Susan.

"Yes, I'm going right after school to play some basketball; our team is going to the tournament. My great-grandpa is going to cheer me on," answered Sharon.

"I'm so glad we have a center," said Sharon. "We learned in school about the very first community center. It was started by two very brave women, Jane Addams and Ellen Gates Starr."

Susan responded, "I don't think I've heard of them."

"They lived way back in the 1800s. Life in cities was not easy," Sharon continued. "Thousands of people worked in factories even kids and received little money in return. Jane and Ellen both wanted to help people. They moved into one of the worst parts of town. They found a big house on Halstead Street. They rented it and turned it into the first community center, Hull House. Hull House offered child care for working mothers (eventually leading to kindergarten classes.) After a while, many classes were offered to people of all ages: art, music, drama, cooking, science, math, and languages. The people of the city were finally brought together in a place where they could socialize, relax, and escape their working lives. Many of the people who came to Hull House went on to lead successful lives and help other people."

"Well, Sharon," said Susan, "today's game should be played in honor of Jane Addams and Ellen Gates Starr!"

Write three sentences about your favorite sporting event, either as a participant or a spectator. Use each of the three types of parentheses in your sentences.

8. _____
9. _____ _Answers will vary._
10. _____

246 Capitalization and Punctuation
Simple Steps • Sixth Grade

Page 247

Chapter Review

Use a dictionary to look up two words with the prefix ex-, two words with the prefix great-, and two words with the prefix self-. Write a sentence for each.

11. _____
12. _____
13. _____ _Answers will vary._
14. _____
15. _____
16. _____

17. Write a review of a movie you have seen or a book you have read. Include at least two of the following uses of semicolons: between independent clauses, to separate clauses that contain clauses, and to separate groups of words that contain commas.

Answers will vary.

Simple Steps • Sixth Grade
Capitalization and Punctuation 247

Page 249

Tricky Verb Usage

Practice

Circle the best verb in parentheses to complete each sentence. Then, rewrite the sentence using the correct tense.

1. Don't (bring, take) the library books out of the building. — (take)
Don't take the library books out of the building.
2. Brian and Matt (bring, take) extra water to the baseball games. — (bring)
Brian and Matt bring extra water to the baseball
games.
3. Last year Lilly (bring, take) cupcakes on her birthday. — (bring)
Last year Lilly brought cupcakes on her birthday.
4. Grover (bring, take) six cookies out of the box. — (take)
Grover took six cookies out of the box.
5. Yesterday, we (bring, take) blankets and towels to the animal shelter. — (take)
Yesterday, we took blankets and towels to the animal
shelter.
6. Don't (lay, lie) in the sun without sunscreen! — (lie)
Don't lie in the sun without sunscreen!
7. It was unusual that the papers were missing; he had (lay, lie) them in the same spot every morning. — (lay)
It was unusual that the papers were missing; he had
laid them in the same spot every morning.
8. Meagan (lay, lie) in bed too long this morning and was late for work. — (lie)
Meagan lay in bed too long this morning and was late
for work.
9. Jean (lay, lie) the covers over the plates before the rain hit. — (lay)
Jean laid the covers over the plates before the rain
hit.
10. Please (lay, lie) the cups and plates at the end of the table. — (lay)
Please lay the cups and plates at the end of the table.

Simple Steps • Sixth Grade
Usage, Vocabulary, and Spelling 249

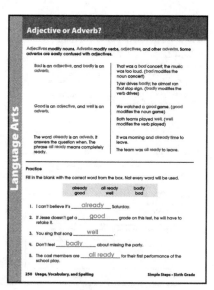

Page 250

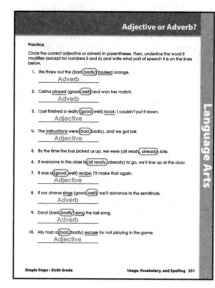

Page 251

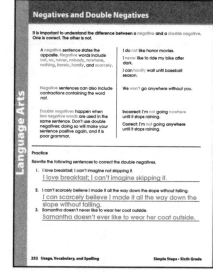

Page 252

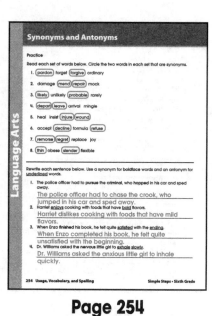

Page 254

Page 255

Page 256

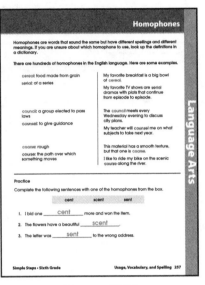

Page 257

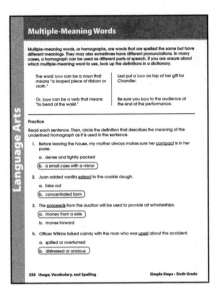

Page 258

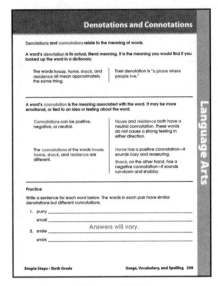

Page 259

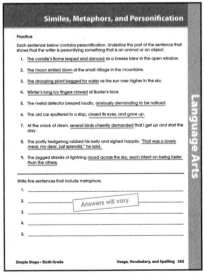

Page 260

Page 262

Page 263

Language Arts

Page 265

Root Words

Practice

Look at each word equation below. The meaning of one part is shown in parentheses. Consult the chart of root words on the previous page to find the meaning of the other part.

Write the meaning in the first blank. Then, combine the two meanings in the second blank. Write the dictionary definition in the space provided. The first one has been done for you.

1. react   re (again) + act ___to do___ = ___again to do___
   Dictionary definition: ___to act or do again___

2. automatic   auto ___self___ + matic (having a mind) = ___a mind___ ___self having___
   Dictionary definition: ___self-acting or self-motivating___

3. transact   trans (across) + act ___to do___ = ___across to do___
   Dictionary definition: ___to carry out a settlement___

4. centimeter   centi ___a hundred___ + meter (meter) = ___meter___ ___a hundred___
   Dictionary definition: ___one hundredth of a meter___

5. aquanaut   aqua ___water___ + naut (sailor) = ___water sailor___
   Dictionary definition: ___an underwater explorer___

6. induct   in (into) + duct ___to lead___ = ___to lead into___
   Dictionary definition: ___to introduce or admit as a member___

Simple Steps • Sixth Grade   Usage, Vocabulary, and Spelling 265

Page 266

Greek Roots

Many words in the English language have Greek roots. Learning the meanings of these roots can help you determine the meanings of some unfamiliar words. Here are some examples of words with Greek roots.

chron means "time"	After Jed's alarm clock broke, he was chronically late to class.
bio means "life"	My favorite class is biology because I enjoy studying animal and plant life.
phon means "sound"	I think this telephone is broken because I can hardly hear you.
cycl means "circle"	A cyclone is a storm that creates a huge funnel of wind that spins in a circle.
therm means "heat"	According to the thermometer, you have a fever of 100 degrees.

Practice

Read the clues below. Then, choose the word with the Greek root from the box that best fits the clue and write it on the line.

| biography | chronological | homophones |
| thermos | | tricycle |

1. ___chronological___ arranged by order of time

2. ___biography___ the story of a person's life

3. ___thermos___ a bottle that keeps liquids hot

4. ___tricycle___ a vehicle that has three circular wheels

5. ___homophones___ words that sound the same but are spelled differently

266 Usage, Vocabulary, and Spelling   Simple Steps • Sixth Grade

---

Page 267

Latin Roots

Many words in the English language have Latin roots. Learning the meanings of these roots can help you determine the meanings of some unfamiliar words. Here are some examples of words with Latin roots.

aud means "hear"	The audience at the rock concert was excited to hear a great show.
vid and vis mean "see"	I recorded a video of the party, so we can watch it later.
ped means "foot"	This street is just for pedestrians and is only open to foot traffic.
ann and enn mean "year"	Each year, my parents go camping to celebrate their anniversary.
liber means "free"	The Statue of Liberty is one of the symbols of freedom in the United States.

Practice

Circle the word with the Latin root that matches each definition below.

1. a large room where people go to hear or see a performance
   (auditorium)   videography

2. freedom
   (liberty)   impede

3. an insect that has many pairs of legs
   pedestrian   (millipede)

4. the part of a bicycle that is operated by the foot
   liberate   (pedal)

Simple Steps • Sixth Grade   Usage, Vocabulary, and Spelling 267

Page 269

Using a Dictionary

Practice

Write the entry word that you would look up in a dictionary beside each bold word below.

1. crickets   ___cricket___   2. contains   ___contain___
3. rubbing   ___rub___   4. dragonflies   ___dragonfly___
5. divided   ___divide___   6. mosquitoes   ___mosquito___
7. found   ___find___   8. soaring   ___soar___

Use the dictionary entries below to answer the questions that follow.

sincere \sin-'sir\ adj. honest; genuine, noun sincerity

squash \'skwäsh\) 1. noun a fruit that is related to pumpkins and gourds 2. verb to crush or press flat

refrigerator \ri-'fri-je-,rā-ter\ noun a machine or appliance that keeps food cold

1. On the line below, write a sentence using the word squash as a verb.
   ___Try not to squash the flowers as you walk through the garden.___

2. Which is an entry word—sincere or sincerity?
   ___sincere___

3. Which guide words would you find on the same page as refrigerator?
   reef • refresh   reflection • regal   refugee • rehearse
   ___reflection • regal___

4. How many syllables are there in refrigerator?
   ___five___

Simple Steps • Sixth Grade   Usage, Vocabulary, and Spelling 269

Page 270

Chapter Review

Circle the best verb in parentheses to complete each sentence. Then, rewrite it using the correct tense.

1. The children were (bring, take) home when it started to thunder.
   ___The children were brought home when it started to thunder.___

2. Marv was (bring, take) to the hospital when he sprained his ankle.
   ___Marv was taken to the hospital when he sprained his ankle.___

3. Grandma said, "Aubrey, (bring, take) me a glass of water, please."
   ___Grandma said, "Aubrey, bring me a glass of water, please."___

4. (lay, lie) on the blanket on the sand.
   ___Lie on the blanket on the sand.___

5. Barbara (lay, lie) her blanket near the bed.
   ___Barbara laid her blanket near the bed.___

6. Maggie (lay, lie) down for a quick nap yesterday.
   ___Maggie lay down for a quick nap yesterday.___

Write a sentence using each of the following words: bad, badly, good, well, all ready, already.

7. _____
8. _____
9. _____
10. _____
11. _____
12. _____

Answers will vary.

270 Usage, Vocabulary, and Spelling   Simple Steps • Sixth Grade

---

Page 271

Chapter Review

Rewrite the following sentences to correct the double negatives.

13. The triplets' parents won't go nowhere without the babysitter.
    ___The triplets' parents won't go anywhere without the babysitter.___

14. Sheila doesn't never wake up before 8 o'clock in the morning.
    ___Sheila doesn't ever wake up before 8 o'clock in the morning.___

15. Nora didn't not like the pizza, but it wasn't her favorite.
    ___Nora did like the pizza, but it wasn't her favorite.___

Complete the following sentences by circling the best answer in parentheses.

16. Sydney likes raisins and granola in his (cereal) serial).

17. Stacy liked the (scent) sent) of the flowers in the window box.

18. Please (ring (wring) out the towels before placing them in the dryer.

19. Zola loved to eat fresh (mussels) muscles) with lemon and butter.

20. Look at the weather (vane) vein) to see which way the wind is blowing.

21. I need to select one more (coarse, (course) to take next semester.

Read each pair of sentences. Circle N for noun or V for verb to identify the part of speech for the word in boldface. Each pair of sentences will have two different answers.

22. Horace dusted the display of books in the store's front window. (N) V
    The schools in our district display student artwork throughout their halls. N (V)

23. Please number your answer 1 through 10. N (V)
    Dr. Patel analyzed the number of tadpoles living in the pond. (N) V

24. Louisa made the goal, evening the score and making the crowd go wild. N (V)
    Later this evening, we will go to my grandparents' house for a party. (N) V

Simple Steps • Sixth Grade   Usage, Vocabulary, and Spelling 271
